Open access edition supported by the National Endowment for the Humanities / Andrew W. Mellon Foundation Humanities Open Book Program.

© 2019 Johns Hopkins University Press
Published 2019

Johns Hopkins University Press
2715 North Charles Street
Baltimore, Maryland 21218-4363
www.press.jhu.edu

The text of this book is licensed under a Creative Commons Attribution-NonCommercial-NoDerivatives 4.0 International License: https://creativecommons.org/licenses/by-nc-nd/4.0/.
CC BY-NC-ND

ISBN-13: 978-1-4214-3356-1 (open access)
ISBN-10: 1-4214-3356-7 (open access)

ISBN-13: 978-1-4214-3354-7 (pbk. : alk. paper)
ISBN-10: 1-4214-3354-0 (pbk. : alk. paper)

ISBN-13: 978-1-4214-3355-4 (electronic)
ISBN-10: 1-4214-3355-9 (electronic)

This page supersedes the copyright page included in the original publication of this work.

BRITAIN IN THE WORLD TODAY

BRITAIN AND CHINA

By the same Author

THE ECONOMIC DEVELOPMENT OF
COMMUNIST CHINA 1949–1960
(With T. J. Hughes)

BRITAIN AND CHINA

Evan Luard

THE JOHNS HOPKINS PRESS BALTIMORE

Published in Great Britain by
Chatto & Windus Ltd
42 William IV Street
London W.C.2

Library of Congress Catalog Card Number: 62-7422

© Evan Luard 1962
Printed in Great Britain

CONTENTS

Introduction   *page*   9

THE PAST

1. The British assault   19
2. The Chinese rejoinder   30
3. Britain and the Kuomintang   42

BRITAIN AND THE PEOPLE'S REPUBLIC

4. The coming of the Communists   63
5. The Korean War   83
6. Missionaries   104
7. Merchants   128
8. Geneva and after   155
9. Hong Kong   176
10. The two Chinas   199

THE FUTURE

11. Chinese aspirations and British interests   217
12. British policy and the future   234

Index   255

This book is the first of a series sponsored by the Leverhulme Trust, designed to examine the change which has come about in Britain's position in the world since the Second World War, and the implications of this for her future. The Trust especially requested that the authors, in writing the books, should seek to take advantage of the first-hand knowledge of some of those who themselves took part in the events they describe. Where possible the present author has tried to do this. He would, therefore, like to express his thanks to a large number of people, including Lord Gladwyn, Sir Ralph Stevenson, Mr. Con O'Neill, Sir Alexander Grantham, Mr. H. J. Collar and Mr. E. J. Price (of the China Association), Mr. John Keswick (of Matheson & Co.), Mr. A. E. Marker (of the Arnhold Trading Company), Mr. P. K. M. Patten (of the Shell Oil Company), Mr. P. Aldworth (of the Hong Kong and Shanghai Bank), Mr. Victor Hayward (of the International Missionary Council), Canon Wittenbach (of the Church Missionary Society), the Rev. A. F. Griffiths (of the London Missionary Society), the Rev. D. W. Thompson (of the Methodist Missionary Society), the Rev. E. J. T. Madge (of the Baptist Missionary Society) and Mr. A. Lea (of the China Inland Mission), for their useful comments and advice; to Mr. A. S. B. Olver, Mrs. Daphne Henwood, Mrs. Coleena Lupton and other members of the staff of Chatham House for a great deal of invaluable help on a number of occasions; and, finally, to Miss Elisabeth Heal for much patient and efficient secretarial assistance.

INTRODUCTION

BETWEEN Europe and China there lies an earth. But it is not miles alone that has made the distance so great. Each, to find the other, had to navigate a sea of steppe and sand, or penetrate a wilderness of ocean. Thus, for long centuries, on either side of these dividing wastes, both lived out quite separate existences, barely even conscious of the shadowed universe beyond. And though, from the time of the twin Han and Roman empires, occasional momentary contacts took place, the two civilizations did not sensibly impinge till the end of the eighteenth century.

Civilizations which evolve in isolation tend to grow more dissimilar with time. For while in practice there has nearly always been, even across the vastest intervals of space, some diffusion of the basic technological equipment which shapes the pattern of primitive communities, the characteristic traits of more evolved societies have not been so readily transmitted. While, therefore, Europe and China each acquired from the Middle East the same basic neolithic, bronze and iron economies, inherited equally plough, pottery, spindle, loom and wheel, the superstructures that they erected over this foundation increasingly diverged as they became more complex.

Other societies had elsewhere, on a similar technical foundation, evolved in the course of time their own forms of civilization. But of these some had lived and died in complete isolation. Others had become fused; or been overlain by newer cultures. And by the end of the Middle Ages there remained on earth only three flourishing and entirely distinct civilizations, those of China, India and Europe.

Each, partitioned from the others by the wall that space erected, had evolved within its own curtilage, almost entirely independently of outside influence, its own system of social organization, its own religion, its own arts, its own state structure, and its own ideology. Each had evolved, through the conditioning of its own language and conceptual structure, entirely distinct patterns of thought. For each, inevitably, both through the natural force of ethnocentricity, and because of the justifications that ideology established for inherited institutions and ideas, native ways became the only right ways, the ways of all others wrong ways. It is not coincidence that, in China as in Europe, strangers from afar came to be "barbarians".

In many fields Europe and China stood at opposite poles. China had emerged from monarchy through feudalism to a highly organized bureaucracy, in which all sovereignty remained with the divine Emperor. Europe had emerged from feudalism through monarchy towards an increasingly self-conscious democracy, in which all sovereignty came to be claimed for the people. China, after a period of great technological fertility during the first thousand years of our era, had, with the development of an increasingly stable, but monolithic, society, fallen into stagnation in matters of science. Europe, after an age of almost complete sterility at the time when China had been productive, had, from the end of the Middle Ages, witnessed an era of unprecedented invention. In China commerce and industry had remained small-scale and backward, and no substantial bourgeoisie had developed. In Europe the rise of a vigorous commercial economy had assured the middle classes of an increasingly powerful position within the state.

Thus, when the first contacts began to be made, each appeared to the other grotesque and strange. Each evolved highly coloured and often distorted images of the other. Because most Westerners possessed few of the refinements of conduct and demeanour to which importance was attached in Chinese society, they often seemed to the Chinese uncivilized, even barbarous. Because the Chinese possessed what appeared to Europeans an inferior material equipment and a less evolved social organization, many in the West were inclined to regard them as backward, even primitive. The West built up a stereotyped picture of China as inscrutable, pagan, changeless; and in each case were mistaken. China painted a portrait of the Westerner as brutal, uncultured, yet cunning; which was equally inaccurate.

Each had no doubt that it could do much to bring the benefits of civilization to the other. It was out of such feelings that the Emperor's Commissioner, Lin Tse-hsu, addressing a communication to Queen Victoria in 1839, warned her of the serious danger to Europe if the Chinese Emperor was to put a stop to the trading contacts of the Europeans, demanding, "If China cuts off these benefits with no sympathy for those who are to suffer, what will the barbarians be able to do to keep themselves alive?" And it was from similarly charitable sentiments that in 1858 the British merchants of Tientsin, in a memorandum to Lord Elgin, declared their conviction that Europe possessed a mission "to develop the vast resources of China, and to expand among her people the elevating influence of a higher civilization".

Britain, more than any other nation, represented the West in the first confrontations that took place between the civilizations of Europe and those of the East. The countries that had come before her, Portugal, Holland and France, had established contacts which were more transitory in time and more restricted in place. They had been able, in an earlier age, to set up trading connexions which did not require them to become seriously implicated with either the people, or the governments, of the lands with which they dealt. England, in the eighteenth century, found herself, willy-nilly, increasingly forced inwards from the seaports towards the interior and, finally, the capitals. In India, discovering herself, suddenly and against all her intentions, burdened with the administration of a vast sub-continent, thousands of miles from her own shore, peopled by strange peoples about whom she knew nothing, she was forced into contact with a culture far older and richer than her own, while she in turn was able to inject into this many of the alien institutions, concepts and ideals evolved in the West. With China, the contact was never as intimate, nor as exclusive, as with India. But the final effect of the British impact was no less shattering.

Two nations could scarcely have been more different. China was, beyond all others, self-centred and self-sufficient. Enclosed by mountain and desert on one side and by sea on the other, immersed in the outwardly unchanging rhythm of her own civilization, the majority of her inhabitants were barely even conscious of the existence of other cultures; and their few contacts with outside peoples gave them some excuse for regarding all other races as, by their standards, barbarian. Britain was perhaps, of all nations of the world, the most outward-turned, the most widely travelled, the most extravagantly diffused. An expanding sea-power, whose people had explored many strange lands, whose dominions stretched into every corner of the globe, whose commercial commitments were scattered among every continent, she often felt her most vital interests to be bound up with events far beyond her own borders. The Chinese were the representatives of an ancient civilization, now perhaps over-refined and almost sterile, bound by a rigorous code of etiquette in all personal relations, and accustomed to veil every expression of opinion in elaborate forms of circumlocution. The British were a bourgeois nation, with a culture that was only recently borrowed and scantily assimilated, adventurous but brash, virile but unpolished, blunt in speech and uncompromising in action. The Chinese, owing allegiance to a divine Emperor, and governed by a super-educated and revered *élite* of mandarins, regarded the workings of the state machine almost as a part of the sacred order of the universe. The British, who had executed their King and attainted their nobility, who took pride in the newly proclaimed ideals of popular sovereignty, were disinclined to pay undue respect to established authority, whether of monarch or official. Above all, the Chinese, both in scientific knowledge and military power, were still a medieval nation. The British, equipped with the technological skill that Western science had made possible, possessed a naval and military might second to none in the world.

Such national differences overlaid the many characteristics that, as individuals, the two races had in common. Both were, more than most other peoples, realistic, matter of fact, often sceptical, in their approach to the universe, suspicious of all that appeared mystical or speculative. Both had, at different periods, by their empirical and practical bent of mind, made valuable contributions to technical and scientific knowledge. Both had keenly developed commercial instincts. Both, though by nature perhaps no less passionate than other peoples, were by nature conditioned to contain their emotions within a becomingly impassive exterior. Both were by temperament fundamentally conservative, resistant to all outside influences likely to infect with the menace of change, and thus often suspicious or uncomprehending of foreign ideas and opinions. Both, in precept as well as in practice, professed the ideals of moderation and of reason. Finally, perhaps most important, each was equally imbued with a profound, if perhaps unconscious, assurance, amounting in the eyes of others almost to arrogance, in their dealings with foreign peoples: and when two such nations confront each other, it is not surprising if the collision is severe.

Both peoples lived within a mental climate that was certain to intensify this clash. Britain at the time of the first governmental contacts at the end of the eighteenth century, had, during the previous hundred years, proved victorious over virtually every other nation of Europe in turn. She had accumulated an empire of huge dimensions, stretching from Canada to India, from the West Indies to Australia. She had perhaps already begun to acquire the subconscious assumption that, in military power at least, the European powers were by nature, even by destiny, masters of all other races. Such ideas were not at first extended to the Chinese Empire, to which for long the utmost deference was shown. But in the last resort it coloured British reactions to the seeming affronts of Chinese officials and court. With the gradual assumption of imperial glory, national pride grew more assertive. The British crown became the symbol of national prestige. An offence to His Majesty's subjects implied an insult to the sovereign himself. And when, in 1839, differences between the two countries finally led to armed conflict, what most provoked the indignation of the British Foreign Secretary was "the affront offered to the British Crown by the indignities put to Her Majesty's Superintendent and by the outrageous proceedings adopted towards Her Majesty's other subjects in China".

But China too had during the eighteenth century passed through a period of imperial conquest. She had acquired dominion over vast territories beyond her western borders and exacted tribute from numbers of her neighbours. She had indeed, throughout most of her history, only rarely come into contact with people who could rival her in military power; still less in civilization. China was the Middle Country; her Emperor, the Son of Heaven; and his divine authority not, like that of European sovereigns, to be shared with other monarchs, since, as Chinese frequently assured each other, "there cannot be two Sons of Heaven". Foreign nations should be thankful enough to be allowed even to visit and trade within the Empire. To ask for more was presumption. And when a British Superintendent of Trade dared to express to the Viceroy of Canton his hopes for the future intercourse between the two nations, the Viceroy was most indignant at the idea that bonds of peace and goodwill could exist between "the Occupant of the Dragon Throne and the ministering servants to whom he distributes his bounty".

There was an equally radical divergence in the two peoples' concept of the manner in which the relations between states ought to be conducted. The British had been accustomed, over hundreds of years, to the system by which the monarchs of European states could communicate with each other through the medium of envoys and ambassadors, specially accredited for the purpose to foreign courts. To them it seemed self-evident that every nation should allow other states the opportunity in this way to make known their views in the highest quarters. It was outrageous that the Chinese should fail to accept the usage current among other civilized nations. It was only natural that when in 1596, Queen Elizabeth dispatched a letter to the Chinese Emperor, it was, as a matter of course, addressed to him in Latin, like all other diplomatic missives of the time; and when in 1859, under a later Queen, British forces were victorious in China, one of the main objects of the British Government in the peace treaty that followed, was to lay down, in the minutest detail, the diplomatic courtesies the Chinese court was in future to observe.

China had no knowledge of the forms of diplomatic intercourse that had been developed in Europe. She had virtually no official contacts with foreign states. Nor did she wish for them. If representatives of foreign governments came to Peking it was only to bear tribute. It was therefore only natural that when the first British envoys made their way to Peking in the late eighteenth and early nineteenth centuries, the Chinese insisted on decking the boats that carried them up the river from Tientsin with flags marked "tribute-bearer"; and demanded, when they reached the Imperial Court, that the ambassadors should prostrate themselves on the ground, knocking their foreheads on the floor, like the other foreign envoys that were received.

British interest in China from the first centred around trade; and the prime objective of British Government policies towards China from the earliest times until the present day has been the protection and promotion of that trade. Yet in no field was the contrast between the attitudes of the two countries more acute. Britain belonged to a community where international commerce formed an important part of economic existence; and where the right to trade had therefore come to be regarded almost as a law of nature. In this world there was no nation whose prosperity was more indissolubly bound up with foreign trade than Britain. The expansion of international trade came to be regarded by many in Britain as the condition of universal progress, the quickest route towards Utopia. And when Lord Palmerston, in the first communication from a British Foreign Secretary to a Chinese minister, expressed his hopes for the future of the "friendly intercourse which has for so great a period of time subsisted between the British and Chinese nations to the manifest advantage of both", he was expressing sentiments that have been shared by all British statesmen and merchants who have had dealings with China since.

China was economically self-sufficient. Her trading contacts with the outside world were at all times tenuous and intermittent. And in such exchanges as did take place she had nearly always been the passive partner. While she had had much that was rare and precious to offer to the West, she had never acquired any commodies that seemed to her of great importance in exchange. So when Chien Lung, in the first letter sent by a Chinese ambassador to a British sovereign, told George III "there is nothing we lack, we set no value on strange or ingenious objects ... and have no use for your country's manufactures", he was saying only what all Chinese of his day accepted as self-evident.

Thus every issue that came between them the two countries approached from an entirely different mental world. Each found it difficult to conceive that any view other than its own could be the right one. Which view was to prevail was settled for a time by British military might. And after Britain had by such means secured for herself in China the conditions of intercourse that she regarded as legitimate, other nations soon sought to acquire for themselves a similarly favourable position. But their aspirations, though not necessarily more self-seeking than Britain's, were sometimes more dangerous for China. And by their pretensions the Western powers served in the long run only to inflame the nationalist sentiment that was eventually to displace them altogether.

This sentiment was not at first armed with the power which alone could give it effective expression. For this reason it was only within the last twenty years that the West began to treat China entirely without discrimination. And it is only within the last ten that she has been able to deal with them as an equal. But the penetration, first undertaken by Britain to make possible the free exchange of goods, had brought with it as well an increasing interchange of ideas. The hazy fairy-tale images each had of the other, exotic kingdom of slit-eyed, mysterious Mandarins and far away island of red-haired, coarse barbarians, sleepy, reluctant dragon and brutal, ravening lion, these began to fade, and more prosaic, but more life-like, contours came to take their place.

Each had much to learn of the other. Slowly the delicate and subtle splendours of Chinese art, poetry and philosophy began to be known in England. China came in time to adopt of her own free will a good many of the institutions and ideas that the British assault first made accessible to her.

But almost as soon as the new acquaintance began to be seriously explored, it was once again to be disrupted. For during the last ten years the institutions and ideas that China has borrowed have come from the eastern rather than the western half of Europe. It is this fact which presents the principal challenge to British policy towards China today.

THE PAST

I

THE BRITISH ASSAULT

THE first British ships to reach Chinese waters, a squadron of four, trading under licence from the Governor of Goa, arrived at the coast in 1637. The Chinese authorities placed difficulties in the way of their onward journey up river to Canton. And when they began nonetheless to enter the river, shore batteries opened fire on them. The British ships returned the fire, silenced the guns, and, sailing up to Canton, exchanged their cargoes and departed.

This first contact between the two countries was symbolic of all that was to follow. From the first it was the British who initiated dealings, while the Chinese remained sullenly indifferent, if not hostile. And from the first it was the British who eventually, if only by force, achieved their purpose. Britain, already beginning to displace the other European nations as the foremost maritime power, was gradually expanding her commercial activity, in Far Eastern waters as elsewhere. The Chinese believed they had little to gain from the trade the Western powers offered. They had already been made wary of European traders by the occasional acts of violence of which these had sometimes been guilty. Europeans were classed with other "outer peoples" as barbarians. There thus began a ceaseless contest between British commercial zeal on the one hand, and the dilatory, often obstructive, always extortionary, tactics of Chinese officialdom on the other.

A number of further engagements followed, in which each combatant occasionally emerged triumphant. In 1685 an imperial edict opened all Chinese ports to foreign trade. But in practice trade became increasingly centred at Canton. In 1689 the East India Company for the first time established a factory at that port. In 1715 this was placed on a more permanent footing, with regular annual visits. And in 1731 the British supercargoes, or company agents, began to stay on at Canton between the voyages of the vessels they represented. As in India at that stage, the Company's policy was to set up such trading posts for commercial purposes only, and to avoid as far as possible more far-reaching involvements. The responsibility for dealing with the Chinese authorities was placed in the hands of a committee of supercargoes.

Thus for long all contacts remained, by mutual consent, on a purely informal basis. The British Government in the early days made no attempt to intervene on behalf of the merchants in their dealings with Chinese officials. For their part neither the Chinese imperial court, nor the Chinese officials, nor the mass of the Chinese people, had any inclination to know more of the lands from which the Western traders had sailed. Indeed they scarcely distinguished between the different peoples involved. All were equally "ocean people", strange creatures from the sea, who, like the Arabs at Canton a thousand years earlier, or the Central Asian merchants of the silk route, emerged briefly from unknown regions to purchase the products of Chinese civilization, but who could themselves be of little concern to the Celestial Empire. All the Emperor and his officials asked was that such people should disturb as little as possible the harmonious ordering of their realm.

During the course of the eighteenth century the Manchu Emperors became, for this reason, more and more concerned to restrict all contacts between those they ruled and the outside world. Chinese subjects were forbidden to emigrate. They were not allowed to travel on foreign ships. They were not allowed to become Christians. To teach foreigners the Chinese language was punishable by the direst penalties. Despite all such efforts, as the trade increased, the foreign traders inevitably impinged increasingly on the life of the Empire. And as the contacts grew, various sources of conflict emerged, each stemming from the divergent world-views of the two peoples.

The first concerned the conditions under which the foreign merchants were permitted to live and trade. As a result of the policy of insulation these had been made increasingly difficult. From 1757 foreign trade was by decree explicitly confined to Canton. The foreign merchants were allowed to live in Canton only during the trading season. After this they had to leave for Macao. They were not allowed to bring their wives with them to China. They were not allowed to learn the Chinese language. They were not allowed to ride in a sedan chair. Nor to row in the river. Nor to walk in the streets. Indeed they were confined almost entirely to the narrow limits of their factories. Within the factories they were free to behave exactly as they chose. All that was asked of them in return was that they should bother the Chinese inhabitants as little as possible. To allow foreigners to mix freely with the Chinese might be not only inconvenient but dangerous. Thus the foreigners, an imperial edict declared, must not "presume of their own accord to go out and in, lest they should try to carry out clandestine dealings with traitorous Chinese". Impatience with such restrictions slowly aroused among the merchants the aspiration for an assurance of such treatment as they were accustomed to receive in other parts of the world.

The second cause of difference was the radically conflicting tradition and outlook of the two peoples on questions of crime and punishment. From very early days the Chinese had evolved for their own people a system of collective responsibility for criminal offences. A family or clan, a group of householders, or a village, were made to accept responsibility for all breaches of the peace committed by any of their members. When a crime occurred the group was made responsible for finding the culprit. If they failed, punishment might be executed on the entire group, or selected members of it. But once a victim had been produced the procedure of investigation and trial might be a mere formality. And in such investigations consideration of the intention of the accused was of the smallest consequence. The Chinese authorities naturally thought it normal to apply similar principles in dealing with the foreign communities who resided within their frontiers. They expressed no concern over any crime in which foreigners alone were involved. But if, as occasionally occurred, Chinese suffered injury at the hands of a foreigner, the foreign community was held collectively responsible. Officials would not concern themselves in investigating the circumstances themselves. This was for the foreigners to undertake. What they did demand was a victim, a ransom, a scapegoat, so that there could be assurance that the crime should be avenged; and be seen to be avenged.

The British had been brought up on different concepts. The ancient procedures of trial by ordeal, by compurgation, by jury, had been devised to ensure, not merely that for every crime committed somebody should be punished, but that the particular individual responsible should be identified. Equally important, it was essential to ensure, by the strict observance of common and case law, by the rigid adherence to established rules and procedure, that no man should be condemned without the most careful and painstaking investigation of the circumstances, in proof of the indictment. Finally it was from very early times accepted that the guilt of the accused lay not merely in the fact that he had performed a certain action, but that he did it with a particular intention or frame of mind. Thus when the British discovered, in a series of incidents in which Chinese subjects were killed and a foreign seaman accused, that the Chinese authorities were little interested whether the accused person was himself guilty of the deed in question, that the procedure of inquiry was frequently of the most perfunctory, and that no account was taken by the Chinese magistrates of whether the crime was the result of accident or intention, they became increasingly reluctant to commit themselves to a system of justice which appeared to them barbarous and revolting. And after a British seaman responsible for the discharge of a salvo of salute, which by mischance caused the death of a Chinese citizen, had been reluctantly handed over to a Chinese magistrate and, after a purely nominal investigation, strangled at his orders, mistrust hardened into defiance. The revulsion that was set up on the British side as a result of such incidents was a major cause of the subsequent British exaction of extra-territorial rights of jurisdiction in cases where British subjects were involved.

The third source of contention concerned the heavy and apparently quite arbitrary levies placed on the trade by Chinese officials at different levels. The British were quite used to customs duties. But they were accustomed to a system in which these were exacted at a regular and unvarying rate in accordance with the prescribed tariff. The capricious way in which the demands of the Chinese officials were imposed aroused first bewilderment, finally resentment.

In China traditions were different. Local officials had always had wide powers in the levying of taxation. One of the most important sources of revenue for provincial administrations was the levy imposed on inter-provincial trade. The exaction of locally determined duties on foreign trade was equally legitimate. And as the distinction between public revenues and private incomes was even less clear-cut in China than in eighteenth-century Europe there was nothing untoward in the highly personal method of assessment adopted by the various authorities in Canton.

Finally, many British merchants were aggrieved at the fact that they were not able, as in other countries, to deal freely with any of the Chinese dealers who chose to do business with them, but only with the Co-Hong, an association of officially approved merchants that they regarded as monopolistic. The grounds for this complaint were perhaps questionable. The merchants of the Co-Hong were probably no more and no less monopolistic than were those of the East India Company. There is indeed a curious parallelism between the two institutions. In each case individual merchants undertook transactions with other individual merchants. They were free to bargain without reservation over prices, quality, or quantity, without any overriding control from above. Yet those who engaged in such dealings were in each case members of a trade association possessing a strangely ambivalent status, half-private, half-official; half-exclusive, half-open; half-independent, half-government controlled. And in each case this association was itself assured of an official monopoly, explicitly recognized and established by Royal Charter.

Within this framework the merchants of both countries were able for long to establish personal relationships that were both friendly and enduring. These were reinforced by the scrupulous integrity of both parties in all their commercial dealings, and by the readiness of each for this reason to be generous in the granting of credit, even on occasion to cancel altogether the debts of a partner who was in difficulties. With all the difficulties that came between them there emerged a sentiment of genuine respect on both sides.

It was in the hopes of remedying some of the grievances harboured by the British trading community that the first diplomatic contacts between the two countries took place. Lord Macartney succeeded, in 1793, in securing an audience with the Chinese Emperor, but did not manage to evoke the slightest response to the various requests which he had been sent to put forward. Lord Amherst, in 1816, managed to reach Peking, but his mission had to be abandoned as a result of differences over questions of protocol. Finally in 1834, Lord Napier, appointed Chief Superintendent of Trade at Canton on the abolition of the East India Company's monopoly, failed, after a prolonged contest, even to obtain an audience of the Viceroy of Canton. This last incident brought to a head the final issue on which the differing British and Chinese viewpoints were producing increasing friction.

One of the principal aims of the Macartney and subsequent missions had been to obtain the consent of the Chinese court to the dispatch to Peking of a permanent British envoy, who might be able to regulate some of the questions at issue between the two governments. After the East India Company's monopoly was finally abolished in 1834, the British Government, in despair of securing this aim, appointed Lord Napier as "Chief Superintendent of Trade", whose function it was to deal on an official basis with the Chinese provincial authorities at Canton. His duty was, in the words of Lord Palmerston, "to place himself in direct communication with the local authorities at Canton in order to offer protection to British subjects, and to be the organ of communication between the British and the Chinese Governments."

The Chinese had no interest in such contacts. They considered that all commercial matters that might arise as a result of the Emperor having permitted foreigners to come to Chinese ports, should be settled with the Chinese merchants of the Co-Hong with whom they had to deal. Mandarins had more important things to do. Thus, in the words of the Viceroy of Canton writing to the Co-Hong merchants on the occasion of Lord Napier's visit, "the Empire of Heaven appoints officials, civil to rule the people, military to control the wicked. But the petty affairs of commerce are to be directed by the merchants themselves. With such matters officials are not concerned."

Within a year or two of the British Government's appointment of the new superintendent the various sources of conflict that had developed between the two countries began to come to a head. At one time the merchants trading with China and the directors of the East India Company had shown themselves surprisingly sensitive to Chinese susceptibilities on many matters, and had been ready to concede much for the sake of securing their position in China. When during the Napoleonic Wars the British Government appeared to be about to occupy Macao, the Select Committee at Canton believing, probably with great exaggeration, that recent British territorial expansion in India had "more or less tended to produce in the mind of the Chinese a dread of the English nation and inspired them with an idea of their aiming at universal conquest in the East", advised the utmost caution. And the Select Committee of Supercargoes, writing in 1831, declared that in earlier days the Chinese officials and merchants "seemed to have been aware that any degradation would be submitted to for the preservation of trade". The British Government themselves had often been ready to show consideration. The official instructions to the new chief superintendent specifically laid down that he was to avoid any conduct, language or demeanour, which might "revolt the opinions or prejudices" of the Chinese people or Government, and to "study by all practicable methods to maintain a good and friendly understanding".

But when the monopoly of the East India Company was abolished in 1834, the new merchants who seized the opportunity to develop the trade between India and China thus opened, were of an altogether different mind from the old China hands of Company days. They were anxious to make this trade as profitable as possible as quickly as they could, and were not at all disposed to be so patient as their predecessors with the various difficulties that Chinese administrative methods placed in their way. The British Government as well, increasingly conscious of its new power and increasingly assertive in its relations with foreign states, became, especially under the forceful Foreign Secretaryship of Lord Palmerston, more and more impatient of Chinese methods and manners. As they began to take on themselves greater responsibility for promoting the interests of British traders in the East, they were less and less prepared to tolerate what they regarded as the humiliations and insults heaped on British subjects—and so on the British crown— by the Chinese Government. For, as Lord Amherst irascibly declared, after he had been carefully kept waiting for two hours by Chinese officials before being refused an audience, China was now dealing with "the officers appointed by His Britannic Majesty, who was by no means inclined to submit to such indignities".

Meanwhile, too, a new issue had emerged to intensify the misunderstanding between the two countries. Towards the end of the eighteenth century the East India Company had assumed a monopoly of the sale of opium in most parts of India, and had established regular auctions of the drug. The auctions became an important source of revenue for the Indian Government. To most people in the West at this time, the habit of smoking opium seemed, like the wearing of strange clothes, the binding of feet, child marriages, pigtails and concubines, merely another quaint and exotic oriental habit. It was different from the practice of the West, certainly; but not necessarily wrong for that. Precisely because the opium habit was scarcely known in the West, little thought was given to the social problems it presented, and there had been no occasion for the hardening of any stereotyped moral attitude towards it. Consequently there was scarcely more revulsion in England at the institution of public auctions of opium in India, or its subsequent sale in China, than there was over the publication in Britain of the unabashed confessions of an English opium-eater.

The merchants who bought the opium traded it to different parts of the East. But during the early part of the nineteenth century it came increasingly to be shipped to China. The West had traditionally had an adverse balance of trade with China. As a result traders had been obliged to export bullion to pay for what they bought there. The voracious demand for opium in China and the existence of convenient sources of supply in the Government of India's auction-sales offered an ideal method of remedying the deficit. Between 1795 and 1834 the total shipments of opium from India rose from less than two thousand chests to about twelve thousand.

Yet again, the viewpoint of the Chinese Government was different. For them the problem of opium addiction had become a grave one. In 1800 an imperial edict had forbidden the import of opium. But the edict was little regarded, either by the ordinary citizens of China, or by the officials whose duty it should have been to prevent the traffic, but who found the drug could in practice serve as a useful source of revenue. And though as a matter of form the East India Company forbade the carriage of opium in its own ships, the British and other foreign merchants, finding Chinese officials so amenable, had neither difficulty nor compunction in carrying on the trade. Both British merchant and Chinese official equally found it convenient to shed his conscience on to the other; each feeling, no doubt, that any responsibility for breaking the Emperor's injunction was not his own.

To the Chinese Imperial Government it was bad enough that their own officials were so venal as to flout the Emperor's edicts. But that the foreign merchants should abuse the privileges they had been granted by evading the laws of the Empire, was intolerable. And when, in 1839, the Imperial Government at last made a determined effort to suppress opium-smoking all over the country, one of the first steps taken was to send an imperial commissioner to

Canton to put a stop to dealings in the drug. For it was generally considered that opium-smoking in China was purely the responsibility of the foreigner. And indeed, principally, of Britain. For as the new commissioner informed Queen Victoria, in a letter which he addressed to her on the subject in 1839, the Chinese official world had "reflected that this noxious article is the clandestine manufacture of artful schemers under the dominion of your honourable nation".

The British Government and merchants, on the other hand, would not accept that the prevalence of opium-smoking in China could be attributed to the foreign traders. And they were by no means persuaded that the Chinese Government, even now, were seriously concerned to stamp out the habit of opium-smoking. They believed, or convinced themselves, that the new measures which the commissioner instituted against them were yet another example of the indefensible and arrogant discrimination of the Chinese Government against all foreigners. And so Lord Palmerston, in a dispatch to the Minister of the Emperor of China, setting out the British complaints against the Imperial Government, declared that the Chinese Government had "left untouched their own officers who were most to blame, and had used violence against foreigners, who were led into transgression by the encouragement and protection offered to them by the Governor of Canton and his inferior officers".

The British certainly never consciously had the intention of imposing the opium trade on China by force. In 1837 the Government warned the British merchants that they could "not interfere for the purpose of enabling British subjects to violate the laws of the country to which they trade". Captain Elliot, the British Superintendent, agreed, under duress, to the destruction of all British stocks of opium at Canton, valued at £2½ million. And later he ordered the masters of all ships in Hong Kong, at the time the only available harbour, to make oath to him that they had no opium on board, on pain of expulsion from the port. But Captain Elliot and many of the British merchants, their national pride affronted by the peremptory methods adopted by the Chinese authorities, refused to sign a bond undertaking not to engage in the trade on pain of death, since they affected to regard this as insulting. And when further sources of conflict with the Canton authorities arose, merchants, superintendent and Foreign Secretary equally began to believe that national honour could never be satisfied, nor tolerable treatment by Chinese officialdom be assured, unless by force.

The war that erupted in 1839, and was terminated in 1842 by the treaty of Nanking, is known among Chinese as the First Opium War, the war by which the opium trade was forcibly imposed on China by foreign aggression. To the British it has been known as the first Anglo-Chinese War, the war by which the Chinese Empire was opened up to commercial intercourse on the normal, internationally accepted terms. In fact the war broke out neither over trading facilities, nor over opium; but over the killing of a Chinese subject by drunken British seamen in a brawl, the subsequent Chinese demands for the surrender of a scapegoat, and the various measures of retaliation, culminating in a clash between British and Chinese warships. But without the tensions that had occurred as a result of the other long-standing matters in dispute the incident would never have developed to the point of war, any more than had almost exactly similar events in the past. The British had certainly never originally contemplated going to war to enforce their demands for better conditions of trade and intercourse. Still less had they had any intention of forcibly resisting the Chinese Government's efforts to stop the opium trade. In his instructions to the British negotiators after the war, Lord Palmerston specifically declared that "H.M. Government make no demand in this matter"; and, if the Chinese Government continued to prohibit the importation of opium "British subjects who engaged in a contraband trade must take the consequences of doing so".

The treaty made no reference to opium. Nor did the treaty concluded after the second war, which arose out of a similarly trivial incident in 1856. But it is an inescapable fact that, after the conclusion of the first war, the trade in opium from India to China rose from about 20,000 chests in 1840, to over 60,000 in 1859; that after the second war the trade, under Western pressure, was legalized; and that it was not finally ended until 1917. It was not an episode that did credit to the British nation. And it is one that no Chinese has forgotten to this day.

Yet in a sense there was some truth in the assertion of British apologists that the true cause of the wars was not the opium trade. For more than a century the two countries had come into increasingly acute conflict over a variety of issues. The clash that took place in 1839 over the murdered Chinese seaman was the culmination of this series. And the British Government, at once exacerbated by long years of mounting frustration in their dealings with an Empire they considered effete and corrupt, and exhilarated by the increasing power and glory of their own Empire, consciously or unconsciously made use of the opportunity it provided to enforce their demands for what they considered their rights.

In the war which followed they secured the opening of five ports to European residence and trade; the recognition of British consular officers who were to be assured of access to the Chinese authorities; the establishment of a "fair and regular" tariff of five per cent on both imports and exports; the abolition of the Co-Hong's monopoly of trade; the cession of Hong Kong; extraterritorial jurisdiction in the Treaty Ports; and the explicit recognition in the terms of the Treaty of Britain's equal status with China. After the second war, the British Government secured the opening of further treaty ports, especially in the increasingly important Yangtze area; the acceptance of a British permanent envoy at Peking with right of access to a minister of state; freedom for foreigners to travel and to trade in any part of the interior; and an assurance of protection, free speech and unhampered movement for missionaries. Thus on all the major matters on which, in the hundred years before, conflicts had arisen, on the conditions of residence in China, on the right to trade, on legal procedures, on commercial levies, on equality of status, on diplomatic intercourse—as well as on opium—Britain ensured that, during the hundred years to follow, her will was to prevail.

2

THE CHINESE REJOINDER

As a result of the two wars relations between Britain and China entered a new era. The most powerful kingdom in the West had, for the moment, subdued the greatest empire of the East. The Empire of Heaven was, for the first time, confronted by foreign conquerors who possessed a civilization of their own; who had no wish to transfer their own seat of government within the Chinese state; and who thus could not be, as other conquerors in the past had been, slowly assimilated into the texture of the Empire.

Its immediate reaction was to retreat once again into the shell that the ancient order of Chinese society provided. The policy of the Chinese Government remained in general to have as little to do with foreigners as they could, to isolate them from Chinese affairs, and to hope that the Heavenly Empire might still, as far as possible, be left to go its own way in peace. They had little curiosity about the ways of the West. While the extrovert and impressionable Japanese, under a newly invigorated government, responded with startling swiftness to the challenge which the sudden manifestation of the West on her shores presented, it took half a century for the self-absorbed and supremely self-confident Chinese to make any serious effort to adjust themselves to the new situation.

In Britain the increasing contacts brought a growing knowledge of China and its civilization, and, with knowledge, a mounting respect. From the days of Marco Polo and beyond, the East had possessed an intense fascination for Europeans. Already in 1686, when British contacts were barely beginning, Robert Hooke had declared to the Royal Society that a better knowledge of China's civilization would "lay open to us an Empire of learning, hitherto only fabulously described". In the eighteenth century the vogue for *chinoiserie* which the first imports of Chinese porcelain, enamelware, and other curiosities had inspired, in Britain as in other European countries, brought with it a good deal of curiosity about the distant civilization of the East. The first books purporting to give an account of Chinese society, political structure and thought, began to appear in that century. By 1850 something like twenty serious and scholarly studies of the institutions and history of the Chinese Empire, many more treating of British dealings with China, besides innumerable travel books and personal memoirs, had appeared. Already in the 1830s there were three English-language journals produced by the merchant and missionary community at Canton, containing, *inter alia*, voluminous articles on Chinese history, literature and travel. In the 1850s the first English newspaper, the *North China Herald* was produced. And in 1857 *The Times* appointed its first correspondent in China.

The British Government too was now prepared to be more generous to the defeated Empire. They had been able, through their victories, to sweep away most of those aspects of Chinese administration and attitudes that had aroused their hostility in the past. The trade with China played an increasingly important part in British commerce. The British Government was only too pleased to send officials to assist the Chinese Government in some of their administrative departments. The increasing number of merchants and officials having contacts with China brought back colourful reports, and often a deep and enduring admiration, of the refined manners and elegant culture of the ancient civilization. The British attitude now became one of benevolent, if sometimes patronizing, goodwill.

The ordinary Chinese, on the other hand, showed little desire for knowledge of, or intercourse with, the foreigners they found amongst them. The ethnocentric standpoint of even educated Chinese was only slowly modified. Only in the 1840s did there appear a Chinese book which gave a sketchy, highly coloured and largely mythical account of some of the West European countries. The Chinese made little attempt to master European languages: in official dealings it was nearly always the Western nations that provided the interpreter. Virtually no Chinese travelled to the West until the last decades of the century. It was not until 1861, at British insistence, that a special Yamen was set up within the Grand Council to be responsible for relations with foreign powers. The first foreign ambassador was sent abroad only just before 1880. And a separate Foreign Ministry was established, again only at the insistence of the Western Powers, in 1901.

There did arise, both among officials and people, a feeling of impatient resentment against the intruders. And among the misty images of the Western peoples that began slowly to form themselves in Chinese minds, that of the British was inevitably among the least attractive. A placard posted by the villagers of San Yuan Li, in Kwangtung, soon after the war of 1839–42, noted that the English barbarians had "formed the habits and developed the nature of wolves, plundering and seizing things by force", and declared that the people of the village would certainly "kill them, cut off their heads, and burn them to death". The Chinese writer of a textbook of Western geography declared that "As to commerce at Canton, the British barbarians are the most fierce and arrogant". And a memorial to the Chinese Emperor in 1861 asserted that "As regards England ... she acts violently and without any regard for human decency".

Only very gradually did the Chinese come to be more receptive to European thought and ways. In 1863 Li Hung-cheng, pointing to the fact that many foreigners learned the Chinese written and spoken language, and even read their classics and history, demanded that Chinese should seek to master the languages of the Westerners so that "all their clever techniques of steamships and fire-arms could be gradually and thoroughly learned". China's first Minister in London, on his arrival in 1877, wrote that England's rise to power had taken place in the course of only a few decades as a result of the adoption of modern techniques. If China wished to become as powerful as the Western nations, the first thing was to "make the Chinese thoroughly familiar with their methods". After the war of 1856–60 the Chinese Government asked the British to build a fleet of gunboats for them. They appointed an Englishman to administer their customs service. The growing number of Westerners coming to China made even the ordinary Chinese man in the street, if not the man in the fields, gradually more aware of the existence of Western nations. Some of the missionaries began to teach the English language. And they translated and disseminated not only religious works, but many other books on scientific, historical and political subjects. By the 90s Chinese translations of Adam Smith, J. S. Mill, Huxley and Spencer could be read by any Chinese who was interested.

The British Government's interest in China had from the start been exclusively for the advantage of British commerce. China was too weak to affect the European balance of power. She was too remote to be of strategic importance. Britain had no territorial aspirations there. All she asked was to be able to trade.

Nor did she demand any preferential treatment. Already in 1841 the British Government, in formulating the terms that the British Superintendent was to demand of the Chinese authorities at the conclusion of the first war, had declared that the British Government "seek for no exclusive advantages and demand nothing that we shall not willingly see enjoyed by the Subjects of all other States". This remained a basic principle of British policy in China. Being first in the field, the British were able in their treaties to secure the conditions they demanded. And it was a matter of indifference to them if similar rights were subsequently obtained by other Western Powers interested in trade with China.

Britain had from the start, because of her dominant position as a commercial power, and because of the importance of the commerce between India and China, possessed the lion's share of the Chinese market. During the second half of the nineteenth century the composition of the trade began to alter. As the world's leading industrial power, Britain sent an increasing volume of manufactured goods to China. By the 1880s cotton piece goods had replaced opium and raw cotton as the principal British export. And when, with the rise of the Indian tea plantations, the tea trade from China began to decline, new Chinese exports such as soya beans, vegetable oil, hides, pig bristles and egg products began to be developed. At the end of the nineteenth century, British trade with China was still worth considerably more than that of all other nations put together.

Thus the Chinese official who wrote of Britain, in a memorial to the Emperor in 1863, that "her purpose was to trade", and that she did not "covet our territory and people" had judged correctly. And when, during the second half of the nineteenth century, the Russians in the north, the Japanese in the east, and the French in the south, each began to make encroachments on Chinese imperial territory, Britain was genuinely concerned about the threat to Chinese sovereignty. Having secured her own purely commercial interests, as well as a base to protect them at Hong Kong, she had no wish to see China become the victim of a general smash-and-grab raid at the hands of the other powers. She was quite content to see the *status quo* maintained. Remaining aloof from the European alliances and holding the balance of power between them, her object was to prevent any other European nation from becoming more powerful at her expense. Thus when Disraeli had magnanimously declared that "In Asia, there is room for us all", there was, possibly, a whispered afterthought, "provided, of course, no one has more room than we do."

When, therefore, after the Japanese defeat of China in 1895, the Russians, the French and the Germans, began to make use of the situation to improve their own position in China, Britain's first efforts were to resist any moves for further European encroachment. She began to adopt an attitude of maternal protectiveness towards the dying Empire. She considerately warned the Chinese Government that the Russian demand for a lease of Port Arthur represented a "standing menace to Peking". In March 1898 the House of Commons passed a resolution declaring "that it is of vital importance for British commerce and influence, that the independence of Chinese territory be maintained". And in the same month the British Ambassador in Washington was instructed to ask the United States Government whether Britain "could count on the co-operation of the United States in opposing action by foreign powers which may tend to restrict the freedom of commerce of all nations in China, either by imposing preferential conditions or by obtaining actual cession of coastal territory".

Britain had good commercial grounds for her reluctance to see China becoming the object of a general spoiling-party such as had just occurred in Africa. For, if large areas of China were to come under the dominance of European powers, these would certainly make use of their authority to grant a privileged position to the commercial enterprises of their own nationals. Britain could maintain her own position without any such artificial protection. And her interests seemed most likely to be served if Chinese sovereignty could be preserved unimpaired. From the start, and long before Mr. Hay conceived the phrase, Britain's policy was that of the Open Door.

Only after Germany had occupied Kiaochow in November 1897, after France had demanded Kwangchouwan in March of the next year, and above all, after Russia had extorted Port Arthur in the same month, did Britain feel obliged to try to keep up with her neighbours. She too asked for a lease of Weihaiwei, for so long as Russia remained in Port Arthur; even then, to demonstrate that Britain's interest was outside rather than inside China, Britain agreed not to build a railway to the leased port. Later she obtained a lease of the New Territories opposite Hong Kong. But the basic British objective remained unchanged. In 1900, therefore, immediately after the Boxer rising, the British Government concluded an agreement with Germany that neither power should "make use of the present complications to obtain for themselves any territorial advantages in Chinese dominions".

But the effect of these successive snatches of Chinese territory was to fan a growing flame of Chinese national sentiment. Already during the second half of the nineteenth century a few officials and others had begun to realize the nature of the challenge which the European penetration of their land represented, and to suggest that China might well need to learn something from the West in order to repel it. In 1862 Tseng Kuo-fan proposed, "We should carefully watch and learn their superior techniques and also learn their shortcomings." There was a movement of "self-strengthening" to ensure that China should be in a position to deal with the foreigners on more equal terms. Some halting efforts were made to improve the equipment and organization of the armed forces. From about 1880 the first railway construction was begun. A few industrial establishments were set up.

After the series of annexations which took place between 1895 and 1900 national aspirations began to take a more coherent form. The two writers K'ang Yu-wei and Chang Chih-tung demanded a movement of reform to save the tottering Empire. Their writings served to inspire a sudden but short-lived attempt to remould the institutions of the Empire on Western lines in 1898. Even the uneducated Chinese began to be increasingly conscious of the humiliations to which their country was being subjected. And at the turn of the century this incoherent sentiment of resentment against the foreigner, both in the villages and at the court, found expression in the bloody violence of the Boxer disturbances.

Thus Britain's amiable, if not entirely disinterested, support of Chinese territorial integrity evoked little answering warmth from the Chinese side. For long Britain remained the most powerful, and therefore the most terrible, of the imperialists. When, after the Japanese victory in 1895, China began to look about for allies against these new enemies, Chang Chih-tung, in a memorial to the Emperor, complained that England "used commerce to absorb the wealth of China". There were equally cogent reasons against alignment with most other powers. France "used religion to entice the Chinese people"; Germany had "no common territorial boundary with us"; and the United States "does not like to interfere in the military affairs of others". He therefore recommended Russia as the most suitable ally. And whether or not on this advice the Chinese Government did at this time begin to turn to Russia as the most useful support against Japanese and other foreign encroachments.

But to Britain Russia remained the supreme menace all over the East. Russian activities in the area were regarded by the British Foreign Office, from Palmerston's day on, with an almost paranoid suspicion. For long Britain's policy in China was aimed, as in Turkey, at bolstering the ailing régime against this dangerous antagonist. She took other steps. She secured consular posts in the wilds of Chinese Turkestan, to watch over the approaches to India. She secured a naval base at Weihaiwei to offset the Russian ports at Vladivostok and Dairen. She undertook an adventure in Tibet to counter Russian influence there.

Thus when, after the Boxer rebellion, Russia appeared about to obtain for herself a still more dominant position in Chinese affairs, the British felt the need to counter this development in some more effective way. In these considerations the need to retain the goodwill of the tottering régime in China seemed of only small importance. Yet by deciding in 1902 to enter into alliance with Japan, Britain was in Chinese eyes, siding with China's principal enemy. And by specifically recognizing in the treaty the right of Japan to take what measures she saw fit to "safeguard her interests in Korea", Britain seemed to the Chinese to be shamelessly encouraging Japan in her pretensions in that area. To the British the alliance was directed to helping Britain against Russia. To China it was designed to aid Japan against herself.

British public opinion, as virulently Russophobe as the Government, acclaimed the pact. They rejoiced still more when, in 1905, their new partners demonstrated their effectiveness by defeating the arch-enemy in resounding fashion. They congratulated themselves on their prescience in allying themselves with the most vigorous and dynamic power in Asia. That Japan obtained by her victory a position in Manchuria as dominant as that formerly held by Russia for the moment worried nobody. While what the people or government of the moribund Empire of China felt about matters seemed of even less significance.

Only when, not long after her victory, Japan acquired control of Korea; began a programme of vigorous development in Manchuria; agreed with Russia on a division of spheres of influence in East Asia; and, finally, during the First World War, presented China with the "Twenty-One Demands" that would have secured permanent Japanese authority over many fields of Chinese internal affairs—only then did the British Government and people begin slowly to suspect that what they had done was to ally themselves with the most dangerous power in Asia against the weakest. The alliance was in fact in basic contradiction with what had always been a prime ambition of British policy in the Far East, to maintain the independence and territorial integrity of China. For the alliance only served to strengthen Japan in her expansionist ambitions. And Britain found herself regarded in China as aiding and abetting in the violation of that Chinese sovereignty, which she had always declared herself determined to uphold.

For the time these considerations brought no change of policy. Britain agreed, as a result of the exigencies of the war, to support Japanese claims to inherit German rights in Shantung. And at the Versailles Peace Treaty, she paid no more heed than any of the other European delegates to the ineffectual efforts of the Chinese delegation to dispute this casual transfer of a substantial helping of the Chinese heartland.

But the provisions of the Treaty created a mood of bitter disillusion in China. A petition, addressed to Britain, declared "that everyone had believed that the design of the League of Nations and the public denunciation by Western statesmen of all the treaties made since 1914, meant the end of power politics, and the termination of secret trafficking among the strong at the expense of the weak: for the nation to be told now that expediency requires China to be sacrificed is to do it mortal hurt, which no blandishments can disguise". And it was this sense of betrayal by the other powers at Versailles that did more than any other single incident to inflame the growing wave of national sentiment in China that was to transform, and eventually destroy, Britain's position in that country.

Growing doubts about the wisdom of the Japanese alliance, the opposition expressed to it in the United States and Canada, and a few twinges of conscience about the way China had been treated, did eventually produce a change in British policy. At the time of the Washington Conference in 1922, Britain let it be known that the Japanese alliance would not be renewed. She even lent her influence to inducing Japan to quit Shantung. Under the Treaties then signed, all special spheres of influence were renounced. The principles of the Open Door, of equality of commercial opportunity, and the safeguarding of Chinese sovereignty and territorial integrity were for the first time explicity recognized by the principal powers involved. And some attempt at securing a balance of power was made in the provision for limitations of naval forces in the Pacific.

The Treaties thus represented a reversion to the publicly declared aims of British policy towards China. During the next decade Britain became in fact the foremost advocate among the Western Powers of a more accommodating attitude towards the national aspirations of China. Already soon after the war Russia, as a result of the revolution, and Germany, as a result of the peace treaty, had given up their special rights and privileges in China. On December 18, 1926, when the Nationalist armies had barely reached the Yangtze in their victorious march to the north, Britain addressed a memorandum to all the other Washington Treaty Powers which, noting the growth in China of a powerful nationalist movement, declared that "any failure to meet this movement with sympathy and understanding would not correspond with the real intentions of the powers towards China". The Western Powers should "abandon the idea that the economic and political development of China could only be secured under foreign tutelage, and should declare their readiness to recognize her right to the enjoyment of tariff autonomy". They should expressly "disclaim any intention of forcing foreign control upon an unwilling China" and should "recognize the essential justification of the Chinese claim for Treaty revision".

Britain was the first of any of the Western Powers to enter into diplomatic negotiations with the new Nationalist movement. She agreed with a good grace to relinquish her concession at Hankow, even before the Nationalist Government was established. Between 1927 and 1930 while the Nationalists were still in the process of conquering China, she gave up other settlements at Kiukiang, Chinkiang and Amoy, as well as the naval station at Weihaiwei.

THE CHINESE REJOINDER

In 1928, the British Government in common with the other Western Powers agreed to the restoration of tariff autonomy to China. In 1931, the Chinese salt administration was returned to Chinese hands. In the same year a British naval mission was sent to China to train and rearm the naval forces of the Nanking Government. Britain even tentatively agreed in 1931 to the abolition of extra-territoriality if other powers would do the same; though as a result of the sudden looming of the Manchurian crisis, this never came to anything. Gradually the British Government and public opinion became increasingly conscience-stricken about their retention of a privileged status in China.

To concede some of the aspirations of Chinese nationalism was one thing. To espouse Chinese causes in the international field was quite another. China was too feeble to be considered seriously as an ally. And though the Japanese alliance had been abandoned in the letter, many in Britain remained faithful to it in spirit. For Japan was still the only nation in the area that could be a reliable support in case of differences with a European power.

When the Japanese began their seizure of Manchuria in 1931, British opinion only gradually became alive to the true facts of the situation. In the East, as in Europe, the British public was unwilling to face the possibility that it might only be possible to contain force with force. "Conciliation" and "arbitration" were the universal panaceas. Few considered what should be done if one of the parties refused to be conciliated. The British people continued to convince themselves that the force of public opinion was such that Japan would never be able to hold on to any territory acquired by aggressive means. The British press continued to be sure that somehow everything would come out all right in the end. The British Government continued to propose resolutions in the League, to make declarations of non-recognition, to support the despatch of Commissions of Inquiry. But further than this neither Government, press nor public were prepared to exert themselves.

The Chinese were quick to note that the British seemed to react considerably more sharply to the Japanese encroachments in Shanghai in 1932 than to the initial thrust in Manchuria. British public statements seemed to express more concern over Japanese readiness to maintain the Open Door in Manchuria than for any effective action to discountenance Japanese aggression there. No Chinese could fail to observe the difference between the resolutely pro-Chinese line of the United States Government and the rigidly non-committal attitude of the British—though the difference was perhaps more noticeable in words than in deeds. It was scarcely surprising that Mr. Matsuoka, the Japanese representative at the League of Nations, after a speech by Sir John Simon, should declare that Sir John had said in half an hour what he had been trying to say for the last ten days. And once again, as forty years before, when Japanese pressure became more intense, it was to Russia, despite the huge ideological gulf that divided the two Governments, that China turned in 1937 for a Treaty of Alliance and a limited measure of military assistance.

All such diplomatic divergences only reflected a more fundamental conflict. In some ways certainly the gulf dividing the two peoples had narrowed. The perpetually increasing flow of British missionaries and travellers sent home an ever-widening knowledge of China to Britain. British scholars occupied an important position among the ranks of the able and devoted foreigners who did so much to open up many aspects of Chinese thought and civilization, not only to their own peoples, but to the Chinese themselves. Even the old China hands, the British business men in the settlements, though they rarely learned the Chinese language and spent most of their leisure time exclusively in the company of fellow-Europeans, over and again fell under the spell of the country, becoming often enthusiastic advocates of Chinese causes.

And the Chinese for the first time began to acquire some knowledge of Britain. The mission schools and universities turned out an increasing number of young people who read English fluently and had some acquaintance with English writing and philosophy. After the First World War though Chinese opinion was in many ways more nationalist and anti-Western than ever, there was a sudden surge of interest in Western literature and thought. Many young people travelled to the West to study. If Britain and China were almost as far apart as ever diplomatically, intellectually they were growing closer.

Closer contacts could not in themselves bridge the political divisions. There was still a huge gap between the halting movement of opinion in Britain and the aspirations of the Chinese. No amount of declarations of friendship could unmake the fact that Britain remained the leading imperialist power; and so a leading target for the rising nationalist sentiment. Already at the time of the 1911 revolution, Britain's apparent sympathy towards Yuan Shih-kai, the Imperial pretender, had aroused the resentment of Chinese liberals. And when, from about 1920 onwards, the Nationalist movement began to form itself around Sun Yat-sen at Canton, Britain vied with Japan as the principal enemy. She had still by far the largest share in foreign trade and investment in China. She possessed the most extensive privileges in the way of settlements and concessions in the treaty ports, and played a dominating role in the exercise of extra-territorial rights. Her nationals were not always among the most respectful in their dealings with Chinese citizens. In 1925, a shooting incident in Shanghai led to a nation-wide anti-British boycott. On various occasions between 1923 and 1927 British naval forces were used in Chinese waters to give protection to British subjects. And the Chinese could legitimately claim that, though a few rights and privileges were abandoned from 1926 onwards, the vast majority were preserved unchanged, apparently unaffected by the advent of a modern and tolerably efficient Government in China.

The national sentiments of the ordinary Chinese increasingly found their focus in the Nationalist Party and Government. For the moment that Government, distracted first by its struggle against the Communists, later by the increasing threat of Japan, was not in a position to make its demands effective. And Britain, though not entirely unsympathetic to its claims, was no more inclined than the other Western Powers to concede all that was asked of her before she was obliged to. But in the long run she was to find, inevitably, that it was no more possible in China than it was to be in any other part of the world to halt the tide of national sentiment then beginning everywhere to flood.

3

BRITAIN AND THE KUOMINTANG

THE position that Britain held in the Far East at the beginning of the Sino-Japanese war was, at first sight, little different from that which she had enjoyed at the beginning of the century. She remained the leading Western commercial power in the area. She still held her naval and commercial base at Hong Kong. She maintained a fleet in Far Eastern waters to protect her interests in the region. She retained, in common with other Western countries, most of the special privileges, leases and concessions that she had enjoyed before. And, as thirty years earlier, she continued, for so long as she decently could, to conciliate Japan, despite her aggressive behaviour, partly with the aim of safeguarding British commercial interests in the region at all costs, and partly through a lingering desire to remain on good terms with the most powerful nation in the Far East.

But such similarities masked a fundamental transformation of the true situation. At the beginning of the century British naval strength, together with the land forces that could be called on in an emergency, had been sufficient to enable Britain to assert her power in the area against all the opposition that she was likely to meet. By the thirties, British naval power had ceased to be a significant factor in the balance of forces in the region. And as the Far Eastern nations, and especially Japan, began to build up modern military forces, comparable in effectiveness to those of the West, naval strength became in any case increasingly less significant in relation to land power. By continuing to rely on naval forces at Hong Kong and on the newly constructed base at Singapore to maintain her interests in the Far East, Britain was devoting her efforts to a form of defence that in the event proved totally ineffective against the type of challenge which she was called on to face; and one which merely served to present the victorious forces with the gift of highly costly and elaborately prepared naval installations at the outset of the conflict.

The effect of this relative diminution of British power was decisive. At the beginning of the century Britain had been able, by

BRITAIN AND THE KUOMINTANG

the deployment of the appropriate forces at the proper moment, to maintain her position effectively in many parts of the world at the same time. But by the end of the thirties the unhappy fact was that she was no longer in a position to fight a war both in Europe and in the Far East at once. It was the growing, but still only half thought out, realization of this fact that accounted for many of the hesitations and ambiguities of British policy in the Far East at this period.

British apprehensions over Japanese pretensions had been momentarily awakened by the attack on Shanghai in 1932. They were revived by the so-called Amau declaration in April, 1934, in which China was, in effect, claimed as an exclusively Japanese sphere of interest. In December, 1934, Japan denounced the Washington Treaties. In 1935 her forces began to move forward into North China. There were a number of incidents affecting British interests. Shanghai, Nanking and Canton were bombarded. British ships were attacked. There was increasing favouritism towards Japanese commercial interests in Manchuria and other Japanese controlled territory. British opinion began to be increasingly unsympathetic to Japanese activities.

Yet British policy remained in general strikingly favourable to Japanese aspirations. In some of her actions, certainly, Britain appeared to wish to maintain her traditional policy of safeguarding the independence and territorial integrity of China. She made various efforts to help the Chinese economy, in particular to stabilize the Chinese currency. In 1935, despite Japanese hostility, an economic mission was sent to China to discuss various economic problems with the Chinese Government and to give advice on financial matters. After the opening of the Sino-Japanese war, Britain agreed to participate in the joint construction of a Burma-Yunnan highway, and a project to connect Kunming with Rangoon by rail. She agreed to use the Boxer indemnity funds for the purchase of railway and telegraphic equipment in Britain. She gave five million pounds to help establish a currency stabilization fund. She provided various export credit loans. And in March, 1939, she guaranteed a loan of a further five million pounds to be made by British Far Eastern banks towards an exchange equalization fund for stabilizing the Chinese currency. Practically all these schemes were, directly or indirectly, of advantage to British commercial interests. But they might, in other circumstances, have been taken to show some measure of British political support for the Chinese Government.

Yet any value which such gestures might have had in this direction was completely nullified by the far more obvious efforts of the British Government to conciliate Japan. In March, 1935, the British Government dropped proposals it had been mooting for international efforts to provide financial assistance to China as a result, apparently, of Japanese opposition. The successive Japanese encroachments in North China in 1931, 1933 and 1935 met with no effective British remonstrance. And when Japan finally attacked in earnest in 1937, though British sympathies were at last overwhelmingly with the Chinese, the British Government barely even went through the motions of protest. A meeting of the signatories of the Nine-Power Treaty of Washington met at Brussels in October, 1937, and unanimously passed a resolution requesting members to "refrain from taking any action which might have the effect of weakening China's powers of resistance", and to "consider how far they can individually extend aid to China". This resolution was subsequently adopted by the Assembly of the League. It was as negligible in its effect as most of the other resolutions adopted by that body. In fact by this time the attention of the British Government was almost totally engaged in the affairs of Europe. They had neither the means nor the inclination to undertake any effective intervention in the Far East. The East was to be left to fight their own battles while the West made ready to engage in theirs.

Japanese aggression did not deter British efforts to conciliate Japan. Nor did Japanese association with Germany in the Anti-Comintern Pact. During 1937 negotiations took place in London to bring about closer Anglo-Japanese understanding. In 1938, a prolonged series of discussions took place between the British Ambassador in Japan and the Japanese Government, mainly on the protection of British interests in Japanese-held areas. They were regarded with great hostility by Chinese public opinion, since it was assumed that they would involve recognition of the Japanese position in Manchuria and North China. In 1938 an agreement was reached with Japan over the servicing of the foreign loans secured on the Chinese customs revenues which appeared to recognize Japanese standing as the customs authority in Chinese coastal ports. In July of that year the British Government declined to grant a direct loan to the Chinese Government on the grounds that China was then "engaged in hostilities". Important British firms with interests in North China, showed themselves quite ready to cooperate with the Japanese authorities there. Nearly all British businessmen in Shanghai attempted to carry on their business, as before, after the Japanese captured the city. To most Chinese it appeared that the gradual swallowing-up of China by Japan was a matter of indifference to most in Britain, provided only that British commercial interests were not affected.

In their public statements the British Government took up an attitude of studious impartiality towards the Far Eastern conflict. On June 27, 1938, the British Government made an offer of mediation between the two parties, without the least suggestion that one side might be more responsible than the other for the outbreak of the war. Mr. Chamberlain, on November 1, 1938, shortly after the conclusion of the Munich Agreement, declared in the House of Commons that he did not believe that, when the Sino-Japanese war was concluded, the new capital to develop China could be supplied by Japan alone; China could not be reconstructed without some help from Britain. This not unnaturally gave the impression that the British Government looked forward with equanimity to the prospect of a Japanese victory so long as an open field for British economic interests in China remained assured. And the protests that the statement aroused, especially from British commercial circles in China, were not made out of any concern at the off-hand way in which the Prime Minister seemed to write off Chinese hopes of victory, but at his innocent delusion that, in a Japanese-controlled China, there could be any real opportunities for British trading interests.

Two days later, on November 3, 1938, Japan announced the establishment of a "new order in Asia", including a tripartite, and apparently exclusive "relationship of mutual aid and co-ordination between Japan, Manchukuo and China". For the first time this roused the British Government to take a rather firmer attitude. Even now British misgivings were at first directed to the apparent menace this declaration represented to British interests, not to any violation of Chinese sovereignty (and so of the Washington Treaties) that was implicit in it. And it was only in January, 1939, after two more somewhat similar Japanese statements, that the British Government began ineffectually to invoke the Nine-Power Treaty, to which both countries were parties, to protest against

Japan's encroachments on Chinese territory. In a Note to the Japanese Government, they questioned the Japanese Government's declared intention "to compel the Chinese people by the force of arms to accept conditions involving the surrender of their political, economic and cultural life to Japanese control"; and asserted that the British Government were "not prepared to accept or to recognize these activities". Such "non-recognition" was the fashionable prescription for the international maladies of the time. By it any Government could absolve its conscience of the responsibility for the ills of others without undergoing the tedious necessity of providing any more effective remedy. And it is perhaps doubtful if the British Government possessed any more faith in its likely efficacy than had the Japanese themselves.

During the course of the next six months a series of incidents in Japanese-occupied China, at Kulangsu, at Shanghai, at Swatow, culminating finally in the blockade of the British concession at Tientsin, brought an intensification of tension between Britain and Japan. The opening of discussions between Britain and Russia from May onwards could have led to a strengthening of the position of both powers in the disputes each were then having with Japan. But when, in July, the danger of a European war became increasingly acute the British Government once again drew in its horns. Conversations were opened between the British Ambassador in Tokyo and the Japanese Government on the Tientsin incident. This led finally to the issue of a statement in which the British Government not only conceded most of the Japanese claims in that particular matter, but recognized the special requirements of Japanese forces in China and their right to "suppress or remove any such acts or causes as will obstruct them or benefit their enemy"; and declared that H.M.G. "had no intention of countenancing any acts or measures prejudicial to the attainment" of these objectives.

It is not surprising that Britain's equivocal attitude towards the struggle between China and Japan from 1931 onwards did not make a good impression in China. Chinese could scarcely fail to observe the radical difference between Britain's rapid reaction to any Japanese move that seemed likely to affect British interests, and her apparent indifference to flagrant violations of Chinese territory. And, almost entirely taken up with their own struggle, they could not be expected to be understanding of Britain's European preoccupations which later gave some pretext, if not justification, for

BRITAIN AND THE KUOMINTANG 47

this policy. Only gradually, as the menace that Japanese aggression represented to both became more intense, did the two countries begin to draw together a little. British public opinion became increasingly sympathetic to China, even while the Government continued to pursue a policy of appeasement towards Japan. And in China, Japan's efforts to arouse pan-Asian sentiment against the West probably only served to inspire among many Chinese a rising hope that eventually Western and Chinese interests would increasingly coincide.

British policy towards China during this period was in fact a mass of inconsistencies. On the one hand Britain continued to pay lip-service to the traditional aim of maintaining Chinese independence, territorial integrity and the Open Door. Yet on the other, by her abject conciliation of Japan, she helped to make the attainment of this end impossible. No longer able herself to play any effective military role, she had more than ever to gain by securing a balance of power in the area. Yet, by refusing to make common cause with China and other powers having a common interest against Japanese expansion, she only made it easier for Japan to secure pre-eminence.

There was in fact no deliberate or consistent policy at all. As so often the policy of the British Government was "empirical": that is, it consisted of belated and half-hearted reactions to the moves of others. Preoccupied with European affairs, British statesmen were disinclined to think out any firm or coherent course of action in the Far East for fear of becoming unnecessarily entangled. They hoped that they could stave off difficulties by so far as possible standing clear of all the squabbles of the area, and from time to time issuing a few ineffectual protests over any matter in which British commercial interests appeared affected. Concern for Chinese sovereignty, however sincere, did not extend so far as to make anybody consider taking action to defend it. Many in Britain were prepared to give China their sympathy; but no more.

Britain's actions indeed only reflected the general mood of the time. It was a period when many statesmen were prepared to mouth the words collective security, but none to give them meaning. All were ready to condemn aggression, but none to prevent it. Britain's attitude to the conflict in China was little different from the mood of detachment with which all the nations of Europe demurely contemplated the successive annexations of Abyssinia, Austria, Czechoslovakia, Albania and Finland; or the attitude of polite indifference with which three-quarters of the countries of Europe looked on for nearly nine months while the three major powers of the area became engaged in a conflict that must inevitably determine the future of the continent. It was only when these conflicts had become worldwide that the sense of identification with all victims of aggression, in whatever part of the world, became widespread.

The profound laceration left in the minds of all, in Britain as elsewhere, by the grotesque nightmare of the First World War, made many ready to clutch at any expedients, in the Far East as in Europe, by which such horrors could for the moment be held at arm's length. At the same time the mood of helpless fatalism was such that the idea that disaster in either area might be averted by some effective move to face it—for example by resolutely concerted action with the Soviet Union or other powers—was barely seriously considered. And even when this was half-heartedly attempted in the summer of 1939, suspicion was such as to bring the discussions to nothing.

This failure forced Britain and Russia equally to seek accommodations. Both were primarily concerned with the danger in Europe. And both equally were determined not to have to fight in Europe and the Pacific at the same time. Thus, while the Soviet Union, at the time engaged in battle with Japan in the heart of Asia, succeeded in reaching a temporary understanding with Germany, Britain finally at grips with that country, continued to seek to conciliate Japan. And when Britain at length found herself engaged in both areas at once, with disastrous results, the Soviet Union, now herself locked in struggle with Germany, continued to achieve her objective by a treaty of friendship with Japan. Europe, like China herself, was obliged to sell space to buy time. But the space which Europe sold was China's.

After the opening of the war in Europe the British Government and people began at last to look on China, engaged like themselves in a struggle against the forces of aggression, with some sentiment of fellow-feeling. Britain's relations with Japan remained correct but cool. For a time, in the summer of 1940, when Britain's position in Europe became critical, she was once again obliged to make concessions to pacify Japan. An agreement was reached with the Japanese Government to close for three months the Burma Road along which China was receiving supplies from the West. This was "to give China and Japan a chance to settle their differences"; once again a curiously impartial form of words. At the end of the three months, however, although Britain's position in Europe was little better than before, Mr. Churchill was able to announce that the road would be reopened. And the gesture evoked a corresponding appreciation in China.

When, in December, 1941, Japan went to war on Britain, the two countries were finally brought into alliance. Two days later, China declared war on Germany and Italy. Britain's war and China's were merged.

Participation in a common alliance might, if circumstances had been more favourable, have served to transform completely the unsatisfactory relationship that had persisted between the two countries over the previous decade. And a very great improvement in relations did in fact take place. But the improvement was only relative and partial. Because of the preoccupation of each with its own struggle for survival and the tenuousness of the physical contacts that survived, it was inevitable that the interests of neither power loomed large in the considerations of the other. The diminution of scale that distance creates continued to devalue in the eyes of each the importance of the other, both to the common struggle in which they were engaged and to the world scene as a whole. Nor could the basic prejudices and conflicts of earlier years be instantaneously erased even when, later, the formal basis of that relationship was altered.

Britain began to do what she could within the narrow limits which her own position prescribed to give the Chinese some assistance in their struggle. Already in December, 1940, after the conclusion of the Triple Alliance between Germany, Italy and Japan, and again in April, 1941, the British Government had made grants of ten million pounds for a stabilization fund to support the Chinese currency. In February, 1942, two weeks after Pearl Harbour, it was announced that the British Government had decided to make available to China, on lease-lend terms, all the munitions and military equipment that it would be possible to supply, and to make a loan to China of fifty million pounds on terms to be agreed between the two governments.

A certain amount of military assistance was provided. In December, 1941, General Wavell paid a visit to Chungking to discuss with General Chiang Kai-shek and Major General Brett, United States Army Air Corps Chief of Staff, questions of overall strategy in the Far East. During most of 1942 Britain was too preoccupied with her own difficulties in the Far East to be able to give much help to China. But from 1943 a certain amount of arms, munitions and equipment were sent to China from India so far as the available transport facilities permitted. Several hundred Chinese pilots were trained in India and Britain. Chinese troops in India and Burma were supplied with British equipment, rations and currency on lease-lend terms. Shipping facilities for arms finally destined for China were provided. But for the most part the British Government left the direct supply of equipment to China to the U.S. Government.

A gift of far more importance in Chinese eyes was the relinquishment by Britain, under the agreement of January, 1943, of all her special privileges in China. Already three or four times since 1939 the British Government had reaffirmed their willingness to undertake negotiations for the abrogation of extra-territorial rights and privileges in China. On October 9, 1942, it was announced that, "to emphasize friendship and solidarity with China", it had been decided to carry out these undertakings at once.

The rights that were still enjoyed by the Treaty Powers were extensive. The nationals and firms of those powers were exempt from jurisdiction by Chinese courts in criminal cases, being subject instead to consular courts which also heard some civil suits. Their houses, ships and other property could not be entered or searched by the Chinese police or other authorities. Even their Chinese servants could not be arrested without the consent of the foreign consular authority. Some of the Treaty Powers had the right to station substantial military guards at their legations in Peking, or to send warships along the Chinese coast and up the Yangtze. In some cities the foreigners enjoyed concessions; that is, substantial areas leased in perpetuity for occupation by foreign nationals. In others there were settlements: that is, areas where foreigners could lease and acquire land, ruled by a foreign-controlled municipal council—in effect little independent republics within the Chinese state.

Under the Treaty, Britain, acting in common with the United States, gave up all these special rights in China. She surrendered her concessions in Tientsin and Canton. She gave up her part in the Shanghai and Amoy international settlements. The Chinese Government undertook to assume and to discharge all official obligations connected with the settlements. At the same time the opportunity was taken to confirm the rights that foreign subjects could expect to enjoy in China and to reaffirm their title to existing property there. Nearly all the other Western Powers soon entered into similar agreements, abandoning the privileges they had acquired under earlier treaties.

So were brought to an end the "unequal treaties" that had been the cause of such resentment against Britain in China in the past. They had long become an anachronism. At the time when they had been entered into they had been not without parallel in other parts of the world where European settler populations were brought into contact with legal systems and administrative methods which seemed to them strange, and therefore barbarous—just as in the Middle Ages English kings had given foreign trading communities, such as the merchants of the Hansa factory in London, the right to try their own nationals in their own courts according to their own laws. A somewhat similar combination of commercial concessions and extra-territorial rights had been established in Egypt and Turkey. Once acquired such rights were only with reluctance relinquished by settler populations, who invariably regarded them as essential safeguards of justice and order.

So though, theoretically, the British Government had since the early years of the century been prepared to abandon the privileges acquired in China as soon as they were satisfied that the Chinese administration was capable of affording their nationals proper protection, in practice, so long as the Chinese Government were not sufficiently powerful to enforce their will, nothing was done. And only the impact of the war, with the upsurge of sympathy with China that it brought—and, incidentally, the temporary abeyance of settler interests in the country—at last jolted the British and U.S. governments into taking the final plunge.

In fact, for many years before this, any justification there once had been for the treaty rights had probably ceased to be valid. A modern Western-style legal system had been introduced by the Nationalist Government, and it is perhaps doubtful if at any time Chinese courts had been more predisposed in favour of Chinese nationals than the consular courts, with mainly European juries, had been in favour of Europeans. While there is no doubt that the administration in the settlements was often more efficient than in other parts of the cities where they were placed, conditions in such areas had for long not been worse than in many other parts of the East where Europeans lived without special safeguards. And the naval and military rights of the Western Powers, though claimed for reasons of protection, usually served in a crisis rather to inflame hostility than to subdue it.

Perhaps more important, the maintenance of these rights, which to nearly all Chinese appeared as a humiliating degradation, served in the long run only to increase Chinese resentment against the Western Powers. Even in the West, the prevailing sentiment about such imposed conditions, matters of commonplace a hundred years earlier, was now transformed. They had begun to arouse twinges of conscience among the Treaty Powers themselves. And to world opinion as a whole they were less and less defensible. Thus even regarded solely from the point of view of national self-interest, the Treaty rights had become by 1941 more of a liability, by the odium they evoked, than an asset for the protection they provided.

For a time there occurred a brief honeymoon period in the relations between the two countries. In Britain an intense feeling of sympathy towards the Chinese cause was accentuated by a certain sense of guilt that the British Government was able to do so little to give practical help to China. This sentiment received expression in many quarters during the war years. One of its most striking manifestations was the support that was given in Britain to the Aid to China Fund, established to send relief to China in her struggle. There was probably no other cause during the war years that aroused such a whole-hearted response. Flag days were organized all over the country; "Aid to China weeks" were held in hundreds of cities and boroughs; trade unions raised special appeals; several hundred thousand British workers undertook over many years to give so much a week to the cause; and working-parties knitted innumerable garments. British statesmen regularly pronounced their sympathy for the Chinese in their struggle.

Such sentiments were to some extent reflected in Chinese attitudes to Britain. Britain's renunciation of her former rights in China and participation in a common alliance brought about some reassessment of the stereotyped Chinese image of the leading

BRITAIN AND THE KUOMINTANG 53

imperialist power. There were demands in the Chinese Press that the Chinese Government should try to reach a closer understanding with Britain. And in July, 1945, the Peoples Political Council, a largely nominated body, passed a resolution urging the Government to conclude a twenty-year military alliance with Britain and other countries.

Almost for the first time in history, some personal contacts between British and Chinese statesmen took place. In July, 1943, Dr. Soong the Chinese Foreign Minister, paid a visit to Britain. A few weeks later he participated with Mr. Churchill, President Roosevelt, Mr. Eden and Mr. Cordell Hull at the Quebec Conference. And in November, 1943, General Chiang Kai-shek himself attended the Cairo Conference with Mr. Churchill and President Roosevelt. This last occasion was perhaps the first time, since the earliest contacts between the East and West, that China had participated at an international conference on an entirely equal footing with the great powers of the West.

But this phase was not to last long. New subjects of difference between the two countries began to emerge. First, Britain, inevitably preoccupied with her own struggle for existence, made no attempt to conceal her belief that the Far Eastern struggle must occupy a secondary place. There had already been some differences between Britain and China on the conduct of the first Burma Campaign. At Cairo the Chinese leader can hardly have failed to be aware of the different degrees of importance that were attached to the Far Eastern sphere of operations by Mr. Churchill and President Roosevelt respectively. Mr. Churchill subsequently recorded his impatience with President Roosevelt's "exaggerated view of the Indian-Chinese sphere", and his irritation with the protracted discussions on the conduct of the Chinese war which "took first instead of last place at Cairo". When Mr. Roosevelt, at the conference, gave a specific undertaking to General Chiang Kai-shek that an amphibious operation would be launched within a few months to occupy southern Burma and relieve the pressure on China, the British Prime Minister specifically dissociated himself from this undertaking. And both he and the British Chiefs of Staff over the next few months consistently opposed the plan on the grounds that all the available landing-craft should be reserved for use in Europe; a view that was, eventually, reluctantly accepted by

President Roosevelt. Thus the Chinese Government was made unpleasantly aware that the British Government attached far greater importance to the successful conclusion of the war in Europe than to any immediate move to relieve the pressure on China.

Then again there were widespread suspicions among Chinese that Britain did not attach to China the weight that she demanded either as an ally or as a great power. There were invidious comparisons with the attitude of the United States. It was felt that Britain tended to think always in terms of the Big Three, the United States, like China, of the Big Four (France at this time counted for nothing). Many were probably aware that Mr. Churchill, as he himself later confessed, did not share the "excessive estimates" of Chiang Kai-shek's power and of China's status held by many in America. And it was widely known that while the United States had pressed that China should be accorded a permanent seat on the Security Council, Britain had been indifferent if not actually hostile to this proposal.

Finally, at the end of the war, Chinese resentment was intensified —though this time Britain alone could not be held responsible— by the terms of the Yalta Agreement secretly entered into between the United States, Britain and the Soviet Union in February, 1945. The meeting was held largely to settle the terms on which Russian entry into the war against Japan might be secured. China was not represented. And the terms of the Agreement were not revealed until February, 1946. Yet it was China that was called upon to pay the largest price for bringing about Soviet participation. Under the Agreement, the Manchurian port of Port Arthur was to be leased by China to the Soviet Union as a naval base; the commercial port of Dairen was to be internationalized and Soviet interests there assured; the Manchurian railways were to be operated by a joint Sino-Soviet company; and the *status quo* in Outer Mongolia—in effect Soviet suzerainty—was to be preserved. These arrangements, it was said, would "require the concurrence of" General Chiang Kai-shek; and President Roosevelt would "take measures in order to obtain this concurrence". In effect there was nothing for the General to do but to acquiesce.

Thus the honeymoon began to turn a little sour. Basically the two countries were divided by a barrier that neither government, for all their efforts, could have made away with, the earth's circumference. There is no doubt that the British Government might have

BRITAIN AND THE KUOMINTANG 55

done more, if they had laid themselves out, to show towards China some of those marks of respect to which Chinese attach such importance. But British governments are no more disposed than British individuals to effusive expressions of their sentiments. And it was perhaps understandable that the British, in the situation in which they found themselves, should have found it difficult to distract their attention from the European scene, where they were so bitterly engaged, sufficiently to do full justice to the susceptibilities of the Chinese; any more than the Chinese themselves ever fully appreciated the magnitude of Britain's own problems, both at home and abroad. British statesmen offered many words of goodwill. British ministers declared with almost parrot-like regularity their desire to see the emergence of a strong, united and prosperous China. A more concrete demonstration of support was shown by the dispatch by Britain of five million pounds worth of U.N.N.R.A. aid at the end of the war. But what China really wanted was the respect due to a great power. And this the actions of British governments failed to provide.

Thus even before the war was finished friction was beginning to re-emerge. As soon as it was over new issues arose to embitter relations further. Throughout the period from the end of the war to the fall of the Nationalist Government British nationals and firms seeking to re-acquire possession of their property, despite the specific provisions included in the treaty of 1943 assuring British nationals of their property rights in China, faced constant difficulties. Already in September, 1945, the first British consular officials, sent to Shanghai to protect the interests of British subjects after the evacuation of the Japanese, were for a time refused visas by the Chinese authorities. When British diplomatic and consular officials did arrive, they found that in many cases British property was occupied by Chinese service or other organizations, which steadfastly refused to budge. An unceasing succession of protests was made to the Chinese Government without effect. In June, 1947, the Chinese authorities set a time-limit, at very short notice, within which all foreign companies and individuals were to submit claims to property in China. Although eventually most of the more important British properties, including those of nearly all the big firms, were returned to British control, some British private owners continued, right to the end of the period of Nationalist rule, to have difficulty in establishing title to their properties.

Friction arose over the decision of the Chinese Government to close navigation in the Yangtze to foreign shipping. In pre-war days, British and other foreign shipping had carried a substantial proportion of the trade between Yangtze ports. As a result of the new regulation, British shipping was not only prevented from taking part in the important trade between one Yangtze port and another, but British ships coming from abroad were obliged to unship their cargoes at Shanghai, where they were transferred to Chinese ships for passage up the Yangtze. In 1946 the restriction was widened to include trade between Chinese coastal ports. The measure, which was designed to protect the young Chinese shipping industry, was obviously most uneconomic, especially in view of the lack of Chinese shipping and of trained crews: even the Chinese shipping interests, who demanded the protection, admitted that British freight rates were very much lower than Chinese. The British Government made repeated representations on the matter, claiming there was ample trade for the shipping of all nations, and that the competition of lower British freight rates would be beneficial to the trade. All such approaches were without effect.

There were difficulties over the provisions of the 1943 Treaty relating to the former municipalities in the foreign settlements. Under the Treaty, the Chinese Government were to take over all the responsibilities of the city councils. They accepted the assets. But they refused to meet any of the liabilities, which included payment of interest on loans, and the payment of compensation, superannuation and pensions to ex-employees. In 1946 a "Liquidation Commission" was set up, including representatives of the Chinese Government, and of the foreign governments concerned. But this made no progress. And by the time the Nationalist Government were overthrown no payments had been made by them to any ex-employees of the municipalities. Meanwhile advances of nearly £1,500,000 were made by the British Government to relieve the difficulties of the British subjects concerned. These sums were never recovered from the Chinese authorities, Nationalist or Communist.

These various issues came to a head in negotiations that took place during 1946 and 1947 on the conclusion of a Commercial Treaty between the two countries. In November, 1946, such a treaty had been signed between China and the United States. Drafts

BRITAIN AND THE KUOMINTANG 57

for a British Treaty were exchanged during the winter of 1946–47. The British Government, however, wished to ensure that the Treaty should safeguard the rights of British shipping in the Yangtze. The Chinese Government declined, pointing to the absence of any such provisions in the United States Treaty. There were difficulties over compensation for British harbour facilities in the Yangtze taken over by Chinese Government agencies at the end of the war, over the pensions of the ex-employees of the former municipalities, and over the default in Chinese Government payments on foreign loans (these had largely ceased in 1938 and had never been resumed). Deadlock was reached and the talks finally broke down in October, 1947.

These commercial difficulties reflected a more general *malaise*. Both countries were largely taken up by their own immediate problems of post-war reconstruction. The other side of the world seemed a long way away; and of doubtful importance. Britain, ready to concede much to the nationalism of colonial peoples, found the nationalism of a sovereign nation puzzling. China, after long years of resentment against imperialism, found that, even when the immediate occasion no longer existed, the habit was difficult to shed.

There was, certainly, some resumption of personal and cultural ties. The old China hands returned to their clubs in Shanghai, Tientsin and Canton. The missionaries went back to their villages. A number of Chinese students went to study in Britain. The tradition of British financial advice was maintained by the loan of a Treasury official. The British Council established centres in a number of towns in China, including well-equipped libraries at Shanghai and Peking; arranged large numbers of visits by university teachers, scientists, educationalists, doctors and others in each direction; and financed many scholarships for Chinese students and university teachers in Britain. The Chinese Government made donations to Oxford and Cambridge universities for the establishment of scholarships in Chinese studies. And there were a number of cultural organizations working to improve mutual comprehension.

The British Government, in their public statements, remained full of warm sentiments for China. They were unequivocal in recognizing the Nationalist Government as the only legitimate authority in China. And though they were not in a position to give much in the way of financial assistance, were able to give some expression to their desire to assist in the rebuilding of China by assisting in the development of the Chinese navy.

This had started during the war when a number of Chinese naval officers had been trained in Britain. At the end of 1945 an agreement was reached for the loan to China of a cruiser, a destroyer, two submarines, a corvette and eight motor launches together with all necessary equipment. Arrangements were made for the crews to be trained in Britain. But even here co-operation did not prove an unqualified success. In March, 1947, shortly after it was handed over to her Chinese crew, the corvette was lost with the loss of 59 lives. The cruiser, *Aurora*, renamed the *Chungking*, the pride of the Chinese navy, defected to the Communists in 1949, and was shortly afterwards bombed and sunk by the Nationalists' own aircraft. Soon afterwards one of the other ships, still in harbour at Hong Kong was handed back to Britain by the Nationalists, perhaps because they feared a recurrence of such events.

In general, on both sides, neither Government nor people made much effort to understand the difficulties of the other. The Chiang Kai-shek Government was still, in a literal sense, a nationalist government, run by a nationalist party. And though the dynamism of that party in so far as it affected internal affairs was now largely dissipated, the sentiments and attitudes towards the great powers that animated its members during the thirties still permeated its thinking during the forties. Despite the change in Britain's position, they still saw her as the wicked imperialist. Despite the abolition of the "unequal treaties", they still harboured resentment against the dominant British commercial position in China and the continued retention of Hong Kong. Despite all Britain's public declarations of friendship, she still, they felt, adopted a patronizing attitude to China. Thus they showed themselves, in many fields, determined to extort their rights to the letter. And very often a good deal more.

Britain, on the other hand, made little attempt to allow for Chinese susceptibilities. Some in Britain gave the impression that they regarded China simply as a profitable field for commercial enterprise. Many Chinese felt that Britain had no interest in the Chinese people, the Chinese nation, even Chinese culture; only in the Chinese market: that, to Britain, Sino-British relations meant only commercial relations. Statements by British Government spokesmen, though possibly designed to disown more sinister pretensions, in effect served to feed such suspicions. In June, 1946, the British Prime Minister declared that "our policy with regard to China is to do everything to secure conditions favourable to our trade". In July of the same year the recently appointed British Ambassador to China, declared that the British Government had "only one ambition in China—to increase trade and mutual prosperity". The leader of a Parliamentary mission that went to China during the summer of 1947 as a demonstration of British goodwill, declared that there was "no better way to improve Sino-British relations than by closer commercial intercourse". And by its strident insistence, throughout its stay, on the obligation of China to respect British trading rights, this mission in fact secured almost exactly the reverse of the effect it was intended to achieve.

Relations between the two countries could never be stable so long as the internal position in China remained so insecure. To many in Britain the disunity in China and the inability of the Nationalist Government to reassert its authority over large parts of the country were merely another cause of irritation against the Nationalist régime. And as soon as the Communists began to have control of areas where a British population was established, unfavourable comparisons began to be made between the integrity and efficiency of administration in these regions and in those held by the Nationalist Government. The Nationalists on the other hand, precisely because of their internal difficulties, felt themselves entitled to call for the sympathy and support of all governments and peoples with whom they were in friendly relations. And the existence in Britain of a substantial and vociferous element which gave its support to the aspirations of the Chinese Communists only served to increase resentment against Britain. This feeling found its most violent expression when Britain finally decided to recognize the Communist Government.

From the start British relations with the Nationalists were beset with difficulties. In its early days the Nationalist Government was the representative of that national sentiment in China which was nourished more than all else by resentment against the position that powers such as Britain had built up in China. Their prime aim was to dislodge these from that position. During the twenties and thirties Britain competed with Japan for the honour of representing, in Chinese eyes, China's principal oppressor. And it was inevitable that, conversely, British settler opinion and, to some extent, opinion in Britain, regarded the Nationalists with undisguised suspicion, even hostility.

The action of the British Government, in entering into negotiations, before any other Western government, with the Nationalists, never fully discounted this basic conflict. During the war relations were improved, but as soon as it was over, and the previously existing propinquity re-established, the same underlying attitudes re-emerged. Though Britain had abandoned her treaty rights, nationalist sentiment in China was not yet fully assuaged. It was quick to take offence at even unintended slights. Many British, on the other hand, were not always tactful in deferring to Chinese susceptibilities. And they were becoming increasingly conscious of the shortcomings of the Nationalist Government, whose defects were always more obvious than their difficulties.

No doubt such misunderstandings would have been resolved in time. But time is just what there was not to be. For the Nationalists made the fatal error of losing the civil war. And Britain was therefore faced with the problem of whether she should continue to maintain relations with a government whose authority was confined to little more than a single island off the Chinese coast; or whether she should seek to come to terms with the power that had now secured control of the entire mainland of China.

BRITAIN AND THE
PEOPLE'S REPUBLIC

4

THE COMING OF THE COMMUNISTS

THERE are always peculiar difficulties in conducting relations with a government that is engaged in civil war. Although international law lays down strict rules for the diplomatic forms to be observed by foreign governments in such circumstances, in practice the policies adopted inevitably tend to be influenced by ideological or other sympathies towards the two sides involved. The differences between the attitudes adopted by Britain and other European nations to the emergence of the South American states at the end of the Napoleonic wars, or between the policies of the various European powers to the establishment of the Soviet Union or the Franco régime in Spain, did not arise essentially out of divergences in the interpretation of their international obligations in such matters, but from differences in the national interest or political sympathies of each individual power.

Britain's attitude towards the civil war in China was complicated by various factors. The initial predisposition in favour of the legal and recognized government of the country was quickly counterbalanced by an increasing disillusion with the ineffectiveness of the National Government. The ideological hostility of many towards the Communist cause was to some extent allayed by the persistently favourable reports of the efficiency, integrity, even the moderation, of the Communist leaders in China. Finally as the war progressed and the Communists secured control of a large part of the country, the instinctively realistic urge of the British public and Government to acknowledge this indisputable fact, had to be balanced against the desire to act, so far as possible, in agreement with Britain's principal partners and allies.

At the end of the war most people in Britain, as elsewhere, hoped that the somewhat fragile understanding established between the Nationalists and the Communists during the war against Japan, could be extended into the peace that followed, so that a unified government for the whole country could be brought into being. The British Government gave its full support to the efforts of the United States Government to bring about some such solution. Already within a few months of the end of the Japanese war, however, fighting had broken out in North China and elsewhere, and it became increasingly doubtful whether this hope could be fulfilled.

The policy of the British Government in this situation was laid down in 1945 and reaffirmed in a series of public statements between then and 1949. It was held that the difficulties in China were matters for the Chinese themselves to settle. Meanwhile the Nationalist Government was the officially recognized government of the country whose authority alone could be respected. On November 28, 1945, Mr. Bevin told the House of Commons that the British Government regarded the civil war as an "internal problem for the Chinese themselves to resolve". On December 13 of the same year, Mr. Noel-Baker, Minister of State, said that while the British Government had "done everything in their power to encourage, so far as they properly could, the settlement by agreement of any internal difficulties", these were in the last resort "matters for the Chinese themselves". The Government would not even pledge themselves to support the holding of elections in China to settle the issues involved. Mr. Noel-Baker declared in response to demands for this, that it would be "overoptimistic" to hope for such a solution in the existing situation.

The principal challenge to the authority of the Nationalist Government at this stage occurred in Manchuria. Manchuria had been occupied by the Soviet Union during her brief war with Japan. After considerable delay, and after stripping the extensive industrial installations of the area bare, the Soviet forces withdrew. But for long they would not allow Nationalist forces to enter the region. And these claimed that when they did get there, Communist forces had already been allowed to obtain effective control of the area.

The British Government supported the Nationalist claim to reentry, declaring that "it would not be in the general interest of the world if anybody attempted to obstruct the reoccupation of Manchuria by the forces of the Government we recognized today". But the situation there made it more than ever important to ensure that other powers, in particular the Soviet Union, should be constrained to give an equally clear acknowledgement of the authority of the Nationalist Government as the legitimate government of China; and, if possible, a public assurance that they had no intention of interfering in China's internal affairs. The matter was discussed at the meeting of the foreign ministers of the United States, U.S.S.R.,

THE COMING OF THE COMMUNISTS 65

and Britain in Moscow in February, 1946. The meeting finally arrived at an agreed formula, and the declaration issued at its end declared that "the three Foreign Secretaries ... were in agreement as to the need for a unified and democratic China under the Nationalist Government, for broad participation by democratic elements in all branches of the Nationalist Government, and for a cessation of civil strife. They reaffirmed their adherence to the policy of non-interference in China's internal affairs".

The reference to "broad participation by democratic elements" was sufficiently vague to bear almost any interpretation either side might wish to put on it. But in the declaration the Soviet Government had been brought to give their unequivocal support for a China unified "under the Nationalist Government". The declaration's terms were to a large extent an endorsement of the policy already adopted by the British Government, and it became the text quoted by British spokesmen on innumerable occasions in support of that policy during the next three years.

There were elements in Britain, however, who were not happy about this policy. Already in August, 1945, immediately after the end of the war, a Labour M.P. urged in the House of Commons that the Government should be very cautious about coming down on one side without having regard to the "vast territories that were administered by another section of the Chinese people, who seemed to have some contribution to make to the future of the world". In December, 1945, an adjournment motion was moved to demand that the Government should ensure that the United Nations or the Big Three should make themselves responsible for conducting free elections throughout China. On January 23, 1947, Lord Lindsay of Berker, initiating a motion in the House of Lords on the Government's China policy, declared that the Chinese Communists were in practice only "radical agrarians", that the Kuomintang were, on general admission, completely corrupt, and that it was monstrous for the Government to stand aside and watch the destruction by a totalitarian and repressive government of an honest, sincere, agrarian community holding a large part of China. The China Campaign Committee, originally formed to lend support to the Chinese war effort, but later re-formed by elements sympathetic to the Communist cause in China, in January, 1948, passed a resolution demanding that the British Government should establish economic and cultural relations with the "North China régime". In the same month in the House of Commons, a Labour M.P. demanded that British policy should be one "of friendship and trade with the liberated areas" and that no encouragement should be given to the effete, corrupt and ramshackle organization, which was the official government of China.

These views were certainly not representative of the bulk of British public opinion at the time. But they did reflect a very widespread disillusion with the Nationalist régime, which was widely regarded as suffering from the double defect of being undemocratic without the redeeming grace of being efficient. The Communists on the other hand, even when their politics were deplored, were widely respected for their honesty and administrative ability. Already on January 6, 1948, a leading article in *The Times* said that while the K.M.T. was "still under corrupt influences", some of the programme and performances of the Chinese Communists had won widespread approval among many in Britain and the United States. A leading article in the *Manchester Guardian* two or three months later declared that "no ally of the West was so weak and disreputable as the K.M.T. Government of Chiang Kai-shek". On October 12 of the same year *The Times* was saying that the Nationalist Government must reform itself drastically before it could hope to become a rallying point for Chinese patriotism.

This recognition of the deficiencies of the Nationalist Government did not mean that public opinion in Britain at this time generally welcomed the prospect of a Communist victory in China. It is true that the popular image of the Chinese Communist régime among most people in Britain was extremely vague, and varied widely according to the predispositions of the observer. This is not surprising since very little was known about Communist-held areas and their rulers. And since what little was known came mostly from those who were, if not Communists, at least inclined to be sympathetic, some of the views taken were inclined to be optimistic. The *Manchester Guardian* believed that Communism in China was chiefly "a movement of outraged tenant farmers". *The Times* declared that the Chinese Communists were unlike those elsewhere, since they did not "try to force popular wishes into a rigid mould"; their system had held together because the leaders had "persuaded the people they ruled that their government was not the olympian agency of oppression". Perhaps the most optimistic section of British opinion was the business community in

THE COMING OF THE COMMUNISTS 67

China, many of whom felt that their life under the Communists could scarcely be worse than it was under the Nationalists, and declared their belief that in the long run the new movement would prove more Chinese than Communist.

The most common view was still that the best hope for the future lay in some strengthening or broadening of the Nationalist Government rather than in a victory for the Communist armies. Such opinions were expressed by many in both parties in debates in Parliament. It was the general consensus of the Press. Already in January, 1947, Lord Jowitt, the Lord Chancellor, while reaffirming the Government's policy of non-interference, said that China "must not be subject to totalitarian rule imposed by any one clique or party"; and that the British Government would welcome the fulfilment of that part of the Moscow declaration referring to "broad participation by democratic elements".

As a Communist victory became more probable, opinion about the likely nature of the régime began to become less sanguine. On November 2, 1948, an article in the *News Chronicle*, while admitting that "it had never been worth a man's while to fight and die for the K.M.T.", declared that it would be "a black day for the democracies if a Communist China were to emerge in the Far East", and demanded that the West should seek out honest and democratic leaders in Nationalist China to strengthen them. On January 20, 1949, the *Daily Mail* said that the British public should not delude themselves into believing that Chinese Communism was different from any other kind of Communism. On February 8, 1949, the *Manchester Guardian*, somewhat retracting earlier judgements, wrote, "There is no evidence that the Chinese Communists are independent of the Kremlin." And it seems likely that the bulk of the British population in so far as they thought about the matter at all, were more impressed by the fact that the challengers to the authority of the Nationalist Government were Communists than that they were, so it was said, good Communists.

Even when it began to look increasingly as if the Communists would prove victorious, the British Government's position remained unchanged. In a foreign affairs debate on December 9, 1948, after the Communists had gained control of Manchuria and much of North China, Mr. Bevin once again declared that British policy was governed by the Moscow Declaration. But the Government were becoming increasingly doubtful about committing themselves towards the Nationalist cause in a civil war. On January 19, 1949, when Britain, in common with the United States, the Soviet Union and France, received a request from the Nationalists to act as mediators to secure a cease-fire, the British Government announced that they had "regretfully declined to intervene". Increasingly the possibility of a Communist victory had to be taken into account.

By the beginning of 1949, when the Communist armies advanced to the Yangtze, many began to take a Nationalist defeat for granted. At the beginning of February the Nationalist Government informed the British Government that as from February 5 the seat of government would be Canton. But although a senior member of the Embassy, with the status of counsellor, was sent to Canton to maintain contact with the Chinese Government there, the British Ambassador, like most of his colleagues, remained in Nanking. Similarly most British consular officers in areas overrun by the Communists stayed on at their posts.

From January to April, 1949, there was something like a ceasefire in the civil war, during which both sides exchanged mutually unacceptable demands with the other, meanwhile taking the opportunity to regroup their forces. In early February the Communist forces reached the Yangtze, and for the next two and a half months the two armies were ranged facing each other on opposite sides of the river. On April 5, peace talks between a new Nationalist Government and the Communist Government in North China began. They made little progress and on April 17 the Communists delivered an ultimatum to the Nationalist Government, stating that if their terms were not accepted by April 20, hostilities would be resumed. At this point the British Government which had always declared their intention of remaining aloof from the civil war found themselves, in a somewhat surprising fashion, implicated in the most direct, and indeed physical, sense.

Since the time of the first British war with China, British governments had traditionally regarded themselves as justified in making use of British warships in Chinese waters for the purpose of protecting British lives. After the Treaty of Nanking in 1842, British warships possessed the right to patrol Chinese coastal waters and the Yangtze. During the Nationalist march to the north in the twenties, British warships had several times opened fire, when it was thought necessary to protect British interests. Although the right to

THE COMING OF THE COMMUNISTS 69

patrol Chinese waters had been given up under the Treaty of 1943, very many in Britain continued to regard such action as normal in conditions of unrest in the Far East. And British naval vessels continued, on occasion, to be sent to Chinese waters with the permission of the Chinese Government.

Already in November, 1948, questions had been asked in the House of Commons about the measures the British Government proposed to take to protect British citizens in Shanghai and elsewhere. At the beginning of December it was reported that, while both British and United States authorities had decided not to send troops to Shanghai, a policy of naval protection in the Whampoa River (the tributary of the Yangtze on which Shanghai stands) was to be adopted. As a result, throughout the early part of 1949, the British had warships at Shanghai without interruption. These included a cruiser and two destroyers.

But in addition it was decided that warships should be sent, with the consent of the Nationalist authorities, up that river from Shanghai to Nanking. This policy was maintained even after the Yangtze became the front line dividing the two armies. The Prime Minister later explained to the House of Commons, that this was done "so that in the event of a breakdown of law and order as a result of hostilities, they would be able to assist in the evacuation" of British nationals. In February, when the Nationalist Government had moved to Canton, they had warned the British authorities that they could no longer accept responsibility for the safety of the ships. Regular trips up the river had nevertheless continued to be undertaken. But no attempt was apparently made to give the Communists, whose armies then held the north bank of the river, any information about such movements.

So long as the truce persisted, no great problems were created by this somewhat unusual procedure. But the Communist ultimatum, after one or two postponements, was finally due to expire on April 20. On April 18, the Flag Officer at Shanghai, after consultation with H.M. Ambassador in Nanking, decided that on the following day, April 19, the frigate H.M.S. *Amethyst*, should sail from Shanghai for Nanking, between the two enemy lines, in order to relieve the destroyer, *Consort*, which was then at Nanking and beginning to run short of supplies.

The *Amethyst* flew the white ensign. And she had a Union Jack painted on her hull. It is perhaps doubtful how many Chinese battery commanders on either side were likely to have recognized the British flag, even if they had seen it. In fact, about 60 miles from Nanking, batteries on the Communist bank opened fire. The ship suffered considerable damage and casualties, and was finally grounded. The Flag Officer, despite the commanding position held by the Communist batteries over all movements along the river, ordered the *Consort* down from Nanking, and a cruiser and frigate up from Shanghai, to come to the *Amethyst*'s assistance. The *Consort* came under heavy fire, suffered considerable damage and casualties, and after making several attempts to take the *Amethyst* in tow, was obliged to withdraw towards Shanghai. The cruiser and frigate also attempted to reach the grounded ship, but met such heavy fire that they too were obliged to withdraw after doing what they could to silence the shore batteries. On April 21 the *Amethyst* was refloated but with only four officers left unwounded, one telegraphist, and her chart destroyed, could go no further, and eventually took shelter in a creek. About 60 of the crew, including wounded, were got ashore, and with Chinese help reached Shanghai overland. Later the ship managed to move about fifteen miles up river, where it was decided she should remain.

During these operations, in the four British ships involved, 42 men were killed, including the Captain of the *Amethyst*, and 53 wounded. The Communists claimed to have suffered 252 casualties as a result of gunfire from the British ships. They said that it was not until the day after the initial exchange of fire that they had become aware that the ships involved were not Nationalist ships but British (Nationalist warships had recently been in the vicinity); and that they had believed that these had fired on their forces to anticipate an attempted crossing of the river. They also maintained that the *Amethyst* had fired first (a claim which the Communist authorities have almost invariably put forward in relation to any international incident in which they have become involved). And Peking radio began to talk of a "joint naval attack by the K.M.T. and the British imperialist navy".

Various attempts were made to make contact with the Communist forces. The British consular officer in Peking was instructed to explain the situation to the Communist Government and to request them to prevent a recurrence of the firing. A Chinese-speaking member of the Embassy at Nanking volunteered to try to make contact with the Communist forces in the field. After passing

THE COMING OF THE COMMUNISTS 71

through the Nationalist lines, he reached the local Communist headquarters on April 23 and asked that the *Amethyst* should be allowed to proceed, either to Nanking or Shanghai, without further molestation. But the local commander, complaining that the ship had entered the war area without obtaining clearance from the Communist military authorities and had then proceeded to inflict casualties on his men, would only allow the ship to proceed to Nanking on condition it assisted the Communist armies in crossing the Yangtze. This stipulation was, not surprisingly, refused.

Before the end of April the Communists had successfully effected a crossing of the Yangtze and defeated the opposing Nationalist armies. The British warship was thus now totally surrounded by Communist-controlled territory. For several weeks discussions continued between British naval officers and the local Communist commander about the terms on which the *Amethyst* might be released. Before allowing the *Amethyst* to proceed down the river the Communist commander demanded an admission by the British naval commander that it was the British ship that had opened fire, an apology, and an agreement to pay compensation for the Chinese soldiers and villagers who had been killed. The British officer demanded that the *Amethyst* should be released before any discussion of such matters. Meanwhile the crew of the ship were allowed by the local army commander to buy food locally. But they were not allowed to bring in replenishments from Shanghai.

In the night of July 30 the *Amethyst* slipped anchor and, avoiding the Communist batteries, started to escape down the river in the wake of a river steamer. The ship rammed a river boom and, after heavy exchanges of gunfire with shore batteries, finally reached the open sea. During the escape, the Communist press claimed, the river steamer and a number of junks were rammed in the darkness and sunk, causing the loss of several hundred lives.

The escape received a tumultuous acclaim in the British press. The commander of the *Amethyst* and several members of the crew received decorations. Spectacular welcomes were organized for the frigate throughout her journey back to the United Kingdom from the Far East. But, even when all allowance is made for the gallantry of the crew themselves, it is difficult to regard the affair as a very glorious episode in British naval history. The century-old convention that, if anything untoward occurred in China, the solution was to send warships to the scene, was one that had died hard. Even after this escapade, dramatic shows of force by the Pacific fleets of the Western Powers continued to take place. A British cruiser was ordered to Shanghai from Hong Kong. Another was sent to the Far East from Bermuda. The United States Pacific Fleet Headquarters announced that two American cruisers would proceed to Chinese waters from Pearl Harbour. It is not entirely clear what these impressive arrays were intended to achieve.

By the time the Communist armies reached the Yangtze a very large number of towns in North China had already been occupied by their forces during the civil war, without the least harm occuring to British lives or property. Indeed they had won widespread admiration for their good order and discipline, which were favourably compared with those of the Nationalists. If serious fighting had broken out in Nanking the existence of British warships was most unlikely to have influenced the situation one way or the other. And in such conditions it is improbable that it would have been possible, or prudent, to evacuate British nationals down the Yangtze. Indeed in conditions of civil war the ship could only have been an embarrassment and a provocation; and would inevitably have become, finally, a hostage to the occupying armies. It was, no doubt for such reasons that the United States, and all other nations, had withdrawn their own naval forces from Nanking well before the Communist armies arrived.

But even if it were believed that the presence of British warships at Nanking could be useful, the decision to dispatch one of them up the river between the two battle lines, within twenty-four hours of the expiration of the latest ultimatum and without notification to one of the two armies concerned, was a strange one. Even if, as was hoped, there had been time for the *Amethyst* to reach Nanking before the expiry of the ultimatum, there would scarcely have been time for the *Consort* to withdraw. In this case two warships would have been stranded in Nanking, instead of one, while the civil war raged all about them. But the decision becomes even more surprising when it is considered that, for the dispatch of supplies to the *Consort*, the only immediately urgent object, no river journey was necessary at all, since there existed, throughout the period in question, alternative communication between Shanghai and Nanking, by road, rail and air. Though admittedly somewhat uncertain, some such expedient could scarcely have been less precarious than the

THE COMING OF THE COMMUNISTS 73

river journey, between two hostile armies, on the very eve of an ultimatum and final expiration.

It is perhaps unlikely that the affair exerted any very permanent effect on British relations with China and its new conquerors. But it no doubt served to convince many, not only in China but throughout Asia, that the gunboat mentality was not yet dead.

As it became more evident that the Communist armies were likely to become victorious, increasing consideration had to be given to the establishment of some contacts with the new régime. Ever since the Communist occupation of northern towns, such as Mukden, Peking and Tientsin, in the autumn of 1948, British consular officers had been trying to reach day-to-day arrangements with the local Communist authorities. On April 29, 1949, a Foreign Office spokesman announced that Britain was trying to establish "friendly relations with the Chinese Communist authorities, though this would not affect Britain's present relations with the Nationalist Government". All such overtures were rejected. This was no doubt because the Communist Government were not willing to enter into any local relationship with British officials until the British Government agreed to transfer recognition from the Nationalist Government to their own. They wanted all or nothing.

Indeed the Communist authorities showed little evidence of any desire for the friendship of the Western Powers. Peking radio continued to put out virulent attacks on British imperialism. On March 25, a statement was issued in Peking and given much publicity by the Chinese Press and radio, attacking in violent terms the policies of colonial governments towards their Chinese minorities. It was claimed that in Malaya thousands of Chinese had been thrown into jail without cause, and whole villages driven into concentration camps. But the unfortunate situation of Chinese in such countries was only temporary, since when the People's Republic of China was established it would be able to give them "all possible assistance". The statement was no doubt intended as one bid in the vital competition about to break out between the Communists and the Nationalists for the allegiance of the minorities in South East Asia. But it was taken by many in Britain and elsewhere as a confirmation of their gloomiest forebodings about the seditious activities of Chinese Communism in the area.

Nevertheless it had been announced by the Communist authorities from an early stage that the Chinese People's Revolutionary Military Committee and the people's governments "were willing to protect all foreign nationals in China who engaged in their normal vocations". On May 1, the authorities declared that they would be ready to enter into diplomatic relations with all the Western Powers, including the United States, on a basis of equality provided that these broke off relations with "the remnant K.M.T. forces". And on June 19, Mao Tse-tung declared, in a speech setting out the foreign policy that the new régime would adopt, that it was willing "to establish diplomatic relations with any foreign country on the basis of equality and mutual benefit, and mutual respect for sovereignty and territorial integrity", provided that that country was willing to sever all diplomatic relations with "the Chinese reactionaries", to cease all further assistance to them, and to adopt a "truly and not falsely friendly attitude to the people of China".

Already in January, 1949, there were reports that the British Government had been consulting with the French and United States Governments on the attitude that should be adopted towards the rapid extension of Communist power in China, and on the effect of this on the situation in Asia as a whole. On May 2 it was reported that the British and United States Governments were in consultation on the whole question of future representation in China. For the moment both Governments decided to maintain their missions in Nanking, by then in Communist hands. Not long afterwards, however, the United States Ambassador was withdrawn for consultations, and did not subsequently return.

At the beginning of June there were further discussions between the United States, British and French Governments about the possible recognition of the new régime. While both the British and French Governments were thought to be in favour of fairly early recognition, the United States Government was reported to have asked a number of friendly governments not to recognize until inter-allied consultations had been completed.

On June 10, Mr. Alexander, the First Lord of the Admiralty, during a short visit to Hong Kong, made the first official statement implying some modification of the policy hitherto followed by the British Government. On the eve of his departure from the colony he said that it was Britain's desire to "establish and maintain

THE COMING OF THE COMMUNISTS 75

neighbourly relations with the people of China" and to continue "the friendliest possible relations with whatever government the Chinese people might choose". There was at this time, when the Communist armies were beginning to approach the borders of Hong Kong, increasing concern over the possibility that the new conquerors, who had never concealed their hostility to all forms of colonialism, would take the opportunity, on reaching the south, to gobble up Hong Kong in the process. Mr. Alexander's visit to Hong Kong was primarily to consider the defensive problems involved. And his statement there may have been partly conditioned by a desire to conciliate the new rulers of China before they took any irrevocable decision. On June 22, shortly after his return to Britain when the Communist threat to Hong Kong was even more menacing, he repeated the statement in almost identical terms in the House of Commons. But he added, to allay the increasing fears about the effect which the new régime might exert on the British position in South East Asia, that the Government were resolved "to prevent the unsettled circumstances in China from putting in peril the people of Hong Kong and Malaya".

It began to be fairly apparent that there would be no comeback by the routed and demoralized Nationalist armies. As a Communist victory became assured, British public opinion began to move in favour of some form of recognition of this situation. On May 5, a leading article in *The Times* declared that "the links between this country and China are ancient and valuable . . . if the Chinese Communists in their turn do come to recognize the gain which their country can get from commerce and friendship with Western countries, the door should not be shut against them". There were increasingly pressing demands from some Labour members in the House of Commons for the establishment of relations with the new régime. In June it was reported that a survey carried out in Shanghai showed that the foreign business community almost unanimously considered that recognition should be accorded as soon as the Central People's Government was established. There was growing respect among business circles in China for the achievements of the new régime. The British Consul General publicly praised "the restraint, moderation and realism" of the military authorities in Shanghai. British businessmen were reported to be determined, under these conditions, to maintain their business connexions in China for as long as possible.

In August Britain was formally asked to look after United States interests in China and the Americans began to close down their Consulates. It came to be generally assumed that they were preparing to withdraw from China completely. Britain on the other hand, announced that, although for special reasons it had been decided to close the Consulate at Swatow, it was the intention to keep other Consulates open and to maintain the Embassy staff, which was still divided between Nanking and Canton. By September less than a dozen nations continued to maintain diplomatic staff at Nanking. The other Embassies either withdrew to Canton or left China altogether.

Early in September there were talks between Mr. Bevin and Mr. Acheson, at which Far Eastern policy was discussed. The communiqué stated that the two powers were "in accord" over their overall Far Eastern policies, but disclaimed any purpose of reaching "specific agreement", and spoke of the "development of policy along parallel lines". This was generally taken as a euphemism to describe a head-on clash of opinion. The British Government were reported to have stressed the importance of British commercial interests in China. Both governments accepted that there was no political future for Chiang Kai-shek in China. The United States Government, however, were clearly not prepared to recognize the Communist régime in the near future. The British Government, it was thought, were preparing to do so fairly soon. But it was accepted that whatever action was taken, recognition would not be granted without consultation.

On October 1 the People's Republic of China was established. Messages were sent to all foreign diplomatic representatives inviting their Governments' recognition of the new régime. On October 2 the Soviet Union (which had maintained her representative with Chiang Kai-shek to the last), announced her recognition. During the next few days most of the East European governments did the same. On December 9 Burma, first among non-Communist countries, announced her decision to recognize the new Government.

British relations with the Nationalists were becoming increasingly remote. In May, the British Government had had to protest to the Nationalist authorities against the use of requisitioned British ships for the transport of troops. On July 20 the legislative Yuan, the Nationalist legislature, had sent messages to the British Parliament and the United States Congress, asking for continued help in

THE COMING OF THE COMMUNISTS

fighting the spread of Communism across Asia. The message was virtually ignored in Britain. In the autumn there was further dispute between the two Governments over the use by Nationalist naval vessels of the coastal waters of Hong Kong for military operations (they had a right, by a convention of 1898, to use them for peaceful purposes). Finally when the Nationalist Government moved from Canton to Chungking in October, another change in British representation took place. The Councillor from the Embassy in Nanking who had maintained contact in Canton did not move with the new Government, and the two British consuls in Chungking and Tamsui, where Chiang Kai-shek (who had resigned the Presidency in January) had his headquarters, were deputed "to maintain contact" with the Government without diplomatic status.

On October 18 the British Ambassador, Sir Ralph Stevenson, left China for "consultations". The next month a conference of British diplomatic and colonial representatives in the Far East, including Sir Ralph Stevenson and the Governors of Hong Kong and Singapore, was held in Malaya under the chairmanship of Mr. Malcolm McDonald, United Kingdom Commissioner General in South East Asia, to consider policy towards the régime. The conference was reported to have recommended rapid recognition of the Communist Government.

In Britain itself, it began to be widely assumed that recognition was imminent. Some doubts were expressed. Some Conservative M.P.s remained hostile to any form of recognition. On October 3, a leading article in *The Times* said that, although British trading interests in the Far East were in favour of recognition, other considerations, such as the Chinese attitude to the outside world, and especially China's recently expressed intention to invade Tibet, would have to be borne in mind. On October 15 the *Manchester Guardian* said that there would be no hasty recognition by Britain: the development of normal relations would depend on the political actions of the Chinese Government. And at a Press conference in Ottawa, Mr. Bevin said that the British Government would have to consider such questions as treaties and obligations: the British position would depend on the treatment of her nationals.

But in general it was increasingly accepted that Britain must acknowledge the fact that the new Government now exercised effective control of the Chinese mainland. It was widely stressed that British commercial interests in China far exceeded those of any other Western government, and that, from a purely practical point of view, recognition was becoming urgent. On October 7 the *Daily Telegraph* advocated not merely recognition, but the transfer of the United Nations China seat to the new Government. On October 22 *The Times* declared that, "providing China recognized her obligations and refrained from provocation, the West were quite ready to do business and to recognize the Communists as the only lawful government of China". On November 5, the *Manchester Guardian* maintained that "the obvious interest of Great Britain in the Far East was to explore", with her allies, the possibility of peace and conciliation with the new China. And in a foreign affairs debate on November 17, many Members of both sides of the House considered recognition inevitable. Mr. Churchill, the Leader of the Opposition, accepted that there was much to be said in the existing circumstances for entering into relations with the new régime.

But both he and Mr. Bevin agreed that it would be best for the British Government to move, if possible, in step with their allies. From October onwards the British Government had in fact been engaged in prolonged consultations with its partners. On October 19, Mr. Bevin announced in the House of Commons that the Government "proposed to consult with other friendly governments" before reaching a decision on recognition. On November 16, while these consultations were in progress, Mr. Bevin said that he was "concerned to act together with the Commonwealth and other friendly governments" so that if possible a number of governments would be able to move together.

But it became increasingly clear that it was going to be extremely difficult to reach any agreement. On October 26, Dr. Evatt, the Australian Secretary for External Affairs, said that he believed that recognition should be conditional on Chinese assurances about the territorial integrity of neighbouring areas, especially Hong Kong, and the willingness of the new Government to carry out all its international obligations. The Indian Government on the other hand were thought to be pressing for early recognition. The French were reluctant to act without the United States. And on December 7, Mr. Acheson, the United States Secretary of State, said that he considered, not merely that recognition would be premature, but that the time had not yet come even to consider the matter.

Thus the British Government had to consider whether the

THE COMING OF THE COMMUNISTS 79

admitted need to consult carried with it the necessity, if agreement could not be reached, to defer absolutely to the wishes of their allies; and if so to which allies they should defer. A decision became increasingly urgent. In December a delegation representing commercial interests in Britain and China urged immediate recognition. The Government's own supporters in the House of Commons were becoming increasingly impatient for a decision. At the end of December the matter was brought to a head.

On December 30 the Indian Government announced their recognition of the People's Republic. Pakistan followed suit on January 4. The British Government decided that they could wait no longer. On January 5 it was made known in London that the United Kingdom would recognize the new Government on the following day. On that night formal notification of the ending of British diplomatic relations with the Nationalist Government was conveyed to the Nationalist Ambassador in London. The following day official notice of recognition was handed to Chou En-lai by the British Consul General in Peking. It was announced that Mr. J. C. Hutchison, previously Commercial Minister at Nanking, had been appointed chargé d'affaires *ad interim*. At the same time the new Government was informed that the British Government had withdrawn recognition from the Nationalist Government; but that the British Consul in Tamsui would continue to keep in touch with the Nationalist authorities on the island.

The Governments of Ceylon and Norway announced their decision to recognize on the same day. Within the next fortnight, Denmark, Israel, Finland, Afghanistan, Sweden, and Switzerland did the same.

The British Press almost unanimously approved the decision. *The Times* declared that there "could be no doubt that the Government had acted wisely"; recognition would enable Britain, and through Britain the other Western Powers, to make their policies known. The *Manchester Guardian* said that the majority view in the country was that "convenience and prudence alike demanded" that the Peking Government should be recognized. Even the popular Press accepted that the decision was merely an acknowledgement of existing realities. Only, in a few cases, was there some criticism of the timing of the move.

Comment abroad was on the whole understanding, even in countries, such as the United States, which had themselves decided to adopt a different policy. The importance of British commercial interests in China was widely acknowledged. But the reaction of the Nationalists was ferocious. On the day of the announcement, the Nationalist Foreign Minister declared that the phenomenon of Great Britain rushing to offer recognition to the puppet Peking Communist régime was viewed with regret and astonishment. The British Consulate in Tamsui was stoned. And Madame Chiang Kai-shek, in a broadcast from New York, said that the decision was that of moral weaklings: Britain had been "taken by its leaders into the wilderness of political intrigue and had betrayed the soul of a nation for thirty pieces of silver".

Criticism of the move in Britain only started to be vocal some time after the event, when it began to be felt in some quarters that recognition had brought little of value to Britain, for example in helping to protect her interests in China. The Conservative leaders, in a later Commons debate, claimed that the British Government should have made greater efforts to act in conjunction with their allies. There was criticism of the decision to recognize without waiting until after the meeting of Commonwealth Foreign Ministers at Columbo, which took place only three days after the decision was announced. Others expressed apprehension over the effect recognition would have on the British position in Malaya and other parts of South East Asia.

Government spokesmen could reply that, so far as seeking agreement with their partners was concerned, there had in fact been full consultations, but that, as Mr. Younger told the House, "in the course of these it became clear that because of the varying attitudes of different members of the Commonwealth, united action was not to be expected". Recognition had been based "on the facts of the situation in China", not on a calculation of immediate benefits. Replying to the Opposition criticisms, Mr. Bevin said that it had not been for the Government to consider the political colour of the new Chinese Government. There had been strong pressure of public opinion in India, Pakistan and other parts of the east which had to be taken account of. There had been similar pressure from commercial interests and Chinese experts in this country. And so far as getting agreement was concerned it had proved impossible to reconcile what some members of the Commonwealth wanted to do with the "very aloof attitude" of the United States.

The Government could fairly claim that they had from the start

THE COMING OF THE COMMUNISTS

made clear how anxious they were to move in step with the United States and other members of the Commonwealth. If it had not been for this desire, recognition would no doubt have come far sooner. But given that there was an absolute difference of opinion between many of those whom they consulted, they had in fact had no alternative but to side with one group or the other. In the circumstances they could scarcely be blamed, having done their best to bring about an agreed course of action, for acting in accordance with their own convictions.

British governments have long tended to take a pragmatic view in their attitude to the emergence of revolutionary régimes. They have never concerned themselves unduly about ideological niceties. This indifference has been particularly pronounced where British commercial advantage was at issue. The attitude of British governments to the emergence of the independent states of South America did not derive fundamentally from conviction of the dangers of meddling in the internal affairs of others, still less from a belief in the right of subject peoples to free themselves from the tyranny of a colonial government—a highly dubious doctrine for British statesmen to vindicate—but from the need to preserve the commercial connexions that Britain had built up since the decline of Spanish power. British sympathy with the confederate cause in the American Civil War was not conditioned mainly by a passionate faith in the sanctity of state rights, still less by any predilection for the institution of slavery, but by the dependence of Lancashire on the raw cotton of the South. The decision, tardy and reluctant, to enter into relations with the Soviet Union, was dictated more by the need to keep up with trading rivals than by any softening of hostility to the Bolshevik creed.

Similar considerations were without doubt an important factor in the decision to recognize the Chinese People's Republic. It was widely hoped that it might still be possible to salvage something of the extensive British interests in the country. Recognition seemed likely at least to facilitate this. Pressure from commercial interests was strong and strident. But this was only one factor among many. Many British residents in China needed to have contacts with the existing authorities, which would not be permitted until recognition had been granted. There is little doubt that the majority of public opinion in Britain approved the step. Nothing could have been gained, and much might have been lost, by deliberately isolating the new China from contacts with the West, and so ensuring that her only foreign contacts were with Communist countries. Finally, recognition was needed, as the Government repeatedly pointed out, merely as an acknowledgement of fact. Whether Western governments like it or not, the Communist régime did in effect control China. To continue to designate the authorities controlling little more than a single island off the Chinese coast as the government of China would have seemed to most in Britain an absurdity.

Indeed some held that, according to a strict interpretation of international law, the British Government had in fact no option but to recognize. Most authorities do not accept that recognition is a discretionary act of policy on the part of the recognizing government. Provided that that government are assured that the new authorities possess effective control of the greater part of the territory of the country concerned, and provided that the normal conditions demanded by international law are fulfilled, there is, it is generally held, a legal duty to recognize.

In fact the arguments in favour of recognition were expressed, in eloquent language, by the Leader of the Opposition himself, Mr. Churchill, in a debate in the House of Commons two months before recognition took place: "Recognizing a person", he pointed out, "is not necessarily an act of approval. One has to recognize lots of things and people in this world of sin and woe that one does not like. The reason for having diplomatic relations is not to confer a compliment but to secure a convenience. When a large and powerful mass of people are organized together and are masters of an immense area and of great populations, it may be necessary to have relations with them. One may even say that it is when relations are most difficult that diplomacy is most needed."

During the ten years since these words were spoken, relations between the British Government and the new masters of China have indeed often been difficult. Certainly they would have been far more difficult if diplomacy had been impossible.

5

THE KOREAN WAR

RECOGNITION of the new régime did not in itself solve any problems. The British Government quickly found that its immediate effect was simply to provide the occasion for the new Chinese régime to demand still further political concessions from Britain. And within less than a year the relations between the two countries were further complicated by the eruption of a conflict in which the armed forces of each were engaged on opposing sides.

It had been almost universally assumed that the British Government's act of recognition would itself automatically bring about the establishment of diplomatic relations. This view was soon proved false. On January 9, 1950, Chou En-lai replied to the British Note announcing recognition. He expressed the willingness of the Chinese Government to enter into diplomatic relations and accepted the appointment of a chargé d'affaires *ad interim* "for the purpose of carrying on negotiations concerning the establishment of diplomatic relations".

The British Government appeared somewhat taken aback to find that, to establish diplomatic relations, it was necessary to conduct negotiations. On January 17, the British Consul-General in Peking was asked to make inquiries about the meaning of this phrase. On January 28, Chou En-lai announced that the discussions with the new chargé d'affaires would concern "preliminary and procedural questions" relating to the establishment of diplomatic relations. It was generally assumed that the discussions would be confined to such formalities as diplomatic immunities, mutual facilities for consulates, and similar matters.

The new chargé d'affaires and most of the remaining staff of the former Embassy at Nanking arrived at Peking on February 13. Negotiations started on March 2. Three main questions were raised by the Chinese negotiators. These were the British Government's decision to maintain *de facto* relations with the Nationalist authorities in Formosa; British abstention, since recognition, in votes taken on the exclusion of Nationalist delegates at the United Nations; and the disposal of various Chinese state properties, previously held by the Nationalists but now claimed by the Communist Government as the successor government: this referred principally to about seventy aircraft flown out to Hong Kong by the Nationalists and at that time subject to legal proceedings in the island.

On March 17, Mr. Hutchison, the new chargé d'affaires, gave a verbal explanation on all these points. The British Government maintained that their *de facto* recognition of the Nationalist authorities in Formosa was purely a matter of convenience based on the undeniable fact that those authorities exercised effective control in the area, and had no bearing on the right of sovereignty of either government in Formosa. They had not so far voted in favour of a transfer of the China seat at the United Nations because they felt it better to make sure that an effective majority existed for this before doing so. And on the question of the Chinese Government property, they said that while most of this would be handed over to the C.P.G. when formal diplomatic relations were established, in some cases the property was subject to legal proceedings and the matter could only be decided by the law courts. These answers did not satisfy the Chinese Government. On May 8, they delivered a Note requesting clarification of H.M.G.'s attitude.

Meanwhile the tone of the Chinese Press and radio hardened. A Peking broadcast on May 22 referred to the "exceedingly unfriendly attitude" of Britain and the "notorious duplicity of British traditional foreign policy"; and warned the British Government that the current talks would collapse unless there was an immediate change in the actions and attitude of Britain. Peking radio became vehement in its attacks on the actions of British colonial governments. There were vague threats that the questions of "British properties and interests in China" and "the situation in Hong Kong" might be raised at the talks. On May 24 a public statement was issued by the Chinese Ministry of Foreign Affairs declaring that the Chinese Government thought it necessary to secure some clarification of the "disparity between the British Government's declarations and its actions".

In Britain there began to be increasing impatience. It had been generally felt that the act of recognition had been a generous gesture towards the new Government and there was some resentment that the Government should now appear to seek to impose conditions on being recognized. Opposition members declared that Britain

THE KOREAN WAR

was being "humiliated" by the negotiations. There were suggestions that a time-limit should be placed on the talks: after this recognition should be withdrawn. Such impatience was to some extent shared by the Government. In a foreign affairs debate on May 24, Mr. Bevin described the questions raised by Communists as "side-issues", entirely separate from the question of the resumption of diplomatic relations.

On June 17 the British chargé d'affaires delivered a reply to the Chinese Government's Note of May 8. This restated H.M.G.'s position on the points that had been raised. But it reaffirmed Britain's willingness to exchange Ambassadors and asked whether the Chinese Government wished to do likewise.

No reply was ever received from the Chinese Government. There was nevertheless a certain relaxation in the Chinese Government's attitude. Though it was never accepted as an official Embassy, the British mission in Peking was granted most of the normal diplomatic privileges and immunities.

On October 1, 1950, Chou En-lai speaking at celebrations of the first anniversary of the establishment of the Republic, said that the negotiations with Britain, though they had gone on for a long time, had proved fruitless, because the British Government had continued to accept Chinese Nationalist representation in the United Nations even though they had recognized the C.P.G. (in fact by this time Britain had started to vote in favour of the transfer of the China seat to the People's Republic). At the same time Britain had adopted an "impermissible" and unfriendly attitude to Chinese nationals in Hong Kong and other places. On November 1, Mr. Ernest Davies, the British Under-Secretary of State for Foreign Affairs, said in the House of Commons that, while it was unfortunate that the establishment of diplomatic relations had not been achieved, it was for the Chinese to take the next step.

The British Government started to vote for China's admission to the United Nations in September, 1950. But with the outbreak of the Korean War in June, and especially after the entry of Chinese forces in November, relations between the two Governments became more difficult. The negotiations for the resumption of diplomatic relations were never resumed. Technically the British representative in Peking is still known as the British "negotiating representative". In Chinese eyes there are still no diplomatic relations between the two countries.

If the British Government attached real importance to entering into formal diplomatic relations, it could be argued that some of the actions which they took in the period immediately after their recognition were not those best suited to serve this purpose. The Chinese Government had from the start been explicit in declaring in all their public pronouncements that a condition for entering into diplomatic relations was the "severance" of relations with the Nationalists. Britain's decision to maintain a Consulate at Tamsui was no doubt designed to secure protection for British trading and other interests in Formosa. Perhaps too it was conceived as some sort of compromise to make the divergence between British and U.S. policy appear somewhat less acute. But it was inevitable that the Chinese Government considered the decision to be in direct conflict with the conditions they had publicly laid down for the establishment of diplomatic relations. It is possible that an attempt to secure British interests in Formosa by some less formal arrangements, for example by asking U.S. Consulates to look after British interests as Britain looked after U.S. interests in China, would have been more easily over-looked by the Chinese Government.

The decision to abstain in votes for the admission of Communist China to the United Nations may also have been intended to minimize the appearance of disunity among the Western Powers until a firm majority for the change-over could be mustered. But to the Chinese leaders it seemed that a sincere recognition of their Government as the legitimate government of China carried with it automatically a recognition of their right to represent China at the United Nations. If the British Government were prepared later, even after China's entry into the Korean War, to vote in favour of admission without the necessary majority in support, they might perhaps as well have done so from the start.

On the Hong Kong aircraft the British Government could not have acted otherwise than they did. But here again, to the Chinese Government the recognition of their right to former Chinese state property seemed to stem automatically from the act of recognition. With the pragmatic approach to justice of all Communists and of most Chinese, they found it inconceivable that the British Government could not, by a simple executive action, declare that all Chinese Government property had become in British eyes, as the Hong Kong Supreme Court at first ruled, by the very act of recognition the property of the newly acknowledged Government.

THE KOREAN WAR

To the British, however, such points appeared irrelevant to the establishment of diplomatic relations. And it was understandably aggravating that the Government they had made some sacrifice to recognize should seek to haggle over relatively trivial issues before agreeing to enter into formal relations. It is in fact doubtful how far the failure to establish official diplomatic relations has affected the subsequent contacts between the two countries. Although the representatives of each country in the other are still formally styled chargés d'affaires, their staff in practice are able to perform all the normal functions of an Embassy. Neither have normally had difficulty in making contacts with the officials with whom they have needed to deal. The negotiations that took place during 1950 concerned shadow rather than substance, name rather than reality. The failure to establish a closer relationship in the years that followed was the result, not of the breakdown of these negotiations, but of new and graver events that intervened.

There had already, in the months that followed recognition, been considerable disillusionment with the new Chinese Government in Britain. The public pronouncements of the new régime remained intransigent and dogmatic. There were many reports of difficulties among British businessmen. Chinese officials showed themselves in many of their dealings with foreigners in China almost as difficult as their predecessors. In foreign policy all hopes that the new China might show herself independent of the Soviet *bloc* were quickly dispelled. And over Formosa, and later Tibet, the new Government proved uncompromisingly bellicose.

The British Government were clearly anxious to make every allowance. In May, 1950, Mr. Bevin declared in Parliament that "we all ought now to co-operate to give China a chance". At the Labour Party Conference later that year Mr. Bevin described China as "that great pacifist nation", and called for her admission to world councils. And in December, 1950, he expressed to the House of Commons his conviction that Britain should seek to keep China in association with the other nations of the world so that she should not feel forced to align herself permanently with the Soviet Union. For the Chinese, he felt, however obstinately they might maintain their traditional antagonism to foreigners, "could not work up any great hostility" to Britain.

Unfortunately by this time Chinese troops were already engaged in battle with those of Britain and other states. The chance of inducing China to enter into a more satisfactory relationship with the Western world was therefore already almost beyond hope. But the British Government could perhaps fairly claim that they made more strenuous efforts than any other Western government to prevent these events from taking on the unhappy proportions they finally assumed.

After the invasion of South Korea by North Korean troops on June 24, 1950, Chinese comment naturally supported the North Korean contention, belied by United Nations observers on the spot, that the war was the result of a South Korean attack. The principal Chinese reaction to these events, however, was directed not to the intervention of United Nations troops in that war, but to the action of President Truman in assigning the U.S. Seventh Fleet to ensuring the neutralization of Formosa. On June 28, the first public statement by Chinese leaders on events in Korea, reserved the brunt of their anger to denouncing this decision. This was designed, Chou En-lai declared, to obstruct the Chinese liberation of Formosa, and constituted "armed aggression against Chinese territory" and violation of the United Nations charter. This remained the dominant theme of Chinese propaganda for the next few months. All the evidence in fact suggests that Chinese forces in mid-summer 1950, were already poised for the invasion of Formosa and the liquidation of the Nationalist Government. The Chinese leaders were far more indignant at being cheated, by President Truman's declaration, of this opportunity, than by the effect of United Nations intervention in Korea.

The situation was altered when the United Nations decided that their forces should cross the 38th Parallel, and so bring about the forcible unification of Korea. The original Security Council resolution, passed on June 25, the day after the North Korean invasion, had demanded that United Nations members should provide South Korea with such assistance "as may be necessary to repel the armed attack and to restore international peace and security in the area". But ever since the end of the Japanese war the United Nations had been endeavouring to bring about the reunification of the country. These efforts had been frustrated by North Korean obstruction. Thus when the United Nations forces finally halted the North Korean advance and began once more to move forward towards

THE KOREAN WAR

the north, it began to be felt that the opportunity should be seized to bring about the long-desired objective.

On August 10, the United States delegate to the Security Council, Mr. Austin, spoke of "the determination of the United Nations to ensure that Korea should be free, unified and independent of outside influence"; and held that "this was what United Nations forces were fighting to uphold". The Indian Government repudiated this concept of United Nations action. On August 30, Mr. Acheson said that the matter was one for the United Nations to decide.

British opinion on the matter was divided. Some foresaw the risks. "What the Russians—or the Chinese—may say or do if fighting . . . oversteps the parallel," stated *The Times* on September 16, "is a formidable riddle." Other newspapers expressed similar apprehensions. But some maintained that a more easily defensible military line could be established at the neck of the peninsula to the north of the parallel. Many hoped in any case, that by the time the parallel was reached, the North Koreans would have been so thoroughly defeated that they would be ready to accept the United Nations terms without the need for any further advance. But it was almost universally agreed that new United Nations authority would be required to cross the line.

For a time the British Government refused to commit themselves on the point. They were reported to be concerned by reports received from their own and the Indian Embassies in Peking that if the parallel were crossed China might intervene. But it was generally believed that China was too preoccupied with her internal problems to be able to risk war on the Korean peninsula. And when the United Nations troops, flushed with victory, began to approach the parallel, the opportunity to bring about a settlement that was final rather than temporary, and to solve the insoluble problem of reunification, seemed too good to miss. On September 29 Mr. Bevin on the eve of his departure for New York said that "if you wish a united and free Korea, the 38th parallel must almost automatically disappear: there should be no artificial perpetuation of that division".

British and United States forces halted when they reached the parallel. South Korean forces, which could legitimately claim that they were not limited by the terms of the original United Nations authorization, continued to advance. On October 1 General MacArthur called on the North Korean forces to accept a cease-fire "in order that the decisions of the United Nations might be carried out with the minimum further loss of life and destruction".

On the same day Chou En-lai declared that "if the imperialists were wantonly to invade the territory of her neighbour, China would not stand aside". The next day he informed the Indian Ambassador that if U.S. forces crossed the parallel China would be forced to intervene. On October 5 the *Kwang Ming Daily* said that "war in its real sense has only just begun", and declared that the North Korean army had "many volunteers at their back". These warnings attracted little attention in the West.

On September 26 the British delegation at the United Nations circulated the draft of a resolution which provided for the reunification of Korea, free elections under United Nations auspices, a United Nations commission to supervise the return to peaceful conditions, and United Nations aid and economic reconstruction. This was presented on September 30. While it made no specific references to crossing the parallel, it declared that "all appropriate steps should be taken to ensure conditions of stability throughout Korea". But it added that United Nations forces should not remain in any part of Korea "otherwise than so far as was necessary for achieving the objectives laid down in the resolution".

On discussion in the Political Committee, the U.S. delegate urged that the artificial barrier of the 38th parallel should be wiped out and steps taken to eliminate the capacity of the North Korean forces to launch further oppression. The British Government, though supporting the decision to cross the parallel, began to show some concern about the possible reaction of the Chinese. In discussion in the General Assembly on October 6–7, Mr. Younger, the Minister of State, emphasized that military operations would be confined to the fulfilment of the resolution's purposes and said: "If China or any other of Korea's neighbours fear that the United Nations forces might carry hostilities further, or remain in Korea longer than these limited objectives demand, I give them my solemn assurance, as one of those powers whose forces are now in Korea, that their fears have no foundation." The resolution was finally adopted by 47 votes to 5. The next day, October 8, United Nations forces began to cross the parallel. On October 9, Mr. Bevin sent a personal message to Chou En-lai, assuring the Chinese Government that Chinese interests in Korea would be respected and that Chinese views would

THE KOREAN WAR 91

be noted by the Commission that was to bring about the reunification of Korea.

On October 1, a Peking broadcast said that a serious situation had been created by the "United States invasion" of Korea, and repeated the statement that the Chinese people could not stand idly by. Such declarations were still generally regarded in the West as empty threats. The British Government, however, were becoming increasingly concerned. They began to believe that it would be best for the northern expedition to halt at the Korean waistline. This would mean the occupation of over a third of North Korea, including its capital, Pyongyang. But it would leave a substantial buffer region to the north. This might serve to relieve China of anxiety about the proximity of United Nations, and especially United States, forces on her borders, and to assure her of continued access to supplies of electricity which she obtained from North Korean power stations. And it would provide a better defensive position for United Nations forces.

The British chiefs of staff presented advice in this sense to the British Cabinet. This was forwarded by the British Government to the United States Government, who were asked to take it into account. Mr. Bevin later declared that he himself had "had sympathy with the argument about halting at the line of the waist in Korea" and leaving a no-man's-land to the north. And when finally, U.N. troops began their last offensive to the northern border of Korea, the British Government became, as Mr. Bevin later revealed, "gravely concerned" that the United Nations forces might by their action be "running their heads into trouble".

The United Nations Supreme Commander, however, was responsible in military matters to the United States Chiefs of Staff. No decision on whether to advance to the Chinese border was either taken or sought at the United Nations. And the United States Chiefs of Staff decided that United Nations troops should continue to advance to the north.

On October 27, United Nations commanders reported the presence of Chinese troops in North Korea. On the next day General MacArthur's headquarters confirmed that Chinese forces were engaged but claimed that this was a face-saving operation and that there was no cause for alarm. By November 2, however, United Nations forces were being compelled to retreat. On November 4 the Chinese radio announced that, throughout the country, Chinese people were "volunteering to resist American aggression, to aid Korea, and to defend their country" which, it claimed, was directly threatened by the United Nations advance. On November 6 the Security Council received a report from General MacArthur confirming Chinese intervention.

The British Government, now seriously alarmed, took steps to bring about some settlement. On November 8 the British representative introduced a resolution in the Security Council inviting representatives of the Peking Government to participate in discussion of General MacArthur's report. They were instrumental in overcoming procedural objections by the Chinese Nationalists. And the resolution was adopted by 8 votes to 2. On November 15 the Chinese Government replied to the invitation, as well as to an earlier one asking them to discuss the Formosa question. They agreed to talk about Formosa; but refused to discuss General MacArthur's report, which was a "perversion of fact", and a "blustering attempt to intimidate China". They later declared that the Chinese people would not be afraid to take action against aggressors. And they demanded the immediate withdrawal of all foreign troops from Korea to facilitate reunification. Peking broadcasts maintained that the existence of an independent Korea and the security of China were closely inter-related. The presence of United States troops in Korea, together with the dispatch of the United States Seventh Fleet to Formosa and the violations of the Manchurian border by United States aircraft represented a threat to Chinese security. Chinese volunteers, in helping Korea, were only seeking to defend their own country.

There is little doubt that the Chinese Government were genuinely disturbed by the feeling that they were gradually being hemmed in on all sides by the forces of a government that was avowedly and outspokenly hostile to them. U.S. forces were already established in Japan and Formosa and other Pacific bases. Their presence on the northern border of Korea, in immediate proximity to the industrial heart of China, was more than Chinese leaders could stomach. Like their imperial predecessors half a century earlier, they felt constrained to take arms, even against all the odds, to ensure that all Korea should not fall under the power of a hostile government. Korea was to them a buffer state which, though it might be permitted to be neutral, even less than neutral, provided it remained solitary and weak, must never at any price come totally under the

THE KOREAN WAR

influence of any other power. Elated with their overwhelming victories in the civil war, conscious of the almost unlimited numbers of troops they could throw into the battle, they no doubt sought to eject the United Nations forces from the peninsula altogether.

Thus the attempts of the British Government and others to assure them that the presence of United Nations troops in North Korea did not threaten Chinese security were unrealistic. For what the Chinese feared was not so much an imminent invasion of Chinese soil by United Nations troops, as the establishment of a united Korea, whose government was likely to be as hostile to China, and as closely bound to the United States, as that of Syngman Rhee. When Chinese broadcasts demanded an "independent Korea", what they meant was a Korea that was not a menace to China.

Their initial successes in the field only made them less disposed to compromise. Both the Indian and British Governments made increasingly urgent attempts to convince them that United Nations action would not threaten China. On November 22 Mr. Bevin sent another personal message to Chou En-lai, through the British chargé d'affaires in Peking, designed to reassure him about the intentions of the United Nations forces. He reminded the Chinese Government of the terms of the United Nations resolutions and of the intention that United Nations forces should not remain in Korea any longer than necessary. In any case, he urged, the presence of these troops would not endanger legitimate Chinese interests in the area. The message was especially intended, Mr. Bevin said later, to relieve any apprehensions the Chinese might have felt, as a result of past experiences, that some aggression against Manchuria was intended.

Once Chinese troops were committed, however, the Chinese Government were unlikely to withdraw them except on terms that offered China the opportunity to save face in the process. And it soon became apparent that the terms she demanded were exorbitant. The Chinese delegate to the United Nations, General Wu Huai-chuan, arrived in New York on November 24. He agreed to take part in discussion of a resolution already presented. This called on all governments to cease assistance to North Korea, and to prevent their nationals from giving such assistance, but declared that no action would be taken which might lead to the extension of the conflict and reaffirmed that United Nations troops would not remain in any part of Korea any longer than was necessary to achieve the declared objects of the United Nations.

The debate took place on November 28. The United States delegate made an uncompromising speech accusing the Chinese Communists of "open and notorious aggression in Korea". General Wu was even more intemperate, accusing the United States Government of aggression against China, Korea, Viet-nam, the Philippines and other Asian countries, and demanding complete withdrawal of American forces from Formosa and Korea, in order to achieve a "peaceful solution" of these questions. The British representative tried to be conciliatory, stressing once again the limited objectives of the United Nations and expressing the hope that the Peking Government would think very carefully before coming to an irreversible decision. He pointed out, in order to provide some inducement, that the Formosa question was not likely to be settled by the United Nations so long as Chinese Communist forces were engaged in military operations against the United Nations. The resolution was passed. But was then vetoed by the Soviet Union.

At the beginning of December, British attempts at conciliation had to be exercised in another direction. On November 30, the day after the discussion in the Security Council, and while the Chinese delegates still remained at Lake Success, President Truman declared at a Press conference that, if the situation called for it, it might be necessary for General MacArthur to extend the Korean war to Manchuria; and that, although he hoped it would not be required, it was possible that during the conflict the atomic bomb might be brought into action.

On the same day Mr. Attlee informed the House of Commons that President Truman had agreed at very short notice to receive a visit from him in Washington. On December 3, immediately before the Prime Minister's departure, Mr. Attlee and Mr. Bevin had discussions with the French Prime Minister and Foreign Minister, at which it was said that "a general identity of views on the objectives of the two governments" in the present international situation had been reached. On his arrival in Washington Mr. Attlee emphasized that he was not there to advocate appeasement and declared the determination of the British Government to stand by the United States. Nevertheless it is evident that the British Prime Minister made clear to President Truman the deep anxiety that his statement about the extension of the war and the use of the atomic bomb had aroused in Europe. It seems certain that he was particularly anxious to secure an assurance that no decision would be reached on either of these questions without consultation with all powers whose forces were engaged in Korea.

The declaration issued at the end of the talks said that "the President stated that it was his hope that world conditions would never call for the use of the atomic bomb. The President told the Prime Minister that it was also his desire to keep the Prime Minister at all times informed of developments which might bring about a change in the situation". On his return Mr. Attlee announced that he was completely reassured by his talks with the President on the use of atomic weapons. The two statesmen had also given consideration to the procedure by which the United Nations Commander received his instructions; and Mr. Attlee was satisfied that the "general directions of the United Nations had been followed".

President Truman's remarks about the possibility of extending the war to Manchuria and of making use of the atomic bomb were made in answer to questions. It is more than likely, therefore, that they did not represent the considered opinion of the United States administration, but were dictated to some extent by the form in which the questions were framed. In so far as any thought lay behind it at all, the statement was presumably designed to frighten the Chinese into a reconsideration of their bellicose and uncompromising attitude, as this had been revealed two days before in the Security Council debate. It may be doubted whether in fact such a threat was not more likely to make the Chinese Government more intransigent than more accommodating. The statement certainly aroused widespread alarm in many countries in the West. There were visions of General MacArthur, with or without the authority of the United States administration, committing the United Nations to embarking on a full-scale, possibly even an atomic, war against China, without even bothering to consult any of the other nations involved. Mr. Attlee's dramatic visit perhaps served to demonstrate to the United States Government, more effectively than the more normal diplomatic channels could have done, the profound anxiety with which this prospect was viewed in Europe.

Even after the breakdown of the Security Council discussions, the British Government continued to believe that some kind of settlement with the Chinese could be reached. They recognized that, to achieve this, some wider political issues, as well as the purely military ones, would probably have to be discussed. On November 29 Mr. Bevin told the House of Commons that he was convinced that it was "on political lines that a solution must be found". He said that he was then working to bring about a solution of this sort. The British representative at the United Nations, Sir Gladwin Jebb, invited the Chinese delegation to his house for lunch. Like his Indian colleague, he took part in discussions with General Wu, under the auspices of the Secretary-General, designed to explore the conditions which the Chinese still demanded. These made little progress. But meanwhile the Korean issue had been placed on the agenda of the General Assembly. On December 6 the United Nations delegates of fifteen Asian-Arab countries delivered an appeal to General Wu that China should halt her troops at the 38th parallel. On December 14 the General Assembly passed a resolution proposed by the same group, setting up a three-man committee to determine the basis on which a satisfactory cease-fire could be arranged. On December 18 this committee forwarded to the Chinese Government the Assembly's cease-fire proposal, stressing that the aim was to prevent the conflict from spreading and to provide an opportunity "to settle existing issues": this at least gave a face-saving opportunity for the Chinese Government to bring up other Far Eastern questions once the cease-fire was agreed. On December 22 the Chinese Government rejected the proposal, demanding once again the withdrawal of all United Nations troops from Korea, of United States forces from Formosa and their own admission to the United Nations. At the new year they launched an offensive across the 38th Parallel. And on January 3 the Indian delegate reported to the Political Committee of the General Assembly the failure of the Cease-Fire Committee's efforts.

Britain took part in one final effort to bring about a settlement. From January 4 to 12 the Commonwealth Prime Ministers met in London. Several of their sessions were devoted to the Korean situation. Reports from the Commonwealth United Nations delegates (the Indian, British and Canadian delegates had all been intimately concerned in the discussions) were considered. The conference then formulated their views on the best ways of resolving the situation and transmitted these to the Cease-Fire Committee. This was perhaps one of the only recorded instances of an attempt by the Commonwealth Prime Ministers' Conference to take part in united action in relation to a specific foreign policy issue.

THE KOREAN WAR 97

Two out of three members of the Cease-Fire Committee, the Canadian and Indian delegates, were representatives of Commonwealth countries. And largely as a result of the discussions at the Commonwealth Conference, the Committee on January 11 put forward new proposals. These provided for an immediate cease-fire, to be followed by a four-power conference of the United States, Britain, the Soviet Union and Communist China for a settlement of all Far Eastern problems, including the questions of Formosa and the representation of China in the United Nations. All non-Korean armed forces would be withdrawn from Korea by appropriate stages and arrangements made for the Korean people to express their own free will in respect of their future government. These proposals were adopted by the Political Committee by an overwhelming majority. The Secretary-General was asked to forward them to Peking with the request that the Chinese Government should say whether they were acceptable as a basis for discussion.

The terms were in many ways more favourable to China than any others that have been offered to the Chinese Government either before or since. If they had been accepted China would have obtained a cease-fire at a time when she was in possession of all North and part of South Korea. She was offered a chance of taking part in a conference at which the questions of Formosa and Chinese representation in the United Nations might have been discussed, an opportunity that has never recurred. Even if her aims at such discussions had not been conceded, she would have had the opportunity to state her own case. And she would have been able to establish herself as an acknowledged power more effectively than she has ever had the chance to do since. So far as Korea was concerned she would still in practice have been in a position to prevent reunification on any terms that were not acceptable to her. And, should the United Nations have been obliged eventually to resume the war, she would have been better equipped to defend the area she then held.

But at this moment the Chinese forces were rapidly pushing back the United Nations troops in South Korea. The Chinese Government's aim was no doubt to eject the United Nations altogether before any talks began. On January 17 they rejected the United Nations offer, declaring that a cease-fire before the opening of negotiations was only designed to obtain a "breathing space for United States troops". They called once again for the withdrawal of all foreign troops from Korea, the withdrawal of "United States troops" from Formosa (at this time the United States had only military advisers on the island), and the entry of the Peking Government to the United Nations.

On the same day Mr. Acheson, the United States Secretary of State, issued a statement saying that the Communist Government's reply was not acceptable to the United States Government and "no doubt to the United Nations generally". The next day, when the Political Committee met to consider the Chinese reply, the United States delegate demanded that China should be condemned as an aggressor. The British, Australian and French delegates all asked for more time to study the Chinese reply before considering this proposal.

The British Government, though they were disappointed by the Chinese reply, did not consider that it finally closed the door to further negotiations. The British chargé d'affaires in Peking was, therefore, instructed to seek clarification from the Chinese Government. Meanwhile the military position in South Korea began to look rather different. By January 20 the Chinese advance had been halted. U.N. troops were being poured in. And it began to be most doubtful whether the Chinese would be able to push the U.N. forces off the peninsula. At the interview, on January 21, the Chinese Vice-Minister of Foreign Affairs outlined conditions which did represent a significant modification of the previous Chinese position. The Chinese Government for the first time accepted that a cease-fire might take place before further negotiations had been opened. The cease-fire could, the Minister suggested, be agreed at a preliminary meeting of the powers (so ensuring at least some international recognition of the C.P.G.) and put into effect immediately, so that further negotiations could then proceed. Afterwards there would be discussion of the withdrawal of all foreign troops from Korea, the future of Korea, the withdrawal of United States armed forces from Formosa, and other problems concerning the Far East. The Chinese Government still demanded that Communist China should be given a place in the United Nations, but did not specifically state that this should be discussed at the conference as a condition of a cease-fire. The Indian Ambassador in Peking received a communication in similar terms.

These conditions were not in fact so very far away from the offer contained in the last United Nations resolution. The main difference was that the cease-fire would take place only after the calling of the conference, instead of immediately and unconditionally. By this time, however, the Political Committee was already considering a United States resolution condemning China as an aggressor and requesting that the Collective Measures Committee should consider urgently the question of economic sanctions against China by all United Nations members. The British and other delegates requested some time to reconsider this motion in the light of the latest Chinese offer. The British Government felt that action of the sort proposed by the United States Government was premature. "We did not think," Mr. Attlee explained to the House of Commons later, "that a motion condemning China as an aggressor and calling for sanctions was likely to promote the object in view." This was still to try to induce the Chinese to accept a cease-fire, after which discussions on other matters might take place. The Government wanted a chance for further consultations with "their Asian friends who still seemed to have hope of arriving at a negotiated settlement".

Thus the British delegate in New York urged that before taking action the ambiguities remaining in the latest Chinese communication should be further explored. In particular he urged that the United Nations ought not at that time to consider imposing economic sanctions which could only exacerbate the situation. These reservations were widely shared, especially among Asian countries. There were further Commonwealth consultations. The British Government sought to get the resolution amended in order, as Mr. Younger later explained, to "keep the door open for negotiations". As a result, the consideration of sanctions against China, demanded in the earlier resolution "as a matter of urgency", was to be deferred until it was known what progress in reaching a settlement had been made by the Good Offices Committee (which was now to be established in place of the Cease-Fire Committee). And the wording of the aggressor condemnation was slightly softened.

Its main purport, however, was unaffected. It still declared that the General Assembly "found that the People's Republic of China . . ." had, through its assistance to the North Korean Government, "engaged in aggression in Korea". On January 31 the resolution in this form was passed by an overwhelming majority. The British representative voted in favour of it. The British Government, it was later stated, still believed that the condemnation was badly timed, but had come to the conclusion that, since no majority could be obtained for the omission of the aggressor clause, they should vote for the resolution as a whole as the best that could be obtained in the circumstances.

On February 4, Chou En-lai denounced the resolution as "illegal, slanderous and void", declaring that the Chinese Government would not receive the Good Offices Committee set up under it. Both the Indian and the Canadian delegates refused to serve on the Good Offices Committee. Burma and Yugoslavia refused to participate in the Collective Measures Committee. The Good Offices Committee made no further progress in its negotiations for a cease-fire. As a result of the failure of its efforts, the Additional Measures Committee (as the Collective Measures Committee came to be called) on May 14 passed a United States proposal calling for an embargo on the export of strategic materials to China.

So ended for the moment the effort to reach a negotiated settlement of the Korean conflict. It is perhaps unlikely that at any stage the Chinese would have been prepared to settle on terms that would have been acceptable to a majority of the United Nations. The negotiations nevertheless followed a somewhat illogical course. In the early stages while the Chinese appeared completely intransigent and unrealistic in their demands, the United Nations were prepared to offer increasingly generous terms to bring about a cease-fire. But as soon as the Chinese leaders, in their communications to the Indian and British missions in Peking, did at last show some signs of making concessions, little serious effort was made to explore these any further. But these terms were not in fact far distant from the terms proposed by the United Nations; and were no doubt in any case, as in any other oriental auction, only China's starting position. And when, at the end of January the United Nations troops at last began to hold and even to push back the Chinese troops so that China might perhaps have been more ready to talk, the United Nations promptly proceeded to pass a denunciatory resolution in severe terms which, though it could no doubt be justified on the basis of the facts, was scarcely likely to enhance the prospects of a settlement.

The British Government, together with the Indian, almost to the end exerted all their efforts to ensuring that the Chinese should be given the maximum opportunity to come to terms. They were perhaps at first over-optimistic in their estimates of the readiness of China to negotiate. At the end, however, at the very moment when

THE KOREAN WAR

there seemed some chance of inducing the Chinese Government to talk, they agreed to support an act of condemnation that added nothing constructive to the position, and could only serve to make more difficult the further efforts at conciliation that were initiated in the very same resolution.

There was no further attempt at negotiation for a Korean settlement until June, 1951, when Mr. Malik, broadcasting in New York, made proposals for a cease-fire to be followed by an armistice and mutual withdrawal of troops beyond the 38th Parallel. The negotiations on the terms of the cease-fire continued for the next two years, while the fighting still went on, before an armistice could be finally agreed. They were conducted on behalf of the United Nations by United States Army officers who acted in their day-to-day decisions largely on instructions from the United States Government (though there existed a committee in Washington on which other governments engaged in Korea were represented). The British Government nevertheless had some opportunities to exert their influence on the course of the negotiations.

In November, 1952, after the Indian Government had put forward a proposal, designed to break the deadlock that had been reached over the disposal of prisoners who refused to be repatriated, Britain gave this her whole-hearted support. She made strenuous efforts to bring about some kind of accommodation between the Indian and United States Governments on the terms of the offer. As a result the proposal, slightly amended, was accepted by the Political Committee by an overwhelming majority and formed the basis of the agreement that was finally arrived at. When, later, a new conflict arose over which government should take charge of the prisoners during the period of questioning that was to be instituted to ascertain their views, Britain supported proposals that the Indian Government, who were known to be acceptable to the Chinese but were at first rejected by the United States, should be chosen to carry out the task. This too formed an element in the final solution. When the United Nations negotiators, probably under pressure from the South Korean Government, for a time sought to insist that the North Korean prisoners should be excluded from the agreement on repatriation, and released where they were, the U.K. Government again joined with India and Canada in resisting the proposal. And it was eventually accepted that the same conditions should apply to the North Koreans as to other prisoners. Finally, when the war was over, and there was conflict over representation at the peace conference to follow, Britain, alone among the nations fighting in Korea, supported the Chinese demand that India should be represented at the conference.

When these and many other difficulties had been resolved, the armistice was finally signed, despite strenuous efforts by the South Korean Government to sabotage it, on July 7, 1953. So the war came to an end with the rival forces no great distance from where they started. It was one of those rare wars where both sides finally agreed to accept a draw. The Chinese had failed in their efforts to evict the United Nations forces from the Korean peninsula. They had suffered a somewhat humiliating defeat, both in their efforts to secure the return of all the prisoners, and in the obvious demonstration, in the final choice of those prisoners, that not all Chinese preferred Communist rule to any other. But they had successfully pushed potentially hostile forces away from their own frontiers. And, perhaps more important, they had demonstrated to the world that an Asian nation, with a backward economy and inferior equipment, could effectively hold at bay the entire panoply that the West could muster against it.

The United Nations also could claim that they had successfully thrown back the North Korean aggressors, so demonstrating to the world that international crime does not pay. They had shown themselves conciliatory but firm in their conduct of the peace negotiations. And they had throughout, by a deliberate act of abnegation, refrained from attacking the Communist positions and supplies in Manchuria and the Chinese mainland, despite the severe handicap to their military operations that this entailed. But perhaps the most important achievement of all was that by fighting a war of resistance—with whatever motives—in the name of an international organization, and with the authority of that organization, a new precedent had been established. Before the Second World War, collective security had been a slogan. After that war it had become a policy.

It might well be argued, however, that having previously passed a resolution specifically calling on the United Nations forces to take such steps as were necessary to reunify Korea, they virtually admitted defeat in finally settling for less than this. It may well be

THE KOREAN WAR

questioned even on grounds of principle, whether the United Nations were well advised in taking the decision to cross the 38th parallel. For in so doing they laid themselves open to the charge that they were converting a war to resist aggression into a war of conquest. And in failing to achieve this object, they exposed themselves equally to the criticism that they had publicly demonstrated that the organization had not the power to impose the authority to which it had itself laid claim.

The British Government supported the decision to cross the parallel. They felt, like many other governments, that an opportunity was thereby presented to achieve the reunification of the peninsula, an object that had been fruitlessly pursued by the United Nations ever since the war. Once the line had been crossed, however, they were more aware than most other governments of the danger of provoking Chinese retaliation that was being run. And once China had intervened they were tireless in their efforts to seek some kind of accommodation.

That these failed was no fault of theirs. The Chinese were in no mood for compromise. And they were at first victorious in the field. Only a long process of attrition eventually persuaded them to accept less, very much less, than they at first hoped to achieve. And they may in retrospect have regretted that they had not been prepared to look, with more favourable eyes, at the efforts at mediation that Britain, with other nations, had attempted.

Throughout the hostilities in which they were engaged, the two governments remained in diplomatic contact. The British mission in Peking maintained a strange existence, continuing to negotiate on many matters vitally affecting British interests with the representatives of a nation with which their own government was to all intents and purposes at war. They were in general treated correctly, if without cordiality. The fact that the forces of the two countries were engaged at the time in ferocious hostilities probably did not much affect the course of their discussions. Nor probably did the conflict exert any direct influence on the subsequent course of relations between the two countries. But that China, in the war, was able, for the first time since the British conquest a hundred and twenty years earlier, successfully to defy the embattled armies of the West, was a symbol of the fundamental transformation that had now taken place in the relations between the two nations.

6

MISSIONARIES

WHEN the British first arrived in China, Christianity had been known there for many centuries. It was first brought in the seventh century by Nestorian missionaries from West Asia, received imperial blessing, and survived in that form for about two centuries before being suppressed. During the Mongol dynasty several Franciscan monks, sent by the Pope, reached China by land. An Archbishop of Peking was consecrated, but it seems that few converts were made and the faith quickly died out. In the sixteenth century Dominicans, Franciscans, Augustinians and Jesuits again made their way to China. The Jesuits in particular were very favourably received at the imperial court, to whom they brought valuable knowledge of astronomy, geography, mathematics, surveying, and the calendar. The missions began to make a fair number of converts to Christianity. But in 1717, after the Pope had forbidden the veneration of ancestors and various other accommodations to Chinese traditional practice which the Jesuits had permitted, Christianity was proscribed by the Emperor. This prohibition was maintained with varying degrees of severity until nearly half-way through the nineteenth century.

It was the British who founded the first Protestant missions. This occurred almost immediately after the sudden upsurge of evangelical activity which occurred at the end of the eighteenth century. During the last decade of that century the London Missionary Society, the Baptist Missionary Society and the Church Missionary Society all came into being. In 1807 Robert Morrison of the London Missionary Society arrived in China. By 1832 there were five workers of that mission in the country.

Proselytization at that time was extremely difficult. Chinese Catholics were still subject to bouts of persecution. Christian missions were still prohibited. Morrison, having obtained employment with the East India Company, was able to translate the Bible and part of the Prayer Book into Chinese. He distributed scriptures and tracts. He prepared a Chinese/English dictionary and a grammar. But the pace of conversion was by no means dizzy. In

MISSIONARIES

the first twenty-five years of the mission he and his colleagues only claimed to have baptized ten converts to Christianity.

As a result of the war of 1839 the position, both for the Chinese Catholics and for the missionaries, was eased. The French, in their treaty, insisted that the Chinese Government should accept a toleration clause. In 1845 an imperial edict extended similar rights to Chinese Protestants. Foreign missionaries were permitted to preach their faith and set up churches, hospitals and schools within the five treaty ports.

As a result missionary activity increased. Other British societies joined the Congregationalists of the London Missionary Society. From 1846 a few missionaries of the General Baptist Mission started work at Ningpo. A year or two later English Presbyterian missionaries began to travel the country around Amoy and Swatow. In 1848 the Church Missionary Society, the Anglican body, established a mission at Ningpo, and in 1849 the first Anglican bishop of Victoria, Hong Kong, was consecrated. In 1851 the Methodist Missionary Society began operations in Canton. In 1860 the Baptist Missionary Society arrived in Chefoo but soon afterwards concentrated their efforts in the northern provinces of Shantung, Shansi and Shensi. Finally in 1860 the China Inland Mission, non-denominational, but in practice highly evangelical in theology, began its work, devoting itself in particular to converting the remoter regions of the interior that had not previously been penetrated. This became the largest single Protestant mission in China, having workers of various denominations, distributed in different districts, and of various nationalities. Unlike the other missions, it established independent local churches rather than a nation-wide organization. Besides all these, there were a good many other smaller societies, representing a variety of sects, including the Scottish and English Presbyterians, the Quakers and the Plymouth Brethren, and a few entirely independent missions.

At the end of the second Anglo-Chinese war in 1860 the position of the missionaries in China was again improved. The Treaty of Tientsin specifically provided that missionaries should be allowed to travel freely throughout the interior to preach their faith, and that Chinese Christians should "enjoy entire security in regard to their persons, their property and the free exercise of their religious practices". This last provision proved a mixed blessing. For the Chinese Christians came to turn to the missionaries to protect them against their own government. And, as the missionaries themselves admitted, Chinese sometimes adopted Christianity purely for the sake of the support that the missionaries were able to provide in the law-courts. Quite often, especially where whole villages adopted a faith, as the Catholics usually sought to achieve, the missionary became almost a civil official, regulating many of the domestic affairs of his own flock.

Before the end of the century the Protestant missions had penetrated every province of China proper. But they had still reached only a small proportion of the whole Chinese population and their activity remained largely concentrated in the east coast and the Yangtze areas. Even in the 1920s four-fifths of the missionaries were still working in those regions; and three-quarters of the Protestant Church membership and two-thirds of the Chinese staff were concentrated in the east coast provinces. There was some geographical partition between the societies. Most refrained from evangelizing where other Protestant societies were already working. Nevertheless to many Chinese the profusion of competing sects was perplexing. There was, first, the wide gap between the Catholic and Protestant missions, who preached cults so divergent that it was difficult to credit a common origin, even describing their deities under different names. Relations between these were never close, and sometimes positively embittered. And there was some mutual competition for congregations. Almost more confusing was the proliferation of Protestant sects, divided sometimes by quite small dogmatic differences (though often by much wider differences of temperament). There was the multiplication of different national societies nominally representing the same sect. Finally, especially during the twentieth century there emerged radical and sometimes embittered divisions between the fundamentalist and the more modernist groups among the missionaries.

There were various attempts to bring about some co-ordination between the activities of the Protestant societies. There were conferences of the Protestant missionaries in China in 1877, 1890, 1907, and 1913. Attempts were made to adopt a common approach to such problems as the opium trade (which was from the start heartily condemned), foot-binding, ancestor worship and other problems. There was some co-ordination of publication work, and of representations to the Chinese Government on matters of common interest. In 1913, after the World Missionary Conference at Edinburgh of 1910, a China Continuation Committee was set up to co-ordinate the activities of the Protestant missions. In 1922 this was replaced by the National Christian Council. The Conference from the start had a majority of Chinese members, and was sometimes criticized by some of the missions for its modernist theology and its manifest sympathy with Chinese Nationalist sentiment. The China Inland Mission and one or two other groups withdrew from it altogether.

Perhaps a more effective move towards unity was the formation during the 1920s of the Church of Christ in China, in which the London Missionary Society, the Baptist Missionary Society and the British Presbyterian missions participated with a number of foreign societies, mainly Congregational and Presbyterian. United synods were established in five mission areas and the Church was believed eventually to include about one-third of all Chinese Protestants. But the Methodists, Anglicans, Lutherans and some Baptists continued to maintain separate churches. And in the nineteen-thirties there were altogether about a hundred different Protestant organizations working in China.

By the beginning of the twentieth century there were about 5,000 Protestant missionaries altogether. This rose to nearly 8,000 in 1926; but fell again after the Nationalist advance, and was under 5,000 in 1936. By that time the missions claimed nearly 500,000 Chinese Protestants and over 2,000,000 Chinese Catholics. At the same time the proportion of Chinese holding office in the churches was increasing. By 1920 the number of ordained Chinese in the churches exceeded the number of Westerners, though the key positions were still nearly always held by Westerners.

During most of the nineteenth century British missionaries dominated Protestant evangelization in China. In 1890 over half the Protestant missionaries were British. But from the beginning of the twentieth century, and especially after the First World War, they came to be increasingly outnumbered by Americans. In 1922 only eighteen per cent of the missionaries were British and more than half Americans.

The British missions in China were normally organized in a series of stations in the cities and country towns, with a number of sub-stations in the rural areas. Each of these could serve a good many separate village churches. The mission station might consist of a church building or preaching hall, reception rooms, residences for the foreign missionaries and sometimes for the Chinese assistants, often enclosed within a mission compound and usually built in the Western style. In the towns there were often street chapels, perhaps in shops that had been rented or bought. The stations built up local congregations, having their own priests, which were periodically visited by the missionary, who would baptize, instruct, examine and perhaps settle local disputes. The missionaries often lived in isolation from any other Western people. And even when they had such neighbours, as in the towns, they frequently formed a separate community whose relations with the commercial and official world were not always cordial.

At the time of the Japanese war some British missionaries retreated to the regions held by the Chinese. More, however, stayed on in their own areas, and, after Britain became involved in the Pacific war, were interned and, during or after the war, repatriated to Britain. At the end of the war, therefore, though the Chinese churches remained intact, the activities of the societies had to start again almost from scratch. By 1949 the total number of foreign Protestant missionary staff in China was about 4,000 out of whom somewhat less than a thousand were British. Of the British missionaries about one-quarter belonged to the China Inland Mission; about the same number to the Church of Christ in China; a hundred to the Methodist Missionary Society; and the rest distributed among a number of denominations, or non-denominational. There were about 700,000 practising Protestants in China. The Church of Christ in China claimed nearly 170,000 communicants, the churches founded by the China Inland Mission about 90,000, that of the Methodist Missionary Society 40,000, and that of the Church Missionary Society 30,000. Of the other missions the American Southern Baptist and the American Methodists were the largest, but only three had more than 20,000 members. The other Protestants in China were divided among more than seventy different sects.

From early times the presence of missionaries had aroused antagonism in China. Thus, between intervals of toleration, Christianity was periodically suppressed by court and officials, whenever it seemed to them to represent a dangerous rival to the official Confucian ideology of the State; just as, during the first milleninium A.D., Buddhism and Taoism were alternately suppressed whenever each represented an antagonist of the officially approved doctrine.

Already in the first half of the nineteenth century some Chinese officials expressed apprehension over the effect of the foreign preachers and their creeds on the stability of the régime. Such fears appeared to have been justified in the outbreak of the Taiping rebellion whose leader, entitling himself the Younger Brother of Jesus, had been deeply influenced by Christian doctrines. With the growth of missionary activity during the nineteenth century, resentment against the missionaries began to spread among the people themselves, especially in the country areas. This antagonism derived partly from natural hostility to anything that conflicted with traditional habits of thought; but more from the growing national sentiment against everything that came from the West. The missionary was one of the tribulations imposed by Western imperialism. Like railways, extra-territorial rights and foreign control of the Customs, he became a symbol of Chinese humiliation; and those who adopted his faith began to be seen as traitors to the Chinese cause.

As a result, during the second half of the nineteenth century there were a number of outbursts against the intruders. Foreign mission stations were attacked. Missionaries were massacred by hostile Chinese mobs. Propaganda of the most scurrilous, and even obscene, kind against the missionaries and their beliefs was circulated. These prejudices received their most violent expression in the Boxer outbreak, in which more than two hundred foreign missionaries and many thousands of Chinese Christians were slaughtered by inflamed Chinese mobs.

During the period of strident nationalism of the early twenties, feeling against the missionaries was rekindled. An "Anti-Christian Movement" was initiated. Missionaries were condemned as disguised imperialists and Chinese Christians as their running dogs. In country areas, missionaries were still sometimes the victims of attacks. Missionary hospitals and other institutions were seized by means of strikes and boycotts. Some K.M.T. officials and their Communist allies were thought to have encouraged, or at least condoned, such activities. As a result, of the 8,000 Protestant missionaries who had been in China in 1926, all but about a thousand withdrew during the period of the Nationalist advance.

And though in time many returned, their number never again reached the previous peak.

It is probable that after the Japanese war, with the growth of China's self-respect in her relations with the Western Powers, sentiment against the missionaries was less hostile than in earlier times. But there was still a considerable body of Chinese opinion that continued to regard them with suspicion or even hostility. Even if there had been no other influences involved therefore, it is likely that the Communists, professing an avowedly atheistic creed and intensely resentful of every manifestation of Western influence, would have sought to displace the missionaries in time.

In fact very shortly after their accession to power, new factors emerged to speed this process. With Chinese participation in the Korean war, and the intense campaign against counter-revolutionaries that followed, the Chinese Government became even more determined to eject from the country the foreign missionaries, frequently living in remote country areas, often avowedly hostile to the creeds professed by the Government, and many of them nationals of the countries against which China was at war. And with the deliberate intensification of hostility towards the West as that war progressed, it became increasingly convenient to the Government to use the campaign against the missionaries, now pilloried as imperialist agents, as a means of whipping up popular sentiment against the Western Powers, and against the United States in particular.

During the period of the civil war, the missionary societies adopted varying policies in the areas that from time to time came under Communist control. The final decision to stay or withdraw was nearly always left to the missionaries themselves. But sometimes the societies' representatives in Shanghai or their headquarters in London would give advice.

It was a difficult decision to make. Missionaries at this period had very little idea of the intentions of the Communists towards religion or towards foreigners; and so no knowledge of what their personal fate might be when the People's Liberation Army arrived. During 1946 and 1947, in some areas at least, Communist policy towards Christians had been far from tolerant. A number of Chinese priests were reported to have been put to death. Some Catholic missionaries suffered violence. In any case it was by no means yet certain what the outcome of the civil war was likely to be. Many missionaries probably felt that they could be more useful in the areas still held by the Nationalists than under Communist rule. If they stayed on they might have difficulty in receiving supplies from their headquarters and so become a financial liability to the local churches. And if the Nationalists were to prove victorious they would be able to return eventually.

In the event different policies were followed. The Baptist Missionary Society, whose activities were mainly concentrated in the three northern provinces of Shensi, Shansi and Shantung, found some of their mission stations already overrun in 1947. During this period, though a few of the Baptist missionaries elected to remain, most left. Thus by the end of 1948 only about seventeen Baptist missionaries remained in these three provinces. The missionaries of the China Inland Mission, who were also working in some of the remote areas that early came under Communist rule, likewise tended to withdraw at first as the Communists advanced. But, as with the Baptists, some returned at a later stage. On the other hand the missionaries of the Church of Scotland Missionary Society in Manchuria stayed on, despite the bitter fighting in that area and the early Communist occupation. But conditions became increasingly difficult, the authorities were apparently less tolerant than in other, less sensitive areas and the last missionary was withdrawn from the region in August, 1950. Missionaries of the London Missionary Society at Tsanghsien in Hopei, which was overrun in June, 1947, also remained at their posts, concentrating for the moment on medical and educational work. And individual missionaries of all the societies often elected to remain.

By the beginning of 1949 the situation was already beginning to change. The Communists were rapidly conquering the whole of the northern half of the country. And it became increasingly likely that they would finally emerge as rulers of the whole of China. At the same time reports from those missionaries who had stayed on in Communist-held areas made it clear that there was now no active persecution, either of the missionaries themselves or of their congregations. Thus during the early part of 1949 most of the China Inland missionaries, who had at one time been withdrawing with the Nationalist armies, were electing to remain at their posts. Some who had withdrawn earlier returned to their own areas. On the other hand some posts were abandoned altogether. Although the mission's own school, with about fifty missionary children, previously functioning in Shanghai, was transferred to Chungking in the Nationalist area, the headquarters organization stayed on in Shanghai when the Communist armies occupied the city in May, 1949, and continued to function after the occupation without hindrance.

Most other missionaries also decided to stay on. In June, 1949, the directors of the London Missionary Society sent a resolution to their workers in China, reaffirming that the final decision on whether to withdraw or to remain must be left to the individual missionary, and addressed to each a personal letter setting out some of the considerations involved. All the Society's missionaries expressed a wish to stay. The experience of the other societies was similar.

At this stage there was still hope among some of the missionaries at least that they might still be able to perform a useful function under the changed conditions in China. The new authorities declared that they intended to practise toleration of all forms of religious worship. The common programme adopted by the Chinese People's Political Consultative Conference in September, 1949, asserted that "the people of the People's Republic of China shall have freedom of thought, speech, publication, assembly . . . religious belief . . ." And it was noted that in the areas that came under Communist control there was no overt attempt to impede religious services or to displace the missionary.

Missionaries were allowed to travel back to their old areas. The distribution of Christian literature by the Bible societies and other Christian societies and the activities of the Bible book-shops were unaffected. Some of the societies reported that their services were as well or better attended than ever. The churches were free to train new workers. For a time the mission schools and universities were untroubled. Many had more pupils than before. The Baptist University at Cheeloo in Tsinan reported that the number of its students increased from 400 to 800 in 1950, that the number of theological students had also doubled, and that seventy per cent of the teaching staff and forty per cent of the students were still Christians.

But most recognized that this policy of toleration was effective only within limits. The London Missionary Society's report for 1949 said that the government's policy of toleration "appeared to

MISSIONARIES

be effective in the cities, where Christian worship and activity continue unhindered. It is not effective in many rural areas where local officials often place many obstacles in the way of the continuance of public worship and other forms of Christian activity". It was reported that in such cases appeals to Peking occasionally brought results. But in some country areas worship could only be maintained in private houses. And many Chinese priests, when local sources of funds began to dry up, were obliged to engage in some form of labour during most of the week.

There was no overt suppression of church services as such. But there were many difficulties, especially in the country. Churches frequently represented the only substantial building in the villages, and were often used by local officials for the purposes of grain storage or to hold meetings. At first they were nearly always made available again on Sundays. When in 1950 and 1951, however, the Land Reform campaign began to be launched in different areas all over the country, public meetings were usually prohibited altogether during the period of the redistribution. This was no doubt primarily intended to prevent illegal meetings of disgruntled landowners or peasants organizing opposition to the campaign. But it had the incidental effect of preventing all church services for a period. And it very often happened that when the stated time had elapsed the scattered congregations, already disorganized as a result of the Communist conquest, the intense propaganda in favour of that ideology, the dispersal of the missionaries and the loss of their funds, no doubt overwhelmed by the number of meetings they were already obliged to attend, were either too timorous or too indifferent to ask that the services should be resumed. In a large number of cases therefore, country churches, once closed because of the Land Reform, or because of an initial decline in support, were never again reopened.

At the same time other activities of the missionary institutions began to face difficulties. The Christian universities were compelled to give time for the study of Communist doctrine. Some of the clinics and hospitals found it hard to get supplies. One or two suffered from labour difficulties. Government-appointed supervisors were placed in some of the hospitals.

The missionaries of their own accord decided that it was wiser to hasten the policy of transferring posts of responsibility to Chinese colleagues. In time nearly all the hospitals and schools came under the control of boards of Chinese Christians—some of the schools had been from the twenties. Later, in most of the medical institutions, these boards, deprived of foreign funds, sometimes faced with labour troubles or forced to take an increasing number of free patients, found themselves compelled to ask the Government to take them over. And during the course of 1950 and 1951 nearly all the Christian schools were absorbed into the State educational system.

There were also important restrictions on the missionaries themselves. They were obliged, like all in China at that time, to obtain permission from the local authorities to travel anywhere outside their own place of residence. Although for a short time a few seem in some areas to have been able to visit the local churches under their charge, and even, very occasionally, to conduct some evangelism, for the most part permission to travel was refused. Activity was thus confined to the town or village where the mission station was situated. Even here the fear of embarrassing the Chinese Christian population made them cautious in what they undertook. Most important of all in the long run was that, except in the case of one or two medical missionaries, no entry permits were granted for missionaries to enter the country from outside. The societies gradually began to realize that, once the existing missionaries left, their activities in China would inevitably come to an end.

Already before the end of 1950, a number of Protestant missionaries were coming to the conclusion that they no longer served any very useful purpose in China and had made up their minds to withdraw. In December, 1950, the House of Commons was informed that a number of British and other missionaries had by then left China "because of the difficulties which they had experienced in carrying out their work". The attitude of the local authorities varied in different parts of the country, and it was not clear how far this was influenced by the Central Government. But up to that time there had been no cases of forcible expulsion of British missionaries. By then there were probably about 450 British missionaries left in the country. By this time, however, a new phase had started in the attitude of the new Government towards the foreign missionaries.

The Communists' policy towards the missionaries fell into three

MISSIONARIES

main stages of development. During the first, lasting until about half-way through 1950, while some restrictions were placed on their activities, no organized campaign was directed against them and no definite policy appeared to have been laid down by the Government concerning the relations between Chinese and foreign churches. During the second between about May, 1950, and the end of 1951, a highly organized and articulate movement was launched, designed to bring about the establishment of Chinese churches that were fully independent of all foreign associations. Finally from the end of 1951 to 1954 this movement was exploited to whip up feeling against foreign missionaries, but especially against Catholic or U.S. missionaries, as an element in a general campaign of hostility towards the West.

Already in October, 1949, the National Christian Council, probably at official instigation, issued a message to all Christians in China, acknowledging the great social contribution that the missionary societies and the churches they had founded had made in China; but stating that in future any such services would have to be rendered under the leadership of the People's Government and be more co-operative in character. In the same month a letter was sent by eighteen leading Chinese Protestants, including the presidents of the principal Protestant colleges, the General Secretary of the Church of Christ in China, the general secretaries of the Christian Literature Society, of the Council of Christian Publishers of the Y.M.C.A. and Y.W.C.A., the Assistant Secretary of the General Synod of the Anglican Communion and others, to the home boards of all missionary societies. This letter recognized that "missionaries have been sent here for no other purpose than to preach the Christian gospel of love and to serve the needs of the Chinese people". But it declared that in the new Chinese society some adjustment of the relations between the Chinese churches and their foreign counterparts would become necessary. In the past the life and organization of the Chinese churches had been modelled on those of similar churches in Britain and America and reflected the denominational differences of those countries. Much of the administration of the churches was still in the hands of the missionaries, and in some cases church policy was ultimately determined by mission boards abroad. For these reasons "the authority of policy determination and official administration must pass over to Chinese leadership where this has not taken place . . .

The principle of self-support [that is, financial independence] must be reiterated and steps taken for its final consummation".

But this did not mean that the activities of the missions were at an end. Missionaries would have to be prepared to adjust themselves to the new situation, to understand the social and political trends then taking place and to accept the new relationship with the churches. Provided these aims were realized, however, there was "nothing in principle which makes the future position of the missionary untenable, or renders his service unnecessary". On the contrary, "the mere presence of the missionary will give articulate expression to the Christian quality of our fellowship which transcends all differences and defies all obstacles". This last sentence might almost be taken, in the prevailing circumstances, as an urgent plea to the missionaries not to leave their Chinese colleagues, whatever difficulties might be placed in their way, without the support their presence provided.

But in the summer of 1950 the second phase of Government policy began. In May, Protestant leaders from all over the country were summoned to a conference in Peking, at which Chou En-lai, the Prime Minister, and other Government leaders outlined to them the general policy of the Government towards Chinese churches, and in particular on their relations with foreign organizations. At first no announcement was made about the result of these meetings. But it soon became clear that during the conference the Government had formulated the principles of the "Three Selfs Movement", that were later to govern official policy towards the churches. The aim of this movement was that all the Chinese churches should achieve as quickly as possible the three basic aims of self-government (administration and control by Chinese), self-support (financial independence of Western societies and churches), and self-propagation (evangelization by Chinese, rather than foreign, missionary activity and publication).

From the start of their activities, the Protestant missionaries had set themselves to build up autonomous Chinese churches. Indeed not only the objectives but even the vocabulary of the new policy came from missionary sources. The famous Baptist missionary, Laughton, writing in 1869, soon after the establishment of the first Baptist mission in China, declared that his objective was to see "the native church self-governing, self-supporting and free from every kind of foreign influence which tends to hinder it from native, natural development and extension". The China Centenary Missionary Conference in 1907 declared that the final aim should be to build churches that could assume "the full responsibilities of self-support and self-government". And in 1913 another missionary conference called specifically for the achievement of "self-support" and "self-propagation" by the Chinese churches.

Thus the Communist authorities were able to claim that what they were calling for was merely the implementation of policies that had been widely accepted in principle for many years. At first they made no attempt to impose such a policy by decree. As in many other fields they sought to bring about the realization of their policies through the instrument of the more compliant among those principally affected, in this case the Chinese Christians themselves.

Not long after the Peking conference, Chinese newspapers published a manifesto drawn up by a group of Chinese Christians, evidently those most sympathetic with the aims of the Government. The statement made a general call for Chinese churches to give their support to Government aims in many fields. They should, under the leadership of the Government, support the Common Programme, oppose imperialism, feudalism and bureaucratic capitalism, and actively preach the evils of imperialism in China in the past, especially of course of American imperialism, which, it was said, was still plotting to use the church for its own ends. The churches today must purge themselves of this imperialist influence. They must build up Chinese churches whose affairs were managed only by Chinese. "All Christian churches and organizations in China which were still relying on foreign personal and financial aid," the manifesto proclaimed, "should immediately decide on concrete plans to realize within the shortest possible time the objectives of standing on their own feet and making a fresh start."

At first it was believed that a period of three to five years was to be allowed for the process of securing independence. But like other Communist campaigns in China, the programme increased in intensity as it proceeded. The manifesto was widely circulated. It received the signatures of thousands of Christian ministers and laymen. There can be little doubt that considerable pressure was put upon Chinese clergy, especially those in posts of authority, either directly by the Government, or by Christians sympathetic to the Government, to give the movement their support. As a result many of the boards of missionary institutions, schools, hospitals and relief bodies declared that they were severing all association with the West. The Church of Christ in China, the Y.M.C.A. and Y.W.C.A. passed resolutions in this sense. The Chinese bishops of the Anglican Church (by this time the English bishops had resigned) declared that they "rejoiced in the liberation which has come to the people of our nation", declared their opposition to imperialism, feudalism and bureaucratic capitalism, and stressed their determination that their church should not be dependent on foreign countries. Individual synods of the Methodist Church passed resolutions "to set up a Three-Self Promotion Committee", and individual churches of the synod formed similar sub-committees. Other synods passed resolutions declaring their financial independence of the Methodist Missionary Society, and their determination to dispense with the services of missionaries.

In November, 1950, the manifesto was adopted by the National Christian Council. By this time Westerners were gradually being withdrawn from this body, and, though the Deputy Secretary-General remained an Englishman until half-way through 1951, he was increasingly powerless to influence decisions. The Council published the manifesto as an official statement of its policy. By April, 1951, 180,000 Christians were said to have subscribed to it.

When, in the same month, China became involved in the Korean War, propaganda against imperialists of all sorts began to be intensified. So far as the missionaries were concerned, there was increasingly insistent clamour in the Chinese press for the implementation of the Three-Self policy. There were demands that religious belief should be "detached from foreign aggression and reactionary activities". The missionaries found themselves more and more identified with imperialist activity.

This campaign, over and above the many restrictions which had already been placed on their activities, finally induced many of the Protestant missionary societies to withdraw all their members from China. In June, 1950, the directors of the London Missionary Society decided that the Mission's activities "should be terminated in the autumn of 1951, by which time the impossibility of securing entry permits would have reduced the number of missionaries remaining to a very few". But any missionary who was asked to stay and wished to do so would of course be at liberty to do this. Only three months later however, in September, the directors decided, after consultation with church leaders in China, to advise all missionaries to leave the country as soon as possible unless they were asked by their Chinese colleagues to remain. In December the Society sent a long and carefully considered letter to the Chinese leaders of the Church of Christ in China, explaining their policy and confirming their trust in the future of the Church under its Chinese leadership. The mission announced that "while the leaders of the Church of Christ in China deeply regretted losing their foreign colleagues", they had considered that the withdrawal of the missionaries for the present was in the best interests of the Church in China. By early 1951 virtually all the Society's missionaries had applied for exit permits.

The other Protestant societies soon followed suit. In December, 1950, the representatives of the China Inland Mission in China sent a telegram to the General Director, declaring that it was no longer possible for the Mission's main objectives of co-operation with the Chinese churches to be realized, and that it was therefore necessary to begin a policy of gradual withdrawal. In January the Mission instructed their provincial superintendents to proceed with an ordered withdrawal of all missionaries. The Church Missionary Society had already instructed its missionaries that they could leave voluntarily if they felt they were likely to be an embarrassment to Chinese Christians; during the second half of 1950 and early 1951 an increasing number adopted this course. The Methodist Missionary Society left the decision to withdraw to the individual districts in which their church was organized. But the Society reported that during the second half of 1950 and the beginning of 1951 nearly every missionary reluctantly decided to withdraw and apply for exit permits. Finally, the Baptist missionaries, of whom only about twenty were left at the end of 1950, also decided to leave during the course of 1951.

In every case the consideration that finally compelled the missionaries to withdraw was the feeling that under the existing conditions they were becoming more than ever an embarrassment to their Chinese colleagues. Already by early 1950, before the Three-Selfs Movement had been launched, the Methodist Missionary Society reported that their missionaries had begun to realize "that their presence was becoming an embarrassment to their Chinese friends, even though in Synod Council, hospital and school they worked under Chinese leadership". The London Missionary Society stated that "it became increasingly perilous for Chinese

Christians to be associated with foreign colleagues, and in consequence missionaries found themselves becoming an embarrassment to the church". The Church Missionary Society said that their missionaries were proving "an embarrassment rather than a help to the Chinese Christians". Every visit by an English missionary to a Chinese friend, or vice versa, might be a cause of difficulty for the Chinese. And some of the leaders of the Chinese churches made it clear, privately if not publicly, that in the existing circumstances they thought it best that the connexion with the West should be completely severed.

For those few who still remained conditions grew worse. In the spring of 1951 the third phase of the Government's policy towards the missionaries began. The effort to bring into being independent Chinese churches was gradually transformed into a virulent campaign against the missionaries themselves. This may have been partly the result of genuine considerations of security. The presence of missionaries in remote areas, at a time when the Korean war was growing in intensity, may have aroused sincere suspicion: a widespread campaign against "counter-revolutionaries", designed to root out every kind of subversive element, from local war-lords and K.M.T. agents to bandits and racketeers, was in progress all over the country at the same period. At the same time the campaign formed a useful contribution to the general effort to stir up feeling against the West. And as the resistance of Chinese Catholics to the establishment of an Erastian church became more evident, the authorities grew more determined to put an end to all foreign influence within the Catholic Church.

In April and May of 1951 a conference of Christian organizations was called in Peking. Lu Ting-yi, the Vice-Chairman of the Commission of Cultural and Educational Affairs, declared that during the previous century religion had been "used by Anglo-American imperialists as an instrument of aggression". The Government's aim now was to wipe out all traces of that aggression. They were therefore obliged to examine the relationship between Chinese Christian organizations and foreign Christian bodies. And they would encourage the movement that had sprung up among Chinese Christians to achieve independence. The statement finally issued by the conference, therefore, besides giving general support to the Government's policies, demanded that all connexions of the Chinese churches with U.S. and other missionary societies should be severed "finally, thoroughly, eternally and completely". At the end of the same month, an order was made by the Prime Minister under which all Christian missions mainly supported by American funds were to cease their activities, and all Chinese Christian churches to sever their relations with American missions immediately.

Regulations were issued under which all churches and organizations that had accepted foreign funds were to apply for registration. Registration would only be cancelled when it could be shown that self-support had been achieved. Foreign missionary societies were to be allowed to donate their property to local churches, provided no conditions were attached. Christian churches and organizations that had funds deposited abroad before December, 1950, and wished to withdraw them had to apply to the Government for permission, and to explain the origin of the funds and the purpose to which they hoped to devote them. A Religious Affairs Bureau was set up to supervise the affairs of the churches.

From this time a series of accusation meetings were organized all over the country at which foreign missionaries and their reactionary Chinese supporters were denounced. The *People's Daily* demanded that "the accusation movement should be widely spread so that all Christians should raise their political consciousness and express the bitterness that they feel against imperialist aggression". A few British missionaries came in for vilification. A number of Chinese Protestants were accused. The General Secretary of the Church of Christ in China and bishops of the Anglican and the Methodist churches were arrested or denounced. But the campaign was directed at first mainly against American missionaries; and later increasingly against Catholics, both Chinese and foreign. And even before it had got properly under way most of the British societies had already withdrawn.

Thus few of the British Protestant missionaries suffered active ill-treatment. One missionary of the Methodist Missionary Society in a country district was for a short time held in prison on a charge of receiving and transmitting wireless messages from Britain. A medical missionary of the China Inland Mission was detained in connexion with the death of a patient. And one missionary of the Plymouth Brethren who was captured during the Chinese invasion of Tibet in December, 1950, and arrested as a spy, was held in prison for three years, during which time he was subjected to a prolonged treatment of brain-washing. While in prison he could neither send nor receive letters from home. But he was otherwise well treated, and was finally abruptly released without explanation. Many, indeed most, British missionaries had, like other Westerners, to wait long months, without explanation, before receiving exit permits. But they did not suffer the detentions, imprisonments, public denunciations, and humiliations before people's courts, to which many of other nationalities were subjected.

There were, of course, a few British among the six thousand Catholic missionaries (including two thousand nuns) who left China between 1949 and 1954. In general the Catholic missionaries adopted an entirely different policy from their Protestant colleagues in the face of the new conditions. Despite all the difficulties that were put in their way, they for long firmly refused to leave, even after the determination of the authorities to get rid of them had been made clear. Thus in the spring of 1951, at a time when the campaign against missionaries was beginning to be intensified and when nearly all the Protestant missionaries were preparing to leave the country, a Catholic spokesman still declared that there were no plans for withdrawing Catholic missionaries.

There were a number of reasons for this difference of attitude. First, while the Three-Selfs policy could be represented to the Protestant missionaries as an extension of what had always been their own aim in China, to the Catholics the policy was in basic contradiction with the essential tenets of their faith; and the physical presence of the missionaries themselves, of the bishops officially designated to the Chinese dioceses, and in particular of the papal internuncio in China, could serve to preserve the link with Rome in a tangible form. Secondly, the aim of most of the Protestant missionaries in China, as elsewhere, had been primarily evangelical, and this purpose had already been largely frustrated by the Government's activities long before the decision to leave had been reached. But the object of the Catholic missionaries was mainly pastoral: from the start they had sought to establish viable Christian communities, and had indeed very often refused to accept converts unless an entire village would accept baptism. In such circumstances priests were naturally unwilling to desert the flocks for whom they felt responsible. Thirdly, since they held that no effective sacrament could take place without the mediation of a properly ordained priest, the withdrawal of a large part of the

Catholic priesthood in China, would in their eyes effectively destroy the Christian life of the country and, eventually, interrupt the Apostolic succession. There were in any case probably a smaller proportion of Chinese priests ready to take over. Finally, perhaps as important as any of these, was a fundamental difference of temperament. For ideological grounds alone, the Catholic missionaries were inevitably, from the start, implacably hostile to the new régime and all it stood for. This attitude was bitterly reinforced by the Government's policies towards the churches. They tended, therefore, to adopt an attitude of impassioned defiance towards infidel persecutors of their Church, an attitude more heroic possibly, but perhaps less realistic too, than that of their Protestant colleagues.

Thus a very large number of Catholic missionaries refused to leave the country until they were physically compelled to do so. Often this was only after public condemnation and humiliation before a people's court, sometimes on fantastic charges (such as espionage for the U.S. Government, the murder of a hundred thousand babies in an orphanage, and, in one or two cases, cannibalism). Many were imprisoned and some physically ill-treated. One British Catholic missionary of the Salesian Order was imprisoned for a few months before being expelled. A nun who had been in charge of a mission at Toishan was held in prison for over a year. And one or two others were held under house arrest before being taken under armed guard to the Hong Kong frontier.

Nearly all the missionary societies made arrangements before they left for their property in China to be taken over by the Chinese churches. In some cases this was a continuation of a policy that had been initiated many years before. Under Government regulations the Christian churches were only allowed to accept foreign property if this was made over as an unconditional gift. Most societies were prepared to do this; and the property was taken over either by the national churches, by the individual synods or by local churches. But the policy of self-support made it impossible for the Chinese churches to accept funds. Thus the Church Missionary Society, for example, still holds a very substantial sum of money, raised by subscription, for the specific purpose of aiding missionary work in China, which they are unable to make over to the Chinese church for this reason. Some of the societies, or the native churches, were permitted to raise funds by leasing part of their property to Chinese Government organizations.

Thus eventually all the links were severed. The authorities succeeded in setting up national churches for each denomination. In August, 1951, the Chinese Methodist Church established their own Conference and broke all former links with the English Conference. In the same month the Chinese Anglican Church declared itself independent of all foreign churches (it had in fact been recognized as an independent, autonomous province since 1912). In time all the other Protestant churches followed suit. And eventually, after embittered resistance, the Chinese authorities succeeded in setting up a schismatic Catholic church, though very many Chinese Catholics, bishops, priests and laymen continued, on pain of death, to offer resistance to this move.

In general the British societies and churches showed a remarkably philosophical attitude towards the circumstances of their eviction from China. In the reports they issued about their withdrawal, none showed rancour at the course events had followed. All expressed confidence in the future of the Chinese churches in the new conditions. The report of the Church of Scotland's Foreign Mission for 1950, reporting the final withdrawal of the society's missionaries, said that "Christians in the West must show confidence in the sincerity [of the Christian leaders] and in their determination not to surrender anything vital to the life of the Church in any accommodation they are allowed to make with the Government". The Methodist Missionary Society, after reporting that one of the Chinese synods had decided to break its relations with the parent society and its missions, declared that they believed "the synod took this step having at heart the best interests of the Church and their missionary friends". The Church Missionary Society passed a resolution assuring the Chinese bishops of the Anglican church in China of their "sympathetic understanding of their intention to become independent of external aid and to assume the status of a self-governing, self-supporting, and self-propagating church", and affirmed their "continued fellowship in the service of our one Lord".

The attitude of the Chinese churches to their former colleagues varied. For a time a few maintained some contacts with the missionary bodies they had been connected with before. Several districts of the Methodist Church in China continued for a time to send reports to the English church. After the Baptist Missionary

Society had finally withdrawn the Executive Secretary of the Chinese church wrote to them, "We wish to express to all our brothers and sisters in the older churches our sincere gratitude . . . Our desire is for the maintenance and permanence of the Christian fellowship between us."

But in practice the contacts have gradually withered away. In 1957 a bishop of the Chinese Anglican church attended the preparatory meetings for the Lambeth Conference in London. But when the time of the Conference itself came, a telegram was received from the six Chinese bishops due to attend, regretting that they could not come owing to "preoccupation with the urgent tasks at home". A few missionaries have continued to correspond with friends in China even up to the present day. By far the greater number, however, have thought it best to avoid even these contacts lest they should prove embarrassing to their Chinese friends.

The Chinese Government have thus succeeded in their aim of breaking all the links that joined the Chinese churches with Christian organizations in the West. At a "National Christian Conference" held in Peking in August, 1954, Y. T. Wu, the principal spokesman and supporter of the Government's policies among the Protestant leaders, claimed that the Chinese Christian churches had for the most part "rid themselves of undesirable imperialist influences". A new National Council of Churches has been formed "to guide the movement for self-government, self-support and self-propagation". Now that national pride has been satisfied it is possible that the Government will come to feel more ready to allow normal contacts with the representatives of foreign churches on a basis of equality. The Secretary of the Chinese Anglican church was recently allowed to pay a visit to Australia. And in 1956 the East Asian Secretary of the World Council of Churches and the Anglican Bishop of Victoria (Hong Kong) attended a conference of Protestant leaders in Peking.

Thus the story of British missionary activity in China, which began with the activities of Robert Morrison 150 years ago, has been brought to a sad end. During that period the foreign missionaries achieved much of which they may be proud. They built up substantial congregations of Catholics and Protestants in China. They played a profoundly important part in bringing some knowledge of the Western world, of Western culture and Western ideas, to many remote areas of China that were otherwise untouched by the impact of the West. They wielded at times a significant influence on a number of important social questions such as opium addiction, infanticide, concubinage, child marriage, and girl slavery. They were the first to bring modern medical knowledge to China: until the Communists came to power over half the hospitals in China were run by missionaries. The educational establishments they set up played a vital part in forming the minds of recent generations of Chinese: before the war something like ten per cent of all secondary and university students in China were at Christian institutions. And some of the most important figures of the last generations of Chinese statesmen, including Sun Yat-sen, Chiang Kai-shek, the Sung family, and K. C. Wu, were brought up as, or became, Christians.

Perhaps equally important, missionaries did more than any other single body of people to introduce China to the West. Many of the most important figures in British sinology, such as Morrison, Legge, Giles and Soothill, began as missionaries. And of the total number of English people who have acquired some knowledge of the Chinese language, at least nine-tenths have probably been missionaries. By virtue of their calling, they came into a far closer contact with individual Chinese than any other section of the British community; and were frequently able to form relationships as intimate and enduring as any between the two peoples.

The British missionaries played a distinguished part in the foreign missionary record. Some of the early British missionaries especially were figures of considerable stature. Geoffrey Hudson Taylor, the founder of the China Inland Mission, perhaps did more than any other single Westerner to spread a knowledge of Christianity in China. Timothy Richard, the Baptist missionary who spent more than fifty years in China and who was a leading influence within the Chinese reform movement of 1898, was perhaps the only foreign missionary to exert any significant influence on Chinese domestic policy. Yet British missionaries today are the first to admit that their activities were not always directed in the wisest possible way. Commenting on the final withdrawal of Western missionaries from China, the Baptist Missionary Society recognized that these "too easily assumed elements of Anglo-Saxon culture and customs to be essential parts of Christianity". The Western missionaries, with the sole exceptions of the early Jesuits, imported into China almost exact reproductions of Western liturgical forms, Western church organization, Western hymns and prayers, even Western church architecture. And until the last few years the Chinese churches remained largely under Western leadership. The missionaries tended, even in the remotest areas of China, to establish small foreign colonies within the four walls of the mission compound, where they carried on a way of life utterly remote from that of their Chinese flocks outside.

One of the results of this was that, to most Chinese, Christianity never ceased to appear as something foreign to China. Thus it was inevitable that when support from abroad was cut off and when the practice of the faith became clearly out of harmony with the views of the ruling party, loyalty began to wither. The situation today appears to be that, while there is no active persecution or suppression of religion of any denomination, many churches, especially in the country areas, are still closed. In the towns the churches that remain are being amalgamated and regrouped, so that only one Protestant church of whatever denomination serves any single area. Today only about twenty Protestant churches are left in Shanghai, out of about 150 that existed before. In Peking there are only four. And this has been accompanied by efforts by the authorities to bring about some kind of merger of the various Protestant denominations. But considerable Christian activity continues. Bible societies still distribute scriptures all over China. Four Christian magazines are published. And something like 500 theological students are believed to be being trained for the Ministry.

Meanwhile the activities of British missionaries in China still continue to bear some fruit. Among the recent publications of the Christian publishing houses in China were *Readings in the St. John's Gospel* by Archbishop Temple, *The Pilgrim's Progress*, Spurgeon's *Evening Readings*, and a Chinese version of Handel's *Messiah*. In themselves such facts may be trivial. But they can perhaps serve as some recompense to the many generations of British missionaries whose devoted services in China were, in the course of the last decade, so abruptly brought to an end.

7

MERCHANTS

BRITISH merchants went to China, in the seventeenth and eighteenth centuries, to buy. During the nineteenth century, they began increasingly to sell. And during the twentieth they came more and more to manufacture.

The first British merchants purchased at the Chinese ports silks and satins, tea, sugar, ginger, gold, copper, chinaware, spices and other goods highly prized in the West, some unobtainable elsewhere. They offered in exchange woollen cloth, firearms, lead, tin, pepper from the East Indies and raw cotton from India. But since the demand for these was weak, they had to make up the greater part of the balance by exports of silver, and later opium. The Chinese goods were mainly dispatched direct to London where they were resold all over Europe. For this reason there was intense competition to buy up as much as possible of the Chinese goods, especially tea, and to send them with all speed to Europe to secure the firmest prices there.

With the conclusion of the treaties in the nineteenth century, and the development of British manufacturing power, China began to attract the attention of British exporters. There grew up a myth, a vision of an inexhaustible market in the interior, which only needed to be opened up to yield vast fortunes to the enterprising merchant. There was an increasing export of British manufactures, especially textiles.

At the same time commercial organization began to take new forms. As a result of the treaties, more direct contact with the Chinese internal market became possible. There were increasing attempts to cut out the long series of middle men who intervened in many trades between the Chinese producers and the foreign merchants. The compradore system was established, by which foreign firms employed Chinese agents, purchasing Chinese goods from the producers in the interior on their clients' behalf, and, often, disposing of Western goods to Chinese merchants and retailers. In time, specialized import-export firms grew up to handle the trade in particular commodities. And eventually British manu-

MERCHANTS

facturers began to send their own representatives to China to study the markets.

British financial institutions too became increasingly involved in Chinese development. From about 1850 British banks began to operate in China for dealings in foreign exchange, and, increasingly, to finance trade. British money played an important part in the financing of the first railways constructed in China. From the beginning of the twentieth century mining operations began to be undertaken by British interests. And before the First World War British finance houses were playing a dominant role in international consortia, formed with the approval of the British Government, to prevent cut-throat competition between the powers for the privilege of making loans to the Chinese Government on the security of tax revenues.

The right to manufacture in China was secured for all the Treaty Powers by Japan, after her conquest of China in 1895. This activity was at first concentrated in the textile industry, especially in Shanghai. The new factories benefited from the proximity of the raw materials and from cheap Chinese labour. Their products could be exported direct to other parts of Asia as well as to the home countries. British interests played an important role in the development of shipping, including the coastal and river trade. They set up processing and packing plants. There grew up substantial communities of foreign businessmen permanently established in the ports of East China and the Yangtze.

Thus by the thirties, when the second Sino-Japanese war broke out, British business interests in China were very different from what they had been a hundred years before. The business community was by then composed of a number of quite separate strands. There were those who were in China, like their earliest predecessors before them, in order to purchase, for import to Britain or elsewhere, individual Chinese products, tobacco, tea, hides, bristles, or other specialized commodities. There were those who were there, often on behalf of individual firms, to sell Western goods, for example cotton textiles, wool, chemicals, oil, textile machinery and other engineering products. There was a much larger number of firms, ranging from huge organizations such as Jardine Matheson, and Butterfield & Swire, to tiny import-export firms, domiciled only in China or Hong Kong, which traded in both directions and in a large variety of products. There were those

I

who were engaged in mining, processing, or manufacture within China, for sale either there or abroad. There were the shipping firms carrying both internal and foreign trade. There were the banks and other financial organizations which financed trade and business without themselves undertaking it. Finally there were some engaged in such other activities as public utilities, the property market, insurance and other trades.

The British still played a far larger part in these affairs than any other foreign community. British investment in China before the war was well over a third of the total foreign investment in China and more than four times as large as that of any other country except Japan. In 1931 this investment was calculated at about £180 million of which about £150 million was in Shanghai. Britain owned fifty per cent of the shipping engaged on the coastal trade. The total British holdings of Chinese Government loans were over £50 million. In addition there was a fairly substantial British ownership of private property in China.

After the outbreak of the Sino-Japanese war, these activities, which were almost entirely concentrated on the east coast and in the Yangtze valley, were carried on for some years within Japanese-occupied territory. As soon as Japan entered the war against Britain the foreign settlements were seized, British businessmen were interned and their properties sequestrated by the Japanese authorities or their agents. The businesses were placed under Government supervision, but they were often kept running as going concerns and the bulk of the staff thus held together. When the war ended, most elements of the foreign business community soon returned to recover their properties and re-establish their businesses. Although there were sometimes initial difficulties in regaining possession, within a year or two most were once again carrying on their former activities so far as existing conditions permitted.

There were many handicaps to overcome. British businessmen felt perpetually frustrated by the activities of the Nationalist bureaucracy, which they regarded as inefficient, corrupt, often deliberately obstructive. Chinese imports were strictly controlled by a committee set up to establish a co-ordinated import programme. There was no stable relationship between sterling and the Chinese currency. At the same time, because of the war some of the Chinese

MERCHANTS

traditional exports had been replaced by alternative sources of supply. Because of inflation Chinese prices were often quite uncompetitive. And because of her own difficulties Britain herself was not at first able to bring about any great increase in exports.

But it was the civil war which more than anything hampered the redevelopment of commercial activity. As a result the country's economy was never fully restored to normal. Over large parts of the country, the Nationalist Government never regained control. Supplies and markets were disrupted. Corruption was rampant. In October, 1946, a British trade mission was sent to China to explore the possibilities of developing trade but was forced to conclude that so long as the civil war continued it would remain impossible to bring about any great expansion. Though in the long run there could be "incalculable development", what was needed first was the restoration of internal peace and the establishment of a sound and honest administration. As a result of these conditions trade grew only sluggishly, and by the time the Nationalists were expelled from the mainland had still not reached pre-war levels even in terms of value.

There were similar difficulties in the way of a revival of British manufacturing industry in China. Though most industrial properties resumed activity after the war, British companies were reluctant to commit themselves to new investment so long as the political situation remained so unstable. Investment was made hazardous not only by the general insecurity over the future but by the instability of the Chinese currency, uncertainty in the supply and cost of raw materials and by labour unrest. The Chairman of I.C.I. announced in October, 1946, that that company was unlikely to invest any further money in China until the situation there grew clearer. Many other British manufacturers followed a similar course. As the war progressed, economic activity was increasingly inhibited. In February, 1947, the British Under-Secretary of State for Foreign Affairs declared in the House of Commons that China was "on the verge of economic and financial collapse", and that trade would therefore inevitably become increasingly difficult. By January, 1949, the Secretary for Overseas Trade said that in the existing circumstances "it was not possible to make any realistic assessment of the prospects for U.K. trade with China". Certainly nothing could hinder trade more than the existing confusion. Many British businessmen began to feel that even under a Communist régime conditions could not be worse than under the Nationalists.

At the end of 1948, when the Communist armies first occupied some of the cities of North China, European businessmen further south received favourable reports about the demeanour of the Communist troops and the effectiveness of their administration. Foreign businesses were not occupied, nor prevented from carrying on their activities. Attempts by the authorities during the truce in early 1949 to restore trading contacts between the north and Nationalist-occupied Shanghai raised further hopes. In March and April trading connexions between North China and Hong Kong were resumed. One ship left Tientsin for the United States.

After the capture of Shanghai the Communist authorities expressed their willingness to co-operate with foreign business interests. They quickly got the harbour working again. They were energetic in their attempts to tackle the urgent financial problems that faced the community. British ships were permitted, as they had not been under the Nationalists, to transport goods and passengers between Chinese ports. As a result of a telegram to Mao Tse-tung taxation imposed on a large British company was reduced by thirty per cent. The Managing Director of Jardine Matheson, the uncrowned king of the foreign business world, praised the realistic approach of the régime to the first problems they had to tackle. And the British Consul-General was outspoken in his commendation of the efficiency and integrity of the authorities in Shanghai. It began to be hoped that there might still be a few more years of activity in China for foreign business. Perhaps it might even enjoy better conditions than before.

By mid-summer of 1949, there were growing doubts. It was clear that an increasing volume of trade was to be channelled through State agencies. Banking business came to be concentrated in the Bank of China. Trade was controlled by means of export and import certificates. In some categories it was prohibited altogether. In July, 1949, all import-export firms, Chinese and foreign, were registered and only about two-thirds of them gained permission to go on trading. Maximum and minimum prices were fixed for all commodities traded.

Businessmen sometimes had difficulties in dealing with inexperienced officials reluctant to take responsibility for a wrong decision. There were large and apparently arbitrary tax demands on many business firms. In some areas there were labour difficulties, demands for "liberation bonuses", wage increases, huge severance payments and other benefits.

Perhaps more serious than any of these troubles was the blockade of Chinese ports which the Nationalists sought to impose from June, 1949. Chinese ports were bombed, Chinese waters were mined, and foreign ships entering Chinese ports were intercepted on the high seas. The foreign business community in Shanghai joined in sending a communication to the United Nations, protesting at the loss of life and damage caused by air attacks on the city. There was a succession of incidents in which British ships were involved. Many were intercepted by Nationalist warships. Others were bombed and machine-gunned from the air. A few were taken by force to ports in Formosa and detained there for a considerable period.

The Nationalist Government, claiming to be the legitimate government of China, denied that such attempts constituted a blockade, calling them a "domestic closure order". Repeated representations by the British and United States Governments proved ineffective. From November, 1949, two Royal Navy frigates were kept off the mouth of the Yangtze to give assistance to British merchant ships. On one occasion a British destroyer succeeded in rescuing a British merchant ship captured by the Nationalists. And one of the reasons that British trading interests were so anxious for recognition of the Communist Government was that it was thought that this would enable the Royal Navy to deal more effectively with Nationalist warships.

Thus for a time the early hopes began to fade. In May, 1949, Mr. Alexander told the House of Commons that it did not appear that normal trading conditions were being resumed in the Communist-occupied areas. In July, 1949, Mr. McNeil, Minister of State, stated that the position of British businessmen was still causing considerable anxiety. And because of the lack of official contacts with the local authorities it was harder for British businessmen to remedy their position.

Even when, by the beginning of 1950, the new Government had acquired control of the whole mainland and conditions began to become more stable, there was little improvement. At this period the Government was making strenuous efforts to halt inflation and these policies brought about something of a recession in China. There were heavy taxes, forced loans and control of the commodity markets. The change of government inevitably brought continuing dislocation. There had been a substantial flight of capital and of experienced businessmen from the mainland. And over and above all this there were serious floods and famine.

Yet British businessmen remained full of hope. A delegation of them told the British Government in December, 1949, that their representatives in China had unanimously reported that there would still be great opportunities for British commercial enterprise in the new China. Things did begin to improve. There was some development of trade between Tientsin and the South. Exports from North China were freed from export duties and a special subvention was offered for firms engaged in the export trade. The restoration of communications and security in the countryside brought some recovery to internal trade.

About half-way through 1950 there was a more dramatic change for the better. The Government's efforts to stem inflation had been largely successful. The currency had been stabilized and they were ready to allow business activity to expand. The severe tax demands previously imposed were relaxed. Labour was exhorted to cooperate with the businessmen in order to boost production. Some foreign firms reported higher productivity than ever before. The Government organized a national Importers and Exporters Conference, which was attended by some merchants from Hong Kong, to promote foreign trade. The authorities announced that while the trade in certain commodities would remain a State monopoly, the rest would be open to private and foreign merchants. Fifty per cent of foreign trade was said to be still in private hands. The leader of the British business community, after a visit to Peking in October, 1950, declared that if the world situation permitted "the Central People's Government was only too willing to trade with the British Commonwealth".

With the opening of the Korean war there was a large demand in China, both from private and State organizations, for many materials from the West. Chinese purchasing agencies in Hong Kong were very active in buying commodities, especially rubber and oil which were not yet embargoed. Another result of the war, and of the neutralization of Formosa that went with it, was that the Nationalist blockade came to an end. As a result there was a sudden

MERCHANTS

boom in trade, especially with Hong Kong. Hong Kong exports to China leapt to nearly £100 million in 1950, three or four times the normal pre-war figure. U.K. exports rose by fifty per cent from the previous year, though at £3·6 million they were still not much more than a quarter of the 1947 figure. The boom benefited the traders rather than the manufacturers. But some foreign businessmen began to believe nonetheless that their earlier hopes were now proving themselves justified.

Such hopes were soon to be disillusioned. The sudden boom was short-lived. With the intensification of the war in Korea new restrictions in trade with China were introduced. And in May, 1951, the United Nations declared a formal embargo on the export of all strategic goods which were, of course, those that the Chinese were most interested in buying. Traders in Chinese goods found it increasingly difficult to obtain the products they wanted. The hopes of merchants in Hong Kong and Britain for a resurgence of trade with China were quickly dashed.

But the position of British business interests domiciled in China was even worse. From the end of 1950 these were subjected to increasing pressures. Indeed it became increasingly doubtful what part foreign firms was to be permitted to play in the new society that was emerging. They quickly became almost entirely dependent on Government organs, both for supplies of raw materials and for the final disposal of their products. Very often they were unable to secure the materials they required. If they did manage to produce anything they frequently had difficulty in selling it at realistic prices. Occasionally firm contracts were suddenly cancelled without warning. They were not permitted to close branches that were at a standstill; nor to sell their assets; nor, with a few exceptions, to lease them.

Even if, despite all these difficulties, they were able to make any profit at all—and there were a few who did—they were not able to remit funds out of the country. On the contrary, to conform with the Government's regulations, the head offices were nearly all obliged to make substantial remittances of sterling in the opposite direction. For in addition to tax obligations, the firms were compelled to maintain all their employees on their pay roll, even if, as a result of the Government's policies, there was no work for these to do. Any attempt to resist such exactions might have repercussions on members of their staff. A manager of one firm which ceased to remit was held under detention for some days until funds were sent and the wages paid. As a result nearly all the firms in practice continued to remit. For the British head offices felt a considerable sense of responsibility towards their staffs, who were living in China in circumstances of considerable strain.

Indeed the conditions under which British businessmen, and indeed all the foreign residents, lived in China at this time began to be reminiscent of those under which their earliest predecessors had existed at Canton two hundred years earlier. Every inhabitant of a Chinese city, whether Chinese or foreign, had to be registered. He was subject to the ministration of his local street committee which, like the groups of households established by the K.M.T. and earlier régimes, had to ensure that every member conformed to Government regulations. He required official permission to travel to any other town; or to change his address; even to go and stay in a hotel.

But foreign residents required, in addition, a residence permit. To obtain this he had to answer a long questionnaire, giving details of his religious faith, political affiliations, occupation, personal income and the names of his friends and acquaintances. The permit had to be renewed at intervals. If he wished to go to stay overnight with a friend, he had to sign off at the local public security bureau in his own area, and sign on in that of the other. If he had a wireless set this must be registered. And if he sold it he had to sign a statement saying who he had sold it to and for how much. Finally, if he wished to leave the country, he needed an exit permit. To get this he was obliged to undergo a thorough-going examination of all his affairs, to ensure that he was not leaving behind him any unpaid debts or other obligations. This invariably took many months—often years.

In addition, from the entry of China into the Korean war at the end of 1950, the British resident, though normally treated with courtesy, lived in what was to all intents and purposes an enemy country. He was surrounded by an intense propaganda of hatred against the West and all imperialist aggressors. During the Five Antis Campaign launched in 1951 against the world of business, the representative of a foreign firm was sometimes subject to a spate of accusation and denunciation, often from his own staff (though it was his Chinese colleagues who bore the brunt of this attack).

MERCHANTS 137

And all the time his business was at a standstill. His pastimes were annihilated. The clubs, the golf courses, the racetracks, and all the other stately pleasure-domes which the foreigner in China had erected for his own diversion, were requisitioned or closed down. The British businessman sat at his desk, idle, dreaming of a golden day that could never again return.

Nor could he obtain any respite from the strange world in which he lived. For to the foreign manager, the Government would grant no exit permit. He was held in China, imprisoned, a hostage, till such time as the Government had, by their policies, succeeded in convincing his employers that there remained no future in the new China, for the foreign businessman.

As a case-history of the type of difficulty that British businesses had to contend with, the experience of the Kailan Mining Administration may be described. This was a part-British, part-Chinese organization, in practice controlled from London, which owned the largest mining undertaking in China. When the Communist armies first occupied the mine area in December, 1948, officials of the company were assured that the company's administration would be allowed to continue and that British capital invested would be protected. For some months there was no attempt at interference. Some difficulties were smoothed out as a result of personal discussion with Government officials in Peking, a form of negotiation that virtually no other foreign business was ever able to achieve. The miners themselves, under persuasion from the authorities, undertook to bring about increased productivity and better labour discipline, in return for higher wages and better safety measures.

But as time went on the company found themselves placed under increasing pressure. They were squeezed from three directions at once: from the tax authorities, from the trading company that purchased the coal, and from the railway administration which carried it. They were obliged to hand over nearly half a million tons of coal in settlement of some alleged liabilities at a valuation that was about a quarter of the cost of production. As a result of these various exactions they fell further and further into debt. They became dependent on a government loan for the payment of wages. In June, 1949, the Communist administration appointed a military supervisor with a staff of nearly a hundred to deal with the company, in place of the various local authorities in different areas. But it soon became clear that the real function of these officials was to prepare to take over the administration of the mines.

Soon after this the British parent company decided to remit no more funds from London and to withdraw their European staff as soon as possible. In January, 1950, the company's manager in China informed the Chinese Government that they intended to withdraw their interest in the K.M.A. In April they received from the Chinese Government a telegraphed request for the remittance to China of £500,000 either as fresh capital or as a loan to the K.M.A. This, understandably, they declined to do. They offered instead to hand over all their interests immediately if the Chinese Government would in return take over any liabilities of the Administration that were not covered by its funds. They would later negotiate for compensation for the British company's share of the assets of the Administration.

In fact no further negotiations took place. But the British staff were soon afterwards permitted to leave. It is perhaps unlikely that the British company ever entertained any serious hopes of obtaining compensation for the Administration's assets. They were content to cut their losses by undertaking an exchange of all their property in China against the cancellation of any liabilities for which they were held responsible by the Government.

The position of the K.M.A. was not altogether typical since their concession in China would in any case soon have come to an end. Nor did the Chinese Government normally attempt any direct control of the running of the foreign businesses they sought to take over. But otherwise the methods used to make business impossible for the company, and so to persuade them to undertake a voluntary withdrawal, were characteristic of the Government's policy in dealing with nearly all the foreign firms. And the terms on which the final withdrawal was made were those that were later followed by almost all the other British businesses, when they too found themselves obliged to leave.

Conditions for British businesses got steadily worse throughout 1951. In March, 1952, the Hong Kong and Shanghai Bank announced that they had decided to close their offices in Peking, Tientsin, Tsingtao and Swatow. In April, 1952, the British-American Tobacco Company reached an agreement with the Chinese authorities under which they were allowed to close down all their activities in China, and handed over assets worth £10 million, in return for an undertaking by the Chinese Government to make themselves responsible for all further liabilities. Finally on May 19 of that year, the British chargé d'affaires delivered a Note to the Chinese Government informing them that the major British companies operating in China had decided, because of the difficulties they were faced with there, to cease operations in China and to apply for the closure, custody, transfer or lease of their businesses. The Chinese Government were asked to co-operate in bringing this about as quickly as possible.

The reply of the Chinese Government in July promised due protection to all British firms dealing in China, and said that questions concerning closure should be directed to the local authorities who would deal with each case "quickly and reasonably", on its own merits. There ensued a period of protracted bargaining in which individual firms negotiated with local officials on the conditions for their withdrawal from China. Both sides were probably aware that in practice nearly all the firms were likely eventually to follow the example of the British-American Tobacco Company, sign away all claims to their physical assets against the grant of permission to close, the consequent release from further tax and wage payments, the acceptance by the Chinese Government, or the purchasing agency concerned, of an agreed list of outstanding liabilities, and the issue of exit permits to foreign staff. But before an agreement of this sort could be reached, officials had to make a thoroughgoing examination of the companies' assets to make sure that they were in good order and that there were no undisclosed liabilities. The managers in China were held personally responsible for any discrepancies. They were not allowed to leave until all such questions had been cleared up. And besides their difficulties with the purchasing agencies, the companies were often faced with huge claims, usually supported by the authorities, for "severance pay" for all former employees (including sometimes some who had not worked since before the war), even if these were to be kept in employment after the change-over. Until all such questions had been settled, firms were obliged to continue to remit large sums in sterling to ensure wage payments.

A particular difficulty faced the three large banks, the Hong Kong and Shanghai Bank, the Chartered Bank of India, Australia and China, and the Mercantile Bank of India. They all held Chinese official funds, banked by the Nationalist Government, and now blocked in the United States as a result of the United States Government's action in freezing all Chinese assets in that country. The Chinese Government demanded that means should be found to bring about the return of these funds; while the United States Government refused to agree to any procedure that would have the effect of evading their freezing order. The banks were allowed to dispose of most of their buildings. But they continued to negotiate, operating from small back rooms, long after all the other firms had finally achieved their withdrawal.

Some of the smaller firms were given permission to close. A few firms were allowed to let certain properties. But in most cases the negotiations proved long and difficult. In January, 1953, the British Government sent a further Note, asking for the co-operation of the Chinese authorities in allowing the firms to wind up their businesses. But in February, 1954, more than a year later, Mr. Eden announced in the House of Commons that the position of British businesses in China was still "in every way unjust and unsatisfactory": if the Chinese Government wished to improve relations with Britain the best thing they could do was to treat British interests in China with ordinary courtesy and justice.

It was only in the summer of 1954 that things began to move more quickly. At the Geneva Conference, during the brief relaxation in relations between Britain and China that occurred then, the difficulties of British businessmen were discussed in private talks between Chou En-lai and the British Foreign Secretary. A representative of the F.B.I. went to Geneva to explain some of the special preoccupations of the foreign firms. The Chinese Foreign Minister undertook to see that the authorities did what they could to speed matters up.

As a result there was a considerable improvement. Replacement visas were granted more easily. Firms were allowed to cut down staffs. And the discussions on closure proceeded more smoothly. By half-way through 1955 most British firms that wished to do so had received permission to close. They had withdrawn all their foreign staff and had effectively abandoned all their assets. The Chinese Government had successfully secured some of the most modern and prosperous business undertakings in China, without incurring either the odium or the financial liability of outright confiscation.

MERCHANTS

These assets were valued by the Foreign Secretary, in announcing the original decision to withdraw, at between £200 and £250 million. Jardine Matheson's alone left property that was estimated to be worth £30 million. To many large firms the assets left behind represented only a part of interests that were world-wide. But some small businesses lost almost everything they had. All equally were compelled to abandon, at the stroke of a pen, assets that had been built up over many years of commercial activity, rather than go on sinking more and more money, without return, as ransom for staffs held, prisoners, in China.

Thus British commercial and manufacturing interests in China came to an end. If there could no longer be trade within China, however, British merchants continued to have hopes for the future of trade with China. But here there were other difficulties.

The first of these was the restrictions imposed on the export of strategic goods to China. This started long before the Korean war. Already in September, 1949, before the formal establishment of the Chinese People's Republic, the British and United States Governments had banned the export to China of machine tools, heavy lorries, aircraft parts, telephone and signal equipment and other items. During the next year a number of further controls were imposed, both in the U.K. and in Hong Kong. In May, 1951, the United Nations passed their embargo resolution. As a result a uniform system of control was established for all those countries taking part in the Korean war, later administered by the Co-ordinating Committee (COCOM) in Paris.

The restrictions were bitterly attacked by the Chinese Government, who for many years maintained a strong barrage of propaganda designed to secure their abolition. As time went on, and especially after the end of the Korean war, the controls also came in for increasing criticism from British businessmen interested in trade with China. They were also greatly disliked in Hong Kong. In November, 1954, the Governor of Hong Kong made an outspoken attack on them, saying that it was of vital importance to the island that the embargo should be lifted or at least eased. One of the chief difficulties was the uncertainty that surrounded it. Orders were sometimes accepted in good faith in Hong Kong; but the goods simply did not arrive, so that penalties for non-delivery became payable to the Chinese. Critics complained that the British

142   BRITAIN AND THE PEOPLE'S REPUBLIC

Government were more strict in their application of the embargo than some other governments. And they felt that the restrictions were being maintained long after they had ceased to be necessary.

As a result of these pressures, during 1955, and again in 1956, the British Government raised the matter in talks with the United States Government. Although the United States Government would not then agree to any revision of the lists, the British authorities began to make some slight relaxations in their administration of the ban through a device known as the "exceptions procedure". In June, 1956, it was decided to permit the export of "reasonable quantities" of rubber to China from Malaya and Singapore. But there was still an urgent demand for a revision of the lists. There was especial criticism of the fact that the China controls were considerably more stringent than those applied to the Soviet Union. The exceptions procedure was slow and cumbersome. And it remained impossible for merchants to be sure whether any contract which they wished to conclude would be permitted to go through.

In early 1957 the pressure for revision grew more intense. The Labour opposition were becoming sharply critical of the continuance of the embargo. The Sino-British Trade Committee addressed a letter to the President of the Board of Trade in strong terms. The matter was discussed by Mr. Macmillan and Mr. Selwyn Lloyd with the United States President and Secretary of State during the post-Suez discussions at Bermuda in March, 1957. In May, 1957, there were protracted discussions on the subject in COCOM. At these it proved impossible to reach agreement. Eventually the British Government announced that, though they regretted the failure to arrive at an agreed policy, they intended themselves to abandon henceforth the differential between the Soviet and the China lists. This example was later followed by most other members of COCOM.

Within the next year there was renewed pressure for a further relaxation of the new joint list. And in July, 1958, that, too, was considerably eased. As a result of these successive moves, civil aircraft and engines, most types of shipping, petrol, electrical equipment, iron and steel, most motor vehicles and tractors, chemicals and machine tools were freed. As a result British exporters were able to sell to China almost any items that were not of direct military value.

The relaxations of the list that were introduced were resisted by the United States Government, which continued to prevent any trade of whatever sort with China by United States nationals, or in U.S. goods. Some of Britain's Commonweath and N.A.T.O. partners were also doubtful about the relaxations. The British Government, however, were probably never happy, on general grounds, to see commercial contacts entirely subordinated to political considerations. Perhaps even more important in influencing their action was the very intense pressure to which they were subjected by British commercial interests. British companies engaged in the China trade represent in fact an extremely powerful and effective pressure group, as influential perhaps though in a rather different direction, as the China lobby in the United States. An interesting comparison might indeed be drawn between the actions of the British Government in seeking to rebuild trade relations with China after the Korean war, and corresponding action in relation to Egypt after the Suez intervention. For the China trade, despite the relatively small volume involved and the fact that no political dividends were to be expected, the British Government were ready, fairly soon after the Korean war was finished, to bring strong pressure to bear for a revision of the strategic lists. And eventually they were prepared to take unilateral action in order to force the issue. With Egypt, although the volume of trade involved was very much larger and though Britain had a powerful political interest in seeking to restore her contacts with the Middle East, no official efforts were directed to reopening the trade until the end of 1959; and until that time the trade was running at only a fraction of its pre-Suez level. This difference is probably to be related more to the relative effectiveness with which British commercial interests in the two areas are mobilized (together with greater Chinese than Egyptian enthusiasm) than to any clearly conceived political decisions by the British Government in the two cases. But it effectively demonstrates how far, as a result, the policies of the British Government towards China remain in practice, as from the earliest times, dominated by commercial considerations.

The second issue affecting the trade which arose between the two countries concerned the channels through which commerce was to be conducted under the new conditions in China. During the Moscow Economic Conference, organized by the Soviet Union in April, 1952, to publicise the benefits to be derived from increased East-West trade, Chinese officials expressed their belief that in the future some new system of organization would be necessary for the conduct of European trade with China. British businessmen themselves began to think that they might be in a better position to deal with the Chinese state trading machinery if they were organized in some form of association which could represent their joint interests, a new East India Company to set up against the Communist Cohong. Thus the British Note of May, 1952, announcing the decision of British businesses to withdraw from China, told the Chinese Government that, to meet the new circumstances, the British Government were ready to form an association representing manufacturers and overseas buyers which could "maintain direct contact with the appropriate Chinese authorities", and act as a permanent trading organization. And the Chinese reply in July said that there was nothing to prevent any such organization entering into negotiations with any of the Chinese trading agencies, "provided that it did not harbour monopoly designs"—a somewhat ironic stipulation in the circumstances.

For some time, however, this idea was not taken up by either side. Despite the offer they had made, the British traders and manufacturers were anxious to ensure that, whatever joint body might be formed, the trade should in practice remain in the hands of the individual firms having a traditional interest in the China trade. The Chinese, on the contrary, appeared anxious to redirect the trade into entirely new channels. On the one hand, they sought to deal direct with manufacturing interests, so bypassing the old-established merchants both in Hong Kong and in Britain. On the other, they tried for a considerable time to conduct negotiations in trade matters through the exclusive agency of various fellow-travelling or politically sympathetic organizations. These, besides being favourably viewed for political reasons, served as useful propaganda agencies for various Chinese themes, especially for the campaign for the removal of the strategic embargo.

During the Moscow Economic Conference, the Chinese Government reached several agreements with groups of variously assorted businessmen and left-wing politicians. Most of these were for goods that were embargoed. And it later transpired that they did not in any case represent firm contracts. They were the pious hopes of politicians rather than the hard-headed commitments of traders. The Chinese Government established a trading agency in East Berlin which became responsible for nearly all Chinese trade with

MERCHANTS 145

East Europe. In the autumn of 1952, an organization called the British Council for the Promotion of International Trade, designed to encourage British trade with China, came into being. Inquiries by British businessmen were forwarded by Chinese agencies to the Council. In the summer of 1953 this body sponsored a visit by a group of British businessmen, including representatives of large and well-known British firms, to China. The mission entered into an "agreement" for an exchange of goods worth £15 million each way. But once again few of the deals represented firm contracts. And the bulk of them concerned items on the strategic list.

Neither the British Government nor many British firms were happy about the situation in which almost all British trade with China was conducted under the auspices of this organization. In November, 1953, Mr. Eden described the B.C.P.I.T. in the House of Commons as a Communist front organization, whose object was to promote Communist international economic policy; and by implication warned British businessmen against taking part in its activities. As a result most of the British firms that had previously participated in it withdrew.

In March, 1954, the China Association, the old-established organization of British firms interested in the China trade, in conjunction with the Federation of British Industries and the London Chamber of Commerce, wrote to the Chinese Minister of Foreign Trade in China, saying that the two organizations were not satisfied with the existing trading arrangements, under which all commercial business was channelled through a small and unrepresentative organization in London. They told him that it was proposed to establish a new and more representative body. And they asked that discussions might take place in order to find ways of increasing trade between the two countries. No immediate reply was received. But during the Geneva Conference discussions took place on various commercial matters in which a representative of the F.B.I. took part. Strenuous efforts were made to persuade the Chinese Government to redirect trade between China and Britain into the traditional channels, or, if they insisted on dealing with a single association, with the new body that it was intended to set up.

In the amiable mood then prevailing in Sino-British relations, the Chinese eventually agreed to accept this. In June the new organization, entitled the Sino-British Trade Committee (later

K

Council) was established. In it were represented the China Association, the F.B.I., the Association of British Chambers of Commerce, the London Chamber of Commerce and the National Union of Manufacturers. It immediately sent an invitation to the Chinese Government to send a mission to the U.K. to visit the British firms it represented and to study the possibilities for extending trade between the two countries.

This invitation was accepted and the mission arrived in Britain at the end of June. Though they clearly showed that they were more interested in acquiring knowhow than in the discussion of specific contracts, the mission was regarded by British trading interests as a success. In November, 1954, and March–April, 1955, return visits were made, under the auspices of the Council, by large and representative groups of British businessmen to China. Although again the total value of trade transacted was not great, the missions had the opportunity to discuss in detail the type of goods both countries might be in a position to exchange and other technical problems concerning the trade. Later various specialist Chinese missions, concerned for example with textile machinery, plastics, metals, railway equipment, electrical engineering, cables, chemicals and many other specialized products came to Britain. British businessmen began to make trips to Peking in an individual capacity. By 1958 it was normally fairly easy for British businessmen to get visas to China. Some began to go regularly to visit the biennial trade fair at Canton.

In general, therefore, the British merchants were successful in asserting their desire that trade should be channelled through an organization that was acceptable to themselves. The status of the Sino-British Trade Council was recognized both by the British Government and by the Chinese authorities. For a time it became the normal body for dealing with the British Board of Trade on behalf of the China merchants. And in September, 1958, the Chinese Minister of Foreign Trade, visiting London, had discussions with the President of the Council on matters affecting trade between the two countries.

In practice, however, the role of the S.B.T.C. soon began to decline. Negotiations on trade were increasingly conducted by individual firms with the Chinese trading authorities concerned.

MERCHANTS 147

Businessmen no longer relied on being members of an official mission in order to make business trips to China. And the China Association remained the organization mainly responsible for promoting the interests of British traders dealing with China, making representations on their behalf to British Government departments, conducting discussions with the commercial section of the Chinese Embassy in London, and providing information and services for British firms. British commercial circles were by no means sorry to see the decline of the body they had founded, for its demise marked the return to the traditional methods of trading by which they maintained their existence.

The third main issue that arose between the Chinese authorities and the British merchants concerned the terms under which individual transactions were to be conducted. During the first year or two of the régime, Chinese organizations adopted normal commercial practice, paying for their purchases by letter of credit on receipt of the shipping documents, but before receipt of the goods themselves. But as a result of the Nationalist blockade, of seizures by the U.S. authorities at the time when exports from that country to China were prohibited, and of the United Nations embargo, some goods for which the Chinese had already paid never reached their destination. The Chinese, therefore, took to demanding payment by letters of guarantee, that is, promises to pay by a Chinese bank, generally the Bank of China, after the goods had been unloaded and inspected in China. For their own exports on the other hand they continued to demand an immediate payment on the presentation of the appropriate documents.

This discriminatory procedure was obviously unsatisfactory to British merchants. In 1954–55 when diplomatic and commercial relations between the two countries began to be more cordial, the matter was taken up with the Chinese trading authorities. As a result of these discussions the Chinese agreed to pay by an irrevocable letter of credit instead of by letter of guarantee, and to adopt various other adjustments to their earlier requirements. Although the terms of individual contracts were not always identical, their methods were then as a rule roughly in line with normal commercial practice elsewhere, and British merchants were on the whole satisfied with the position. In 1958, however, the Chinese once again altered their methods of payment, perhaps as a result of uncertainties arising from the off-shore islands dispute, which was then flaring up once more. They began to ask for documentary credits of 30, 60 and 90 days for each transaction, and to settle mainly by unconfirmed letter of credit payable only at the place of issue in China. Neither of these were uncommon trading requirements, but they were strongly resisted by most British merchants, since these had little confidence in being able to secure redress in case of any dispute over payment.

Many of the contracts provided for heavy penalties in case of any breach. And the British merchants were probably also, like the Chinese, concerned about what would happen if cargoes were lost as a result of hostilities in the Formosa Straits, or action by the Nationalist navy. In 1956 the Chinese Government set up a Foreign Trading Arbitration Commission in Peking to judge commercial disputes. Most Chinese contracts now provide for arbitration by this body. British traders have sought to persuade the Chinese to accept arbitration in a neutral country. But so far the Chinese have agreed to accept this only in exceptional cases.

These issues have still not been settled. But in fact no trading dispute has yet been sent to arbitration, whether in China or elsewhere. Until 1959, in fact, British merchants were agreed that the record of the Chinese inspection stations examining their cargoes were beyond reproach; and that, with one or two exceptions, the commercial record of the Chinese trading agencies themselves less excellent. Within the last year or two there have been some important lapses which have increased the foreign businessmen's apprehension. These troubles derive partly from current Chinese difficulties. But the difficulties over terms of payment stem basically from the unhappy fact that no solution has yet been reached in the Chinese Civil War.

Despite these various difficulties trade between the two countries steadily increased. Even while the embargo was in force there was a gradual improvement. British exports to China in 1951, the first year it was in force, were about three-quarters as high as the year before. But the next year they doubled again. And they continued to rise steadily until by 1957 they had reached about £12 million, roughly the same as in the late forties and considerably more in value than before the war. The initial sluggishness was partly due to the reorientation of Chinese trade to East Europe, to the need for

MERCHANTS 149

China to devote her agricultural exports to repayments for Soviet economic aid and to the disruption of the previous trading channels as a result of the Communist accession to power. But it remains true that the embargo did effectively prevent China from buying in the West those goods in which she was most interested.

After the removal of the embargo an intensive trade drive was conducted by British exporters. There were huge estimates of potential Chinese demand for tractors, motor-cars, machinery and other goods. A large British motor manufacturer placed a quarter-page advertisement in the *People's Daily*, six times the size of any normal advertisement in that paper, and probably the first by any British manufacturer in a Chinese national newspaper. Another large Chinese mission was received in Britain and received assiduous attention from official, financial and business circles. In September, 1957, Mr. Errol, the Parliamentary Secretary at the Board of Trade, paid a three-week visit to China—the first visit by any British Minister of the Crown to that country—toured industrial establishments all over the country and had talks with Chinese ministers and officials including the Prime Minister, on the best ways of increasing trade. Talks were held with the Chinese authorities about holding a British Trade Fair in Peking, though the project never materialized as a result of Chinese prevarications.

A considerable growth in the volume of trade did in fact take place. In 1958 the first full year after the embargo was relaxed, British exports were doubled, while Chinese exports rose by a third. A more gradual increase has continued since. In terms of value British trade with China is now about three times what it was before the war. Yet for all the fuss that has been made about its potentialities it is still quite insignificant in its proportions. Britain does more trade with Singapore alone than with China; twice as much with Venezuela; and about five times as much with Sweden.

As a result of the events of the last few years, the organization of British trade with China has undergone a complete transformation. Most of the small import-export firms, often domiciled in China or Hong Kong, that formerly played a large part in the trade have now gone out of business. The Chinese authorities normally prefer to deal direct with manufacturers, so cutting out the profits of the middleman. And many of the largest British manufacturers are themselves happy to deal direct with the appropriate Chinese agencies. Nevertheless the greater part of the trade between the two countries is still probably handled by merchant firms. Some of these are quite new organizations, formed only within the last few years, dealing with a wide variety of goods and handling a very large volume of business on a commission basis. They are able, through their established contacts with the appropriate Chinese organizations, and by their knowledge of Chinese needs and prices, to provide services that it would be expensive for individual manufacturers to have to supply for themselves. The Chinese Government seem to have no hesitation about dealing with such firms. Indeed they appear to have established stable, and sometimes exclusive, connexions with some of them. One or two British firms have been granted a virtual monopoly in some valuable lines of Chinese exports.

Conversely, there has also been some modification of the Chinese trading mechanism. In the early years virtually all foreign trade was conducted by a single organization, the China National Import and Export Co-operation. Later this was divided up into a number of separate trading agencies, dealing with individual lines of goods, and often making use of the expertise of former private Chinese merchants dealing in such products. These organizations are responsible for carrying out the programmes of foreign trade laid down in the annual and five-year plans. Since they acquire substantial supplies of foreign exchange by their own dealings, they are normally willing to make independent transactions with exporters or importers without requiring a barter deal in each case. Since 1958, however, a proportion of foreign trade is carried out by provincial and other local authorities, dealing in locally produced goods, at the Canton fair or in Hong Kong. They receive special encouragement from the Government to engage in foreign trade. But since they receive no allocation of foreign exchange, they must usually demand direct barter or back-to-back deals when making purchases. Sometimes foreign exporters are obliged to purchase, or to find a purchaser for, Chinese produce that is unattractive, expensive or difficult to sell. Nevertheless, in general the Chinese authorities have in recent years reverted to very much more flexible methods in conducting their foreign trade.

Some British businesses for long maintained a foothold on Chinese soil. A number of British firms elected to stay on in China,

MERCHANTS 151

even after the majority withdrew in 1952–4. One or two manufacturing and other firms managed to hang on for a while, undertaking processing work for the Government, sometimes under the management of *émigré* Russians or Chinese staff. For the most part they made little, if any, profit. Most eventually decided to withdraw on terms similar to those obtained by other firms. One large British textile firm continued to run their own knitting factory in Shanghai, under British managers, until late in 1959, long after all Chinese businesses had been effectively nationalized. During this time the factory was able to continue working at full capacity with the co-operation of the authorities. The management maintained cordial relations with local officials. And when the final decision to close was made, they were granted relatively favourable financial terms for the final hand-over of assets.

One or two shipping firms continue to maintain offices in China. One of the major British oil companies still has an office functioning in Shanghai. This company, with one or two others, is in a slightly different category from the other British firms. Most of their property (though not the Shanghai office) was requisitioned by the Chinese Government in retaliation for the confiscation by the Hong Kong Government of Chinese oil tankers of disputed ownership. As a result, their assets, though at present in the hands of the Chinese authorities, represent almost the only British commercial property in China that has not been formally relinquished by its owners.

The principal British organizations still functioning in China are the Far Eastern Banks. Early in 1955, at a time when their negotiations over the blocked Chinese official funds in the United States were still deadlocked, the Chinese authorities hinted that they would welcome some form of representation by the banks in China. The Shanghai branches of the banks were allowed to resume banking business. This is of a limited nature, mainly remittances for Embassies and other foreign organizations. They have no Chinese depositors. Meanwhile, however, though the Mercantile Bank was permitted to close and withdraw (it has since been absorbed by the Chartered), the other two British banks have never reached a final settlement in their dispute over Chinese official holdings in the United States. Although the Chinese Government have expressed themselves ready to accept payment in sterling, the U.S. Government are still unwilling to release the frozen dollars to the banks.

Until a settlement about this has been reached, the banks are unwilling to discuss with the Chinese authorities any extension of their activities in China.

The rights of British private property-owners in China were never formally abrogated. They have, however, now become extremely problematic. In 1951 the Chinese Government published regulations providing for the registration of all foreign-owned property, surface rights and mortgages in China, announcing that all property not registered would be treated as ownerless and placed under the control of the Government. Many British owners did ask the British consular authorities to register their property for them and continued to receive rent payments in Chinese currency. Under later regulations they were obliged to appoint agents who would be responsible for dealing with the Government authorities. Since no rents could be remitted abroad this was not a very profitable undertaking for the foreign owner. And from 1958 the Government provided that the actual collection of rents could be carried out only by State or municipal management agencies, who would deduct a fixed proportion of the rent for dilapidations and collection expenses. British property owners received notice from their own agents or attorneys in China saying that they no longer wished to represent the owners, and suggesting that a new power of attorney should be made out in favour of the appropriate State agency.

Some British owners did this and still theoretically receive rent for their property to their accounts in China. But the principal foreign owners who had thought it worthwhile to retain their legal rights to property in China were one or two large estate companies owning considerable assets mostly in Shanghai. In November, 1958, however, the Shanghai manager of the largest of these, Sassoons, who still owned about 60 large properties in China, handed over the company's assets to a State organization. The Hong Kong office of the firm declared that this action was unauthorized and invalid. But it seems likely that in any case, under the control of the State agencies and subject to heavy demands for taxation and repairs, property in China will become so unprofitable to foreign owners, even in terms of Chinese currency, that few will think it worthwhile to cling to their titles.

Similarly, in some cases, British shareholders in Chinese companies that have, likea ll private companies in China today, been taken into "joint state-private operation", have continued to receive

MERCHANTS 153

the statutory five per cent in Chinese currency to accounts in China. But such payments are in any case to cease by 1963 (when the "socialist transformation" of such enterprises will have been completed). And once again the proceeds cannot, of course, be remitted out of China.

Thus British financial and business interests on Chinese territory, if not yet utterly extinct are at least now only vestigial. During his century of activity on Chinese soil, the British businessman had built up thriving commercial centres in many of the East coast and Yangtze ports of China. He had played a large part in the establishment of a modern manufacturing industry in China. In Shanghai he had helped to raise out of the mud the largest city in China and the third seaport of the world. He had provided, here and in other cities, modern municipal services and a pattern of Western administrative methods which were certainly not without their value for those who finally took them over. All the assets that he had built up in this process, worth hundreds of millions of pounds he was eventually obliged to bequeath, without recompense to the new rulers of China.

His activities had not been conducted out of benevolence. During his stay in China the foreign businessman received as a rule a handsome return for his investment. He lived a privileged and in some ways luxurious existence within the heart of Chinese cities, forming there wholly foreign colonies, insulated from the great tide of Chinese life that seethed about him, factory areas such as both he and his hosts had favoured from the start. Though he frequently became a genuine admirer, even lover, of China and her way of life, in many cases preferring to settle permanently in the East rather than return to his homeland on retirement, his contacts with her people were minimal, and his knowledge of their language, life and culture, rudimentary. The hostility that his activities evoked among many Chinese dated from long before the coming of the Communists. And it is probable that even without their advent, the role of the foreign businessman in China must inevitably soon have taken some different form.

During the century that it had lasted, the foreigner's business activity in China had brought much that was of benefit to both countries. A part, at least, of his profits was reinvested in the country. His influence was killed in part by ideology, perhaps more by national pride. British merchant and Chinese official alike continued to hope that, in the field of commerce at least, contacts between the two countries might continue to bring mutual benefit. But in future the trade was to be conducted only at a distance, each transaction negotiated across twelve thousand miles of ocean.

8

GENEVA AND AFTER

EVEN in the most favourable circumstances the relationship between countries of sharply conflicting ideology is seldom an ardent one. But the acquaintance between Britain and the new China opened at a period when the cold war had already achieved its iciest temperatures. It started too at a time when the Chinese rulers, inheriting the same mood of bitterness and resentment towards the Western intruders as their forerunners, began to feel the power and confidence to give such sentiments effective expression; and when after twenty years of isolation in the wildernesses of North China, they were still unsoftened by any diplomatic graces which might have induced them to temper the expression of such emotions. The temperature of the relationship remained therefore, throughout its early years, a chilly one.

Realistic opinion in Britain had never assumed that dealings with the new State were likely to be cordial. Events quickly confirmed this judgment. Already in the months immediately following recognition a succession of small incidents served, taken together, to arouse disquiet in Britain about Chinese intentions. There was a series of clashes around the Hong Kong border. Chinese batteries opened fire on a British destroyer. The military head of the Kwangtung Provincial Government accused British warships, aircraft and infantry of violating Chinese territory. A part of the British Embassy compound in Peking was seized without warning by the Chinese authorities. Various British commercial properties were confiscated in retaliation for action taken against Chinese property in Hong Kong. A Chinese semi-official organization, accusing the colonial Government in Malaya of "inhuman treatment" and "barbarous atrocities" against the Chinese population, sent a telegram to the Colonial Secretary demanding visas to enter Malaya to investigate conditions there; and declared that all the Chinese people would support the persecuted people of Malaya in their struggle against colonialism.

There were a number of incidents involving British consulates in China. After the Communists first came to power, most of the existing British consulates carried on as before. Thus at the beginning of 1950 Britain had, in China as in no other Communist country, about a dozen consulates in action, some in quite remote parts of the country. But in November of that year, when China entered the Korean war, the British consul in Mukden was expelled by the local authorities for having sought to prevent Chinese workers from constructing an air-raid shelter inside the grounds of the Consulate-General without his authority. In February, 1951, the British Consulate-General at Tihwa in Sinkiang was searched by armed Chinese and the Consul-General and his staff deported (both these moves were no doubt largely security measures designed to remove British representatives from sensitive regions). In April, 1951, the British consul in Nanking was interrogated by the authorities there and forced to write an apology in humiliating terms for seeking to intervene on behalf of a British subject outside the normal office hours of the bureaucracy. The British Consulate-General in Canton was searched and some United States equipment removed.

There was in any case less and less that the consuls could usefully do. There were few British subjects left in China, especially in the remote areas. Most of the British firms were doing little business. And it was, besides, proving almost impossible to get entry visas for replacements. Thus in time more and more of the consulates had to be closed. One or two of the less important went out of existence soon after the régime came to power. In March, 1951, it was decided to close those at Chungking, Kunming, Hankow, Nanking, Tsingtao and Amoy. In February, 1952, the Consulate-General at Canton was closed (though it was long before the Consul-General was finally given permission to leave). And in November, 1952, the same decision was made for Tientsin. Only Shanghai remained. And though it has never been officially recognized as a Consulate-General, this office has continued to function, as best it can in the prevailing circumstances, until the present day.

An even more serious aggravation of relations at this time was brought about by the detention of some British residents in China. Between 1950 and 1954 a large number of foreign residents of all nationalities were placed under detention, more or less rigorous, on a number of charges that were either fabricated or trivial. A large proportion were missionaries. Others were businessmen or other Western nationals who had, for whatever reason, aroused the

GENEVA AND AFTER 157

suspicions of the Chinese security authorities. Seven British subjects were at one time under arrest, besides one who had been tried and condemned under the Nationalists. None of them, so far as could be ascertained, received any trial or definite sentence, and the Chinese Government persistently refused to give any information about the whereabouts and welfare of those concerned. They could receive no letters. And the normal consular access to them was not permitted. One was a Catholic nun who had been in charge of a mission at Toishan; another a missionary of the Plymouth Brethren who was captured in Tibet; and a third a wireless operator, employed by the Tibetan Government, captured by the Chinese after their invasion, and imprisoned for four years on the picturesque, if implausible, charge of poisoning a Tibetan lama.

But Britain, since she had been asked to represent the interests of the United States, Canada and one or two other countries in China, was also concerned over the nationals of those states held in Chinese prisons. Because of the fanatical Chinese hostility to the United States, American nationals suffered more than those of any other nation. At one time over forty Americans were in Chinese prisons, as well as some under house arrest. Many of these were missionaries. The arrests seem to have been entirely arbitrary. Those concerned had mainly been guilty of no offence more heinous than their own nationality. There were about half a dozen Canadians in a similar situation. The British Embassy made a long series of representations, both in general terms on behalf of all those detained, and in relation to individual cases. These produced little discernible effect; normally not even a reply. But gradually, especially from 1953 onwards, most of the detained foreigners were deported. By 1955, the last British subject had been released.

These events, superimposed on the eviction of British missionaries and British business, could scarcely fail to create a mood of disillusionment. Perhaps even more disappointing ultimately were the foreign policies of the new Government. Some in Britain were prepared to make some allowance for Chinese intervention in the Korean war. Many at least understood the fears that underlay that action. They could even sympathize with the Chinese Government's fulminations over Formosa. But these had to be taken within the context of other Chinese actions. There was the Chinese intervention in Tibet, which aroused mild British protest; though since Britain had for over fifty years acknowledged ultimate Chinese suzerainty, the British Government apparently accepted that such protests were impossible to sustain by direct representations, let alone to support with effective action. There were the never-ceasing onslaughts against imperialism and, in particular, the almost hysterical hatred let loose against the United States. There were the periodic diatribes against the governments of colonial territories such as Hong Kong, Singapore and Malaya. And there was the suspected support being given to colonial revolutions in Malaya and Indo-China. All these events in combination had the effect that, after two or three years of the new Government's existence, opinion in Britain was considerably less hopeful about the possibility of entering into a satisfactory relation with them than it had been when they first overthrew the Nationalists.

When, in November, 1951, the Conservative administration assumed power in Britain, there was some speculation on how far this would affect British policy towards China. It was felt that the new Government might adopt a somewhat more rigid attitude towards the Communist régime. It was even suggested in some quarters that the new Government might withdraw recognition from the People's Republic.

Sir Winston Churchill's Government soon showed that they were indeed anxious to do what they could to bring British policies more into line with those of the United States. In January, 1952, soon after their return to power, the Prime Minister and Foreign Secretary paid a visit to Washington during which such problems were discussed. In a speech to a joint session of Congress Mr. Churchill said that in future British and American policy in the Far East "would be marked by increasing harmony". He asserted that Formosa must stay safely in non-Communist hands. And Mr. Eden, in a speech to Colombia University gave a stern warning against Chinese activities in South East Asia, especially Indo-China and Malaya.

There were insistent reports that during the visit the Ministers had agreed that should an armistice in Korea be reached and subsequently broken by the Communists, hostilities should no longer be confined to Korea, and that, in these circumstances, United Nations forces might embark on a blockade of the Chinese mainland and the bombing of Chinese bases. Such rumours were strengthened by Mr. Churchill's declaration in a speech to Congress that the United

GENEVA AND AFTER 159

Nations' response in such an eventuality should be "prompt, resolute and effective".

The Chinese reaction to these statements was violent. The press declared that Britain had given her "open support for the United States war policy in the Far East", and had "publicly affirmed their friendship with the K.M.T. bandit remnants in Formosa". The statements also aroused some apprehension in the British press and particularly among Labour members of Parliament. One left-wing Member declared that the United States had decided on war with Communist China and that Mr. Churchill had not resisted this intention. On February 26 the Opposition formally moved a resolution "that this House takes note of the Foreign Secretary's statement, welcomes his adherence to the policy followed by the previous administration with regard to the Korean conflict and the relations between Great Britain and China, but regrets the Prime Minister's failure to give adequate expression to this policy in the course of his recent visit to the U.S.A.".

The Conservative Ministers denied that in fact there was any appreciable difference between their policies and those of their predecessors. Mr. Churchill himself accepted that it would be most undesirable for United Nations forces "to get bogged down in allout war with China". And they were able to reply to the Opposition charges about extending the Korean war by showing that the Labour Government had itself agreed, in secret exchanges with the United States administration, that in certain circumstances, such as heavy air attacks from bases on the mainland, the United Nations might have to have recourse to action "not confined to Korea". The Government claimed that all they had done was to confirm that policy.

In fact it seems that Conservative Ministers in their public speeches in the United States had perhaps tended to overstate the degree of agreement reached over Far Eastern policy. When challenged by Members of Parliament in Britain they had, conversely, been inclined to minimize it. The truth would appear to be that the Conservative administration were more concerned than their predecessors to present an appearance of Anglo-American unity to the outside world, but that the substance of British policy towards China was little changed.

So long as the Korean war continued there was indeed little scope for a distinctive British policy towards China. Chinese public statements remained bellicose and intransigent. When Mr. Eden paid another visit to the United States in March, 1953, during which Far East policy was again discussed, the *People's Daily* declared that the British Government had shown themselves "number one lap-dog of the American aggressors", and had openly proclaimed their intention to support them in a policy of enmity towards the Chinese people. Things were little better after the armistice was signed. There was an ugly incident in September, 1953, when a Chinese vessel, without provocation and without warning, opened fire on a naval launch from Hong Kong which, they claimed, had violated Chinese territorial waters, killing a number of British seamen.

The British Government expressed the wish to bring about an improvement in relations. In a debate in the House of Commons in November, 1953, Mr. Eden said that "it was the policy of Her Majesty's Government to work for peaceful relations with China" and they would be the first to welcome a reversal of current Chinese policy. He expressed the conviction that it must be "in China's own interests to keep open the lines of contact with the Western world" and declared that Britain would be ready to help her to do so. During the next year Britain did in fact have the opportunity to perform some such service for China.

The Korean armistice agreement had provided for an international conference at which China should be represented, to discuss the question of Korean reunification and other outstanding Far Eastern problems. As a result of disputes about representation and agenda at the meeting such a conference was never held. But during the Berlin conference early in 1954 Mr. Molotov made a new proposal—to convene a five-power conference, including China, to discuss world problems. The United States Government at first resisted this suggestion, being anxious not to admit the status of China in the discussion of matters not immediately affecting her. The British Government however were much in favour of the meeting and were supported by the French. It was finally agreed that a conference should be held, but that it should be confined to discussing Far Eastern questions. The principal matters the conference was to discuss were the "peaceful settlement of the Korean question"; and the situation in Indo-China.

But before the conference opened a new crisis had arisen in

GENEVA AND AFTER

Indo-China. The position of the French garrison at Dien Bien Phu became perilous. It began to appear that the Vietminh forces might conquer the entire country. The United States Government became intensely alarmed at this prospect. Mr. Dulles in a speech on March 29 declared that the imposition of the Communist system on South East Asia "should be met by united action". At the beginning of April he proposed to the British Ambassador in Washington that the Western Powers should issue a joint warning to China to desist from supplying aid to the Vietminh, under threat of naval and air action against the Chinese coast. Several aircraft-carriers sailed from Manila to the Indo-China coast. And Admiral Radford, the Chairman of the United States Chiefs of Staff Committee, was reported to be urging United States intervention in the Indo-China war by air and naval bombardment.

The British Government believed that a joint warning to China such as had been proposed was likely to be ineffective. The alliance would then be faced with the choice between risking world war by intervention, or a humiliating withdrawal. They informed the United States Government of their view that it might be more realistic to consider the possibility of some settlement in Indo-China than to risk finding themselves suddenly forced by military events, without time to co-ordinate their views, to accept some less favourable settlement as soon as the Geneva Conference opened.

At the beginning of April Mr. Dulles flew to London and Paris to discuss these differences. Mr. Eden informed him that the British Government had become extremely doubtful whether the Indo-China situation could any longer be solved by purely military means. They would be ready to co-operate in long term plans for some kind of collective defence in South East Asia. But they were reluctant to consider any suggestion of military intervention, or even a warning announcement to China, while the Geneva Conference was pending. British public opinion would certainly be opposed to any commitment that might involve Britain in the Indo-China war. The British Government therefore considered that the most that could be done at the present stage was to give a vague warning that the Western Powers would not allow the work of the conference to be prejudiced by Communist military action.

Towards the end of April Mr. Dulles, while in Paris for a N.A.T.O. meeting, told Mr. Eden that the French Government had received a request from the general commanding their forces in

Dien Bien Phu, asking for a powerful strike by United States air forces within the next seventy-two hours. He asked Mr. Eden whether the British Government would join in an undertaking to the French Government which would, in the last resort, have pledged the two nations to commit their troops to the defence of Indo-China. Mr. Eden was dubious. He flew back to London to consult the Cabinet. The Cabinet supported his own recommendation that the suggestion should be turned down. And a day or two later a similar request from the French Government to join with several other governments in a declaration proclaiming determination to resist further Communist expansion was similarly rejected.

The United States Government regarded the war in Indo-China as one element in a world-wide conflict with the forces of Communism. They saw the Vietminh purely as puppets of China. A warning directed primarily at the Chinese seemed to them an essential element in preventing any further deterioration of the situation that had arisen through Vietminh successes in the field. To the British, however, it was precisely the danger that the West might gradually find themselves increasingly entangled in all-out war with China, and perhaps beyond, which made a direct threat to China of the sort envisaged by Mr. Dulles so dangerous. They were no means as convinced as he that those who tread boldly to the brink of war always step back in the direction they intend. They realized that a threat, once made, would inevitably impel the parties towards its final execution. They were aware that world opinion, especially in Asia, would have seen such intervention as designed to bolster a tottering colonial régime. They knew that British public opinion itself would not have supported British involvement. And they felt that action of the sort proposed at a time when peace talks at Geneva were imminent would have appeared particularly provocative.

It does indeed, in retrospect, seem possible that, if the British Government had acceded to the proposal made to them, the West might have found themselves once more engaged in a struggle as bitter, as protracted, and perhaps as inconclusive, as that which had only recently ended in Korea. And, as then, they might well in the end have discovered themselves at war, not with North Vietnam, but China.

The Geneva Conference opened on April 26. The British and Soviet representatives were elected Co-chairmen. The first dis-

GENEVA AND AFTER 163

cussions centred principally on Korea. The Chinese and North Korean representatives put forward a proposal for the rapid withdrawal of foreign troops, and the holding of elections under a formula by which the existing North Korean régime, though having not much more than a quarter of the population of the country, would exercise an effective veto on the form such elections would take. The United States and South Korean delegates called for elections, under United Nations auspices, in the north only, and for the withdrawal of Chinese troops in that area. Mr. Eden suggested a solution about midway between these two proposals. He called for elections under international supervision, throughout both parts of Korea; for the formation of an all-Korean government that would reflect the balance of population between north and south; and for the discussion of conditions under which "foreign troops" might be withdrawn—he did not specify that the proposal should involve Chinese troops only.

It proved impossible to establish any agreement between these divergent views. Indeed the Communist Powers, by demanding the reduction of the armed forces of both north and south to exactly equal numbers and the abrogation of the South Korean defence treaty with the United States, moved even further from the position of the West. And on June 15, discussion of the subject had to be abandoned. The sixteen nations which had participated in United Nations action in Korea issued a communiqué reaffirming that unification should be attained by free elections, under United Nations supervision, for a national assembly in which representation should be in direct proportion to the population numbers in the two halves of Korea.

In Indo-China an entirely different type of situation was faced. In the first place the military position had become so critical for the French that a settlement began to be an urgent necessity. Next, discussion was made more difficult by the somewhat aloof attitude towards the discussion taken up by the United States representatives: Mr. Dulles in particular made no attempt to conceal his distaste for the entire proceedings, appearing with only the greatest reluctance at the same table with Chou En-lai, and in effect left discussion mainly in the hands of his deputy, General Bedell Smith. Thirdly, there was also a certain ambivalence about the position of China in the negotiations; for although not overtly a participant in the Indo-China war, it was generally accepted that her views would be crucial to the attainment of any solution. Finally, a problem arose over the form in which the indigenous Indo-China states, all three of which were disputed between official French-recognized governments and by Communist, or Communist-supported rebel organizations, should be represented at the conference.

On this final point it was finally agreed that the three Associated States and the Vietminh should all participate in the discussions. The delegates next had to consider the political basis of a possible settlement. Mr. Eden had a number of private meetings with Mr. Molotov, his fellow chairman, and with Chou En-lai. Mr. Molotov was moderate in tone and seemed anxious to bring about a settlement. Chou En-lai was at first harsh and intransigent, but mellowed during the course of the conference.

Many of the important advances were made not at the plenary sessions but during the course of private discussions between the principal delegations. The British delegates, together with Indian representatives, had an important part to play as intermediaries between the two Communist leaders, particularly Chou En-lai, on the one hand, and the French, United States and Associated States representatives on the other. On May 29 the conference unanimously adopted a British plan for bringing about a preliminary cease-fire in Vietnam by direct negotiations between the military commands on the spot on both sides. As a result of a meeting between Chou En-lai and Mr. Eden, an agreement was reached by which the Vietminh were to withdraw from Laos and Cambodia, and the authority of the two royal governments recognized there, provided no United States bases were established in the two countries. And on June 19 there was agreement for a cease-fire in Laos and Cambodia on the same lines as that arranged for Vietnam. Between June 20 and July 10 the conference adjourned. After the conference reconvened on July 10 there was intensive discussion on the composition of the supervisory commission for the armistice, the provision for elections in the three states, and the line of demarcation in Vietnam. Compromise settlements on all these points were reached and on the night of July 20, which M. Mendes-France had set as a dead-line for coming to a settlement, agreements were signed covering all three countries.

The settlement provided for the establishment of an international supervisory commission, consisting of representatives of India, Canada and Poland, to police the cease-fire agreement in the

GENEVA AND AFTER 165

three states. Elections were to be held throughout Vietnam in July, 1956, to secure the unification of the country. Vietminh forces would be withdrawn from Cambodia. In Laos the Pathet Lao forces were to be regrouped in two north-eastern provinces. Both Laos and Cambodia declared that they would not enter into an alliance that was not in conformity with the "principle of the cease-fire agreements". Declarations by France, Cambodia and Laos provided that French troops should be withdrawn from those states by the agreement, and that free elections would be held in them during 1955.

The United States would not subscribe to any of these agreements. Their government issued a statement "taking note" of them, but at the same time did not conceal the disfavour with which they viewed a settlement that was regarded both by the administration and by a large number of the United States people as a moral victory for Communism.

The settlement that was finally arrived at provided in effect for the neutralization of Laos and Cambodia and for the partition of Vietnam. In his discussion with Mr. Eden, Chou En-lai had made it clear that he attached the greatest importance to ensuring that the states of Indo-China should remain "independent, sovereign, and neutral". That a final settlement was possible was no doubt due to the evident fact that China was more anxious to see these states neutral now than to seek to ensure, by a prolongation of the war, that they might later be Communist. Thus their Pathet Lao, Khmer, even to some extent their Vietminh allies, had to be sacrificed in order to reach a settlement on these lines. The most important immediate aim for China was to ensure that her own borders were surrounded by buffer states which could not serve as bases for potentially hostile United States or other Western forces.

But while China was able to insulate these immediately outlying areas from world alliances, she could not prevent the formation of a Western military pact further afield. The possibility of some kind of defence organization in South East Asia had been vaguely discussed between the United States, British and French Governments in June, 1952. In April, 1954, when the situation in Indo-China began to look precarious the idea was revived by the United States Government. The British Government in resisting United States requests for joint intervention in the Indo-China war made it clear that they would have no objection to the establishment of a defence organization. They were anxious, however, that such a proposal should be discussed with the Governments of India, Pakistan, Burma and other countries in order to act in co-operation with the peoples of the area. The United States were not especially concerned whether the so-called neutralist powers joined the organization or not. But they were anxious that the committed anti-Communist nations of the area should be organized together as quickly as possible. The Governments of India, Ceylon, Burma and Indonesia in fact rejected the approaches that were eventually made to them. The pact was nevertheless concluded and at the beginning of September the South East Asia Treaty Organization, comprising the Governments of the United States, Britain, France, Pakistan, and Philippines and Siam was established.

The Chinese Government did not conceal their hostility to these proceedings. The preparations for the establishment of the Organization became known during the Geneva Conference. Chou En-lai told Mr. Eden that the Western Powers were splitting South East Asia in two by an anti-Communist alliance. The Chinese Government were especially apprehensive about the suggestion that the Indo-Chinese states might be included in the new Organization. If this had been done it is unlikely that the Geneva Agreements could have subsisted, since it would have violated the basis of the Agreements, the neutrality of the Associated States. Even without them, the pact aroused a violent reaction in the Chinese Press, which has been continued sporadically ever since.

In the event the Organization has achieved little. Military co-ordination has been of the sketchiest. There have been some attempts to co-ordinate anti-subversive activity in the member countries. The alliance may have had some effect in boosting the confidence of some of the countries of the area in face of Chinese expansion. But the most powerful and influential nations of the area have remained outside it. Many others regard it as a vestige of colonialism. And it is questionable how far it has acted as an effective deterrent against Communist aggression, since the Chinese must well have known that the countries that are members are those that would in any case inevitably have joined in any war in which they became involved in the area.

Britain had a particularly important role to play at the Geneva Conference. Partly because public and official attitudes in the United States both towards Communism in general and towards China in

GENEVA AND AFTER 167

particular, were at this time so impassioned, she played a key part in presenting a more moderate and realistic Western position. Having no national interests either in Indo-China or in Korea, she could perhaps see more clearly than those more intimately affected, or more emotionally committed, the advantages to be gained through some stabilization of the position in South East Asia. A failure to achieve an armistice in Indo-China at this stage could in fact only have meant an indefinite prolongation of the war. This would have led to a prolonged period of unrest and the increasing identification of Communist activity with national aspirations. And it could well have led eventually to the loss of all Indo-China. Thus even from the narrow standpoint of the Western tactical position, there was much to be gained by a settlement. A more important attainment was the abolition of the last important area of armed conflict then existing.

For relations between Britain and China the Geneva Conference was important for quite other reasons than the settlement of the war in Indo-China. During the conference Mr. Eden and Chou En-lai had discussions on a number of other questions affecting relations between the two countries. Chou En-lai showed himself ready to make concessions on a number of points. The Chinese Press and radio became more affable. There was a period almost of cordiality in the relations between the two countries.

Chou En-lai agreed that China should open a mission in London, under a chargé d'affaires, corresponding to the British post in Peking. He undertook to see if something could be done to help British businessmen in China to close their businesses and leave the country. He agreed to review the case of a British subject, captured in Tibet and still held in a Chinese prison; and to inquire into the fate of a party of British sailors from Hong Kong who had disappeared while on a yachting cruise. And the month after the Conference ended, when a British civil aircraft was shot down by Chinese aircraft with the loss of ten lives during a period of tension in the Formosa Straits, the Chinese Government surprised the world by publishing an immediate apology and paying in full the claim for compensation subsequently put forward by the British Government.

One effect of this relaxation was a considerable increase in contacts between the two countries. From the beginning of the régime these had almost entirely withered away. Visits in either direction were almost entirely confined to those known to be sympathetic to the Chinese authorities. In September, 1950, an informal delegation of Chinese, led by Liu Ning-i, a leading member of the Chinese Communist Party, had come to Britain, had been carefully shepherded by pro-Communist organizations and issued various statements attacking British policies. From that time there had been virtually no visits of any sort from China to Britain. In the opposite direction almost the only people able to visit China had been a few prominent British personalities ready to pronounce in favour of the Chinese cause (for example over the Korean war, or the accusations of germ warfare made against the United States), one or two left-wing trade union delegates and an occasional Labour M.P. The British Council, though for a short time they reported that their offices were as well patronized as ever, were finally obliged to withdraw from China in August, 1952.

From the time of the Geneva Conference visits became much more frequent. There were regular delegations for the Chinese National Day and May Day celebrations. There were visits by Members of Parliament of both parties, businessmen, trade unionists, theatrical groups, university delegations and specialists in many fields, regardless of political beliefs. And there were a few visits of the same sort in the opposite direction.

The most important of these exchanges was probably the visit made by leaders of the Labour Party, including Mr. Attlee, Mr. Bevin, Dr. Summerskill (the Chairman of the Party), Mr. Morgan Phillips (the Secretary), and others, as a result of an invitation from the Chinese delegation at the Geneva Conference in August, 1954. The party had talks with Chou En-lai and Mao Tse-tung. Chou En-lai for the first time attended a dinner party in the British Embassy given in the delegation's honour. Both sides agreed on the need for an increase in trade and diplomatic contacts. And after the visit Mr. Attlee made a statement declaring his belief that Formosa should be neutralized for a period before a final decision was taken on its future.

One or two visits were refused from the British side. In May, 1956, the Standing Committee of the National People's Congress, the Chinese Parliament, invited a British parliamentary delegation to visit China. This invitation was turned down by the British Government. The British Government similarly rejected sugges-

GENEVA AND AFTER 169

tions that a parliamentary delegation from China should be asked to visit Britain.

The more amiable mood of China's policy towards Britain from 1954 was a reflection of a general relaxation in her attitude towards the outside world at that time. This was exemplified in her readiness to reach some accommodation with many governments of the area that were by no means congenial in ideology. The Chinese leaders continued to cultivate relations with the major neutral powers of Asia. They even extended this policy to the royalist and anti-Communist Governments of Laos and Cambodia. And it received its clearest expression at the conference of Afro-Asian Powers at Bandung where Chou En-lai succeeded in impressing many with his conciliatory and undogmatic approach.

On matters that they considered of vital national importance, however, the Chinese Government continued to take up an intransigent, and even belligerent attitude. Thus, during the autumn of 1954, in the hey-day of the spirit of Bandung, they launched a heavy bombardment from Chinese coastal batteries against some of the islands off the mainland coast still occupied by Nationalist troops. They reaffirmed their determination to liberate Formosa. And they declared that they would "brook no foreign interference" in their efforts to carry out this intention.

The Nationalists replied with attacks by aircraft and warships on Communist gun-emplacements and other targets. A Nationalist destroyer was sunk by Communist torpedo boats. On August 24 Mr. Dulles issued a statement, pointing out that the United States 7th Fleet was committed to the defence of Formosa, and declaring that a number of other islands were "so intimately connected with the defence of Formosa" that the United States military authorities would be justified in defending them as part of their overall strategy. In December the United States Government signed a defence treaty with the Nationalist Government. But neither the terms of the treaty nor the various public statements made by United States spokesmen made it unambiguously clear whether the United States would intervene to defend the islands at that time under attack. It was evidently the policy of the United States administration to leave the matter in doubt in order to deter any possible attack without undertaking an irrevocable commitment.

On January 18, Communist forces captured Yikiangshan Island, about 200 miles north of Formosa, and close to the Tachen Islands which were also under attack. On the next day President Eisenhower expressed the wish for a cease-fire under United Nations auspices. On January 27 the United States Senate at the President's request passed, by an overwhelming majority, a resolution giving the President authority to employ United States armed forces as he thought necessary for securing Formosa and the Pescadores, as well as "related positions and territories of that area now in friendly hands", against armed attack from without.

British public opinion had from the start of the fighting almost unanimously taken the line that, whatever the merits of the Chinese Government's claim to Formosa, the situation in which the Nationalists continued to cling to small islands, sometimes only a few miles from the mainland coast, though often a great distance from Formosa, could only be provocative; and that the best solution would be one that brought about a Nationalist withdrawal from such islands. There is little doubt that the British Government shared such views. Thus, while the United States Government sought so far as possible to obscure any clear distinction between the islands and Formosa itself, the British Government in all their public statements sought, on the contrary, to underline the differences in the status of the two. Thus Mr. Eden, speaking in the House of Commons on January 26, drew a careful distinction between the Government's attitude towards Formosa, which during the present century had never legally belonged to China, and the offshore islands which "had always been regarded by us as a part of China". In a written reply a few days later he went further, saying "the Nationalist-held islands in close proximity to the coast of China are in a different category from Formosa and the Pescadores, since they undoubtedly form part of the territory of the People's Republic of China". And later he stated in categorical terms that he "would like to see the Nationalists withdraw their forces" from the coastal islands.

But though the British Government were more free than the United States authorities to express openly their views as to the action the Nationalists should take, they were, for the same reasons, less likely to influence them towards the course of action they advocated. There is little doubt that the United States Government, whatever they said in public, did what they could behind the scenes to induce the Nationalists to withdraw from their more exposed positions. Meanwhile the British Government sought in the interna-

GENEVA AND AFTER

tional field to bring about a relaxation of tension. Mr. Eden, while he went out of his way to say that he "understood the position of the Chinese Government" and did not expect them to withdraw their claim to the islands, publicly declared that the first need was to stop the fighting. On January 28, the British Ambassador in Moscow was instructed to call on Mr. Molotov to ask him to use his influence to induce the Chinese Government towards moderation. When a meeting of the Security Council was called and the Chinese Government invited to attend, the British chargé d'affaires in Peking, informing the Chinese Government of the decision, similarly urged the need for a peaceful resolution of the dispute. When Mr. Eden paid a visit to South East Asia in the spring he discussed ways to bring about such an outcome with the Prime Ministers of Burma and India. And throughout the period the Government were reported to be doing all in their power to persuade the United States Government to use their influence with the Nationalists in favour of withdrawal.

The situation was still tense at the time of the Bandung Conference in April, 1955. During the conference Chou En-lai offered to sit down with United States representatives to discuss ways of relaxing tension in the area. Initial United States reaction was somewhat surly. The British Government were reported to have used their influence to bring about a reconsideration of this attitude. The British chargé d'affaires took part in discussions with the Chinese Government in Peking to find a form of words specifying the scope of the talks in terms acceptable to the United States Government. And Britain played an important part, with the Indian Government, in getting the talks going. These were finally successful. In July the negotiations were opened in Geneva; and have been proceeding, in desultory fashion, ever since. In the same month the British Prime Minister raised the subject with both U.S. and Soviet leaders during the Geneva Conference; trying, as he later wrote, "to persuade those present, and absent, of the peaceful intentions of the other side".

Meanwhile the situation in the straits had become calm again. But their discussion with the U.S. at Geneva brought the Chinese no nearer to the attainment of their demands. And in the summer of 1958 they again launched an attack on the islands. Again there was heavy bombardment of those islands nearest the Chinese coast and of convoys of ships sent to supply them. Mr. Dulles issued a statement suggesting, in considerably more categorical terms than in 1955, that the United States might intervene to defend Quemoy and Matsu. While the President had not made any final decision to make use of the powers that he had been vested with by Congress, "we have recognized that the securing and protecting of Quemoy and Matsu have increasingly become related to the defence of Taiwan". A considerable United States naval force was sent to Formosa. United States warships were deputed to escort Nationalist supply convoys to the islands.

British public opinion again expressed its concern that the Western Powers might, if only by accident, find themselves involved in a war which, though it could be presented as a war against aggression, would in effect be interpreted as a war to secure the continued control by the Nationalists of a few small islands within a few miles of the Chinese coast. The British Government made clear that they had no obligation or commitment to take military action for the defence of Quemoy, Matsu or Formosa. But the British Foreign Secretary, now Mr. Selwyn Lloyd, made little attempt on this occasion to distinguish the position of the islands from that of Formosa. Nor is there any evidence that the British Government made any attempt to bring about a Nationalist withdrawal from the islands. British ministers in general supported the statements made by the United States Government. A Foreign Office statement regretted "the current indications that the Chinese Government wished to settle the problem of the offshore islands by force". The Prime Minister rejected a suggestion by Mr. Gaitskell, the Leader of the Opposition, on September 15, that the British Government should make plain that Britain would not join in a war for the defence of Quemoy, or if necessary, fly to Washington to make these views plain to the United States Government.

This alteration in the attitude of the British Government in part no doubt reflected the fact that the Government of Mr. Macmillan and Mr. Selwyn Lloyd were less willing than that of Mr. Churchill and Mr. Eden, especially since the sorry escapade at Suez, to adopt a policy independent from that of the United States. But it was in part a reflection of the general deterioration in the mood of British relations with China since the brief honeymoon period after Geneva. The more conciliatory attitude of the Chinese was maintained up to 1956. In July of that year the *People's Daily* said that there were "pleasant signs that Britain was taking the realistic path

GENEVA AND AFTER 173

of peaceful co-existence". The Chinese Prime Minister attended the celebrations of the Queen's Birthday at the British Embassy in Peking, and proposed the health of the Queen and the happiness of the British people.

He did not attend them in 1957. During that year the Hundred Flowers that were allowed briefly to blossom for a few spring weeks in China, were, from June, once more savagely cut down. A fierce anti-rightist movement was introduced. Early the next year Chou En-lai, usually considered pliable and conciliatory in his diplomatic dealings, was replaced as Foreign Minister. The alteration in the strategic balance between East and West from the end of 1957 may have encouraged a more forward policy. Mao Tse-tung declared his belief that "the East wind prevails over the West". Chinese attitudes to a number of external questions, both in Asia and beyond, showed a notable lack of the spirit of Bandung. Conversely, Britain continued year after year to support United States moves to postpone consideration of the admission of the People's Republic to the United Nations. The British Government, Chou En-lai complained in an interview with a British correspondent, had abandoned the efforts of Sir Anthony Eden to improve relations, and now toed the American line on every matter. British goodwill perhaps began to seem of little value to the Chinese Government.

Chinese propaganda became considerably more hostile. It once again became difficult for any but congenial British visitors to get visas to China. The Chinese Prime Minister, in his annual report to the nation at the National People's Congress in February, 1958, said that "if Britain does not change its double-faced attitude towards China . . . Sino-British relations would inevitably be adversely affected". At the time of the revival of the offshore islands dispute, the Chinese Press claimed that "Lloyd and his like were openly conniving with and backing the United States policy of aggression and provocation against China". There was particular indignation that the British Government, which had recognized China, should now make no attempt, as Sir Anthony Eden had done, to recognize the validity of Chinese claims to the islands. At the time of the British attack at Suez, the Chinese Government issued a statement, reminiscent of those published at the time of the Korean war, saying that China "could not stand idly by" while Egypt's sovereignty was threatened; 250,000 Chinese "volunteers" were said to have registered at offices set up all over China. Huge demonstrations were organized outside the British Embassy in Peking. When Britain sent troops to Jordan at the request of the Jordan Government in July, 1958, more massed gatherings took place and the Chinese Government presented a Note to Britain warning her that she faced "grave consequences" if she failed to withdraw her troops. And today the British are once more abused, in customary terms, as unregenerate imperialists.

British relations with the new Government of China have passed through three phases. At the time of recognition there were some in Britain who hoped that it might be possible, by preserving so far as possible previously existing ties and seeking to draw China into the world community, to establish with her a more satisfactory relationship than had proved possible with other Communist countries. In September, 1950, Mr. Bevin declared that Britain "did not intend to break her long-established friendship with China"; and would be ready to help China fulfil her destiny as one of the great powers. Chinese treatment of British business and other interests, her intransigent approach on many world problems, the ruthlessly totalitarian nature of her internal policies, and the opposition of the two countries in the Korean war for a time frustrated all such hopes.

By 1954 the war was over. China's policies began to be more conciliatory. British interests were now largely displaced, but there seemed a chance that some of the old contacts could be re-established on a new basis. From the time of the Geneva Conference therefore, there seemed once more an opportunity to put relations between the two countries on a better footing.

But this phase too did not last more than two or three years. From 1957 China's mood hardened again. The period of conciliation had not led to any improvement in her international status. She remained an exile from the world community. Whether for these or other reasons, her whole approach to the international scene became increasingly shrill and assertive. With Britain she had few subjects of common interest. Relations became once more remote. Neither any longer had much to gain from the friendship of the other.

The difficulties that have persisted derive partly from ideological divergences. These have necessarily entailed membership of opposing power blocks. Partly they reflect the strident and uncompromising mood of China's new rulers. Still in an early, Stalinist phase of their own revolution, the Chinese leaders have tended to regard the world scene with a stern and unaccommodating eye; and they have perhaps sometimes, for purely internal reasons, welcomed the opportunity to beat the drums of nationalism. Partly the differences that remain are those of national self-interest. But as British power has begun to recede from the Far East, such clashes of material interest have become less acute than they were in former times. Though, therefore, the two countries today are in many ways more remote than they have been for over a century, they have perhaps, for this very reason, less immediate cause for altercation than at any time in their history.

9
HONG KONG

WHEN Lord Macartney, Britain's first envoy to China, arrived in Peking in 1793 he had instructions that, if he could not obtain some assurance of better conditions for the foreign merchants in Canton, he was to seek to secure from the Chinese Government some small island or minor port where Europeans might live and trade, subject to their own laws, throughout the year. To this request there was no more reply than to any of the others that he put forward. In 1834 Lord Napier, during a similarly abortive mission, suggested that the British Government might consider the desirability of occupying a small and rocky island, known to Chinese as Hsiang Kang, the Fragrant Harbour, situated about sixty miles from Canton just outside the mouth of the Pearl River. After Captain Elliot and the British traders had been successively forced out of Canton and Macao by Commissioner Lin in 1839, they took to their ships and found shelter in the harbour formed by the island. And when, at the beginning of 1841, preliminary negotiations took place for the settlement of the war then in progress, Captain Elliot obtained a cession of the island since, as he later wrote to the Governor-General of India, "the palpable impossibility of entrusting our merchants at Canton, and the utter hopelessness of efficient and avowed protection or liberal arrangements at Macao has cast upon me . . . the absolute necessity of providing a secure seat for the trade, without loss of time under our own Flag."

Lord Palmerston, though he too had earlier demanded some island base, saw little value in the acquisition of this "barren island with hardly a house upon it". And his successor, Lord Aberdeen was prepared to forego the demand for an island station altogether. Thus it was only because the British negotiator, himself convinced of its value, exceeded his instructions that the treaty finally arrived at on the conclusion of the war made provision for the cession to Britain of the Fragrant Harbour.

Lord Palmerston's misgivings seemed at first to have some justification. Trade did not flourish in the new colony in the early years. A British merchant writing in 1850 said that "several English

HONG KONG 177

mercantile houses were established here when the colony was in its infant state, but the number of such is now reduced to ten or twelve". Most of the British merchants preferred to deal direct with Canton or the ports newly opened up by the treaty. Few of the Chinese merchants came to the island. It was in theory only open to trade through the five Treaty Ports, and subject to Chinese customs duties. Its approaches were infested by pirates. It had a generally unsavoury reputation. It was principally important as a centre for opium smuggling and for the trade in Chinese coolies to South America, the West Indies and different parts of the Pacific. And the first bishop of the colony, during a preliminary visit, wrote that the foreigners were hated for their "moral improprieties and insolent behaviour", while the Chinese were the "last dregs of native society", who had "flooded to the British settlement in the hope of gain or plunder".

In 1860, by the Treaty of Tientsin, a strip of the mainland opposite the island, near the old Chinese city of Kowloon, was acquired. The island began to become more prosperous. The establishment of more Treaty Ports and the effective opening of the interior made Hong Kong a useful operating centre for firms having dealings in many different parts of the country. Entrepôt trade began to be developed. Import-export firms, British and Chinese, were established in the island. Western banks set up offices there to finance the trade. Trading connections with Japan, Siam and other parts of South East Asia were developed. The number of ships clearing the harbour annually rose from 700 in 1848 to 4,500 in 1864, and to 11,000 by 1898, of which about two-thirds were British. The European population rose from about 700 in 1853 to 2,000 by 1865, and nearly 10,000 by the end of the century. The Chinese population which had been about 5,000 before the British arrived reached 125,000 by 1865 and 250,000 (including the mainland population) by 1898. By this time the total value of the colony's trade was £50 million and included something like forty per cent of China's imports and exports.

As British commitments in the Far East were extended the island's military importance increased. Soon after the colony was acquired the strength of its garrison had been about a thousand, and the only naval forces had been a frigate and one small "steamer". By the end of the century a naval dockyard had been built, the garrison had increased to about 7,000 and the island had become

178 BRITAIN AND THE PEOPLE'S REPUBLIC

Britain's principal naval station in the Far East. But there were increasing doubts about how far the base could be defended against attack from the mainland. Even when the island was first acquired, Palmerston had suggested that to make it defensible the opposite coast would have to be demilitarized. Towards the end of the century there were increasing demands—from the Chamber of Commerce in Hong Kong, from the China Association in London, from the Navy League, as well as the Hong Kong Service chiefs—that a further area of the mainland should be acquired for this purpose. And in 1898 after demands for territory from Russia, Germany and France had been met by the Chinese Government, Britain acquired a ninety-nine-year lease of the New Territories, stretching for a distance of about twenty miles into the Chinese mainland beyond Kowloon.

The colony was provided with the administration and services that colonial rule normally afforded. The Government's revenues rose from about £30,000 in the early 1950s to about £500,000 by the end of the century. While in the early years the home Government had to undertake all the costs of the garrison as well as some subsidy for the administration, by the end of the century the Hong Kong Government not only paid for all its own needs but had to give about one-fifth of its revenue for defence. Roads were built, sanitation provided, schools constructed, a water system created. During the twentieth century much was done to eliminate disease such as plague (which remained endemic until the 1920s) and malaria. Some welfare services were provided. By the middle of that century the colony was, on the assertion of many foreign observers, probably the most efficiently administered territory in the whole of the Far East. The Hong Kong Government could boast something of the same achievement, in miniature, as that of the Government of India. A tiny strip of East Asia was furnished with all the administrative and technical benefits that Europe could provide.

Economically the island continued to prosper. A smattering of light industry began to be set up. Hong Kong banks, and the Hong Kong Government itself, participated in railway development on the mainland. Trade began to be world-wide. After the First World War, the colony's trade suffered, like that of British merchants on the mainland, from Nationalist boycotts and strikes, from the world slump, and from the Sino-Japanese war. While imports from China

HONG KONG 179

remained high, exports to that country dropped sharply, and by 1929 represented only fifteen per cent of the colony's exports. But the population continued to rise. By 1925 it had reached 700,000, by 1927 1,000,000, and by 1941 after an influx of refugees from the Sino-Japanese war, to 1,600,000.

The development of the colony brought prosperity to Chinese as well as British. In 1855 more than half the residents of the colony rated at over £40 were Chinese, and in 1881 of eighteen rate-payers rated at over 4,000 Hong Kong dollars, only one, Jardine Matheson and Company, was not Chinese. Yet except in affairs of commerce the two communities had little intercourse. The Hong Kong Club admitted no Chinese members. The Chinese merchants lived a detached existence, remaining essentially a part of China within a political and administrative entity that was wholly European. For the most part the Chinese population successfully resisted the Government's half-hearted efforts to legislate against gambling, insanitary living conditions, child bondage and other tiresome Chinese habits. And in 1895 the then Governor, Sir William Robinson, had to admit sorrowfully that it was "extraordinary—not to say discreditable—that after fifty-three years of British rule the vast majority of Chinese in Hong Kong should remain so little anglicized". The Governor did not say whether this lamentable state of affairs was more discreditable to the Hong Kong Government or to the Chinese population.

Although in time Chinese unofficial members were nominated for the Legislative Council and the Executive Council, the Chinese population in practice were no more able, nor more eager, than their European counterparts to exercise any effective control over the way they were governed. The constitution of the island remains today in all essentials exactly what it was when it was introduced on the colony's establishment in 1843. The two councils are still, as then, controlled by official or nominated members. And when during the nineteenth century one Governor in his reforming zeal dared to suggest that elections with a limited franchise should be introduced for the Legislative Council, he was told by the Colonial Office that "great commercial interests and the future progress of civilization throughout the East are to a great extent involved in the maintenance of British rule and of orderly government in Hong Kong". A colonial secretary today might well advance somewhat similar arguments for resisting precisely the same innovations.

180   BRITAIN AND THE PEOPLE'S REPUBLIC

Relations with the Chinese of the mainland were almost uniformly unhappy. For long the Chinese provincial authorities regarded the island merely as a centre for the illegal distribution of opium and other contraband. Although for this reason they had demanded in the initial treaty that only registered Chinese merchants from the Treaty Ports should be allowed to trade at Hong Kong, this provision was soon ignored by the Hong Kong Government and merchants, and the mainland became the centre of a widespread trade by Chinese junks from the mainland, evading duty. The Chinese Government also resented the fact that, by registration in Hong Kong, Chinese ship-owners were able to acquire all the immunities of British owners. At a later date the colony was sometimes the refuge of Chinese revolutionaries (though both Sun Yat-sen and Kang Yu-wei were at one time banished from the colony in deference to the Chinese Government's apprehensions). After the British acquisition of the New Territories, there was dispute over the status of the old city of Kowloon, where, under the agreement, the Chinese officers then stationed were to "continue to exercise jurisdiction except so far as may be inconsistent with the military requirements for the defence of Hong Kong". The provision was ambiguous as well as impracticable, and only invited dissension. In 1900 a Colonial Office official minuted, "we have definitely decided not to allow the city to fall under Chinese jurisdiction, and have told the Chinese Government so, and have passed an order in Council including it in the new territory, and the matter is at an end." So simply, in 1900, could a junior British official dispose of the weightiest representations of a Chinese Government.

But the affair was not at an end, any more than was Chinese resentment against other British usurpations. With the swelling flood of Chinese nationalism during the next fifty years, feeling against continued British occupation of the island became increasingly intense and vocal. During the 1920s the colony was subjected to strikes and boycotts. The Nationalist movement became the focus for all such aspirations. Nationalist ministers demanded the return of the island to China. And in so doing they said only what was in the hearts of all educated Chinese of the time—except possibly some of those who lived within the colony.

HONG KONG

The Second World War, with the temporary expulsion of British power from the island, gave a new impetus to such aspirations. Many Chinese began to hope that the time had now come for the colony's return to China. Some felt that it should have been given up under the 1943 Treaty, with other fruits of the "opium wars". It was generally known that President Roosevelt wished to see the territory returned. And as the war drew to its close, there were suggestions that the subject might be discussed at the peace talks.

The Nationalist Government made full use of this opportunity. On August 16, 1945, immediately after the Japanese capitulation, a spokesman at Chungking announced that the Chinese Government would accept the surrender of Hong Kong. On August 20, Mr. Bevin announced in the House of Commons that steps had been taken on the British side to accept the surrender, but warned that "there might still be difficulties" about this. It was reported that British and Chinese forces were engaged in a race to reach the island. On August 22 the United States Secretary of State, Mr. Byrnes, announced that the question of Hong Kong would be discussed at the coming London conference of foreign ministers, a statement that was greeted with consternation in London. On the same day Chinese surrender terms to the Japanese provided for Hong Kong as one of the areas to be reoccupied by Chinese troops. And on August 23, General Wedemeyer, Commander of the United States forces in China, said that "since the outbreak of war Hong Kong had been regarded as within the Chinese theatre", and it was therefore natural that the Chinese should want to accept the surrender.

On the same day, Mr. Attlee announced that plans for the resumption of British administration were fully prepared. He reaffirmed previous declarations, including the Cairo communiqué, that His Majesty's Government did not contemplate any modification in the sovereignty of British territories in the Far East. And he reiterated that arrangements were being made for the Japanese surrender in Hong Kong to be accepted by a British commander. There were hurried and apparently strenuous exchanges between the British, Chinese and United States Governments. The forces on both sides continued to make preparations to receive the surrender. On August 24, it was announced that General MacArthur had sent a message to the Japanese imperial headquarters ordering the Japanese forces to surrender to a British naval commander. And on the same day Chiang Kai-shek announced that "China would not send troops to accept the surrender of Hong Kong lest this should arouse allied misunderstanding". But he hoped that China and Britain might by legal procedures and in accordance with the demands of the times, reach a reasonable settlement of the Hong Kong question. And on the next day he declared that "now that other leased territories had, one after the other, been returned to China, Kowloon [apparently he meant the New Territories] should not remain the exception".

There was no immediate outcome to this demand. But throughout the remaining period of Nationalist rule there was continued agitation in China for the return of the colony. In January, 1946, there were student demonstrations in Nanking and Shanghai. When the R.A.F. began to construct an airfield in Hong Kong this was taken as a sign that the British were intending to dig in. The Chinese Government made representations, complaining that the British action "violated Sino-British unity". On September 19, 1946, the Shanghai City Council sent a telegram to Chiang Kai-shek urging that negotiations should be started with Britain to secure the return of both Hong Kong and Kowloon to Britain. And in 1947 the Chinese Foreign Office reported to the People's Political Council that a "rational solution"—a rational solution was presumably one favourable to China—"of the Hong Kong sovereignty problem was within the bounds of possibility".

There were difficulties over the activities of some Nationalist organizations in Hong Kong. The K.M.T. party machinery attempted to acquire direction of the trade union movement and the teachers' organization in Hong Kong. They sought to control the newspapers of the colony. On one occasion the Government of Hong Kong were obliged to suspend the principal K.M.T. newspaper in the colony for inciting its readers to violence against another Chinese language newspaper. This action provoked the Chinese Government to make strong representations.

Nationalist officials revived the century-old allegation that large-scale smuggling into and out of China was carried on in Hong Kong. In August, 1947, the Chinese Vice-Minister for Foreign Affairs said that China had repeatedly sought the co-operation of the British colony but had had no response. In fact, though there may have been some smuggling from Hong Kong, this trade seems to have been mainly the result of the inefficiency of the Chinese Government prevention services and the corruption of Chinese officials, together with the penal rates of duty imposed on many commodities. Eventually, in June, 1948, an agreement was reached between the Chinese and Hong Kong authorities, under which the Chinese customs service was allowed to establish inspection centres in Hong Kong and to clear all ships leaving the harbour. Chinese customs vessels were allowed to patrol in certain Hong Kong waters. The import of Chinese yarns and textiles to Hong Kong without an export licence was made a punishable offence in the colony. The Chinese continued to complain of currency smuggling from China to Hong Kong. But this was the effect of the catastrophic depreciation of the Chinese currency. And it is unlikely that given the conditions existing in 1948 and 1949 any measure of control would have prevented a large-scale flight of capital from China to Hong Kong.

These disputes reached a climax early in 1948. At the end of 1946 the Hong Kong Government, in the course of a clearance programme, made an order for the eviction of about 2,000 Chinese squatters who were living in ramshackle wooden huts on a site near Kaitak aerodrome. The Hong Kong authorities claimed that the huts were overcrowded and without proper sanitary arrangements, and that the evictions were necessary in the interests of public health and the danger of fire. Chinese on the island and on the mainland, quoting the 1898 agreement covering the lease of the New Territories, which provided for the administration of the old city of Kowloon by Chinese Government officials, declared that the Hong Kong authorities were exceeding their powers. Strong representations were made by the Nationalist Government on behalf of the squatters, and for several months the eviction orders were suspended pending the result of diplomatic negotiations. Finally the eviction order was confirmed, although alternative accommodation was offered. Some of the Chinese concerned forcibly resisted eviction, were arrested and were later imprisoned.

This sparked off a violent reaction in China. In Canton, several thousand Chinese, many of them students, attacked and burnt down the British Consulate-General, the private houses of some of its staff and the premises of a British business firm. The British Vice-Consul and three other British subjects were injured. Other demonstrations took place in Shanghai. All British women and children in Canton were flown out to Hong Kong in British aircraft, and the district was immediately placed under martial law by the Chinese authorities.

The British Government made strong protests about the incidents. The Chinese Prime Minister expressed deep regret and gave orders to the local authorities to bring those responsible to book. But when the British Government presented a claim for compensation for the damage, the Chinese presented a counter-claim for full compensation for the eviction of the Chinese squatters. They reaffirmed the Chinese claim to jurisdiction within the walled city of Kowloon. And they held that responsibility for the riots should "clearly be borne by the Hong Kong Government". A few youths were later imprisoned for their part in the incidents. But despite repeated representations to both National and Communist Governments no compensation was ever paid for the damage caused in the riots.

As in many other fields, Chinese agitation over Hong Kong during the Nationalist period was strident but ineffectual. The British Government, confident in its ineffectiveness, were able to ignore the stridency. When a new and more powerful government emerged on the mainland in 1949, the accents became in some respects less menacing than before. But the threat that lay beyond these new antagonists was a far more serious one to the administration in Hong Kong than any they had yet had to face since the British occupation of the island.

The first concern, as the Chinese armies began to advance towards the south, was for the defence of the colony. Already at the end of 1948, after the Communist victories in Manchuria and North China, it was announced that reinforcements were to be sent to the garrison at Hong Kong. On December 10, Mr. Mayhew, the Under-Secretary of State for Foreign Affairs, said that "it was the intention of H.M. Government to maintain their position in Hong Kong". At the beginning of May, 1949, when the Communist armies forced a crossing of the Yangtze, further reinforcements were sent. The land forces were increased to bring them to the strength of two brigade groups, with tanks, field-guns and anti-aircraft guns; more fighter aircraft were sent; and two cruisers, a destroyer, and two frigates joined the naval squadron, with an aircraft carrier on call if the need arose. Hong Kong organized its own defence force, a militia force, open to members of all races. A

HONG KONG 185

defence council, consisting of the highest officers of the three services, together with local political representatives, was set up at the beginning of June. Mr. Alexander, the Minister of Defence visted the island, and, although he made various political pronouncements that were distinctly conciliatory in tone, reiterated British determination to defend the colony.

Nobody, least of all the Chinese, can have supposed that the island could in fact have been defended for more than a few days against an onslaught from the mainland, any more than it could against the Japanese. Even with the new reinforcements, the police and the militia, the total strength of the forces available was at most 25,000. And even with naval supremacy, the lines of communication were hopelessly extended. The purpose of the dispatch of forces, and the statements that accompanied them, was not to frighten the Chinese Government, but to serve notice that it would be impossible for them to occupy the colony without undertaking a clear-cut act of aggression. In fact when the Communist armies arrived at the border, watched with bated breath from within the colony, they undertook control of the frontier areas without incident. They appeared to be under strict orders to avoid any chance of misunderstanding, and took over the posts from the Nationalists only after these had withdrawn.

But it was recognized that the danger of Chinese political activity in the colony was at least as great as that of direct military assault. During May and June, the Government took powers to tighten the ordinance on the control of societies, so that registration might be refused to any society affiliated with political movements established outside the colony. In August, new powers were taken to expel non-British subjects suspected of being likely to promote sedition, or disturb public order. Later the possession or carriage of arms, ammunition or explosives was made punishable by life imprisonment, and steps were taken to exercise some control of Press and radio. A few schools that had become the centre of Chinese propaganda and agitation were closed. One or two trade unions were suppressed. And some deportations took place.

Some of these actions came in for severe attack from the mainland. Hong Kong was described as a police state, its Government "oppressors of the Chinese people", and its "anti-Chinese policies" as a "challenge to the Chinese people which would lead to serious consequences". Unless the grievances of the population were heeded, the Hong Kong Government would have to "eat the fruit of their own actions".

In fact the powers that had been taken were used sparingly and with discretion by the Hong Kong Government. They were directed impartially against K.M.T. and Communist organizations —indeed the former faction often proved the most troublesome. Deportations were not common. They were mainly for criminal rather than political offences. One or two Communist newspapers continued—and continue—to be published until the present day. And one that was temporarily suspended for insinuating that the colonial government were responsible for starting a disastrous fire which occurred among squatter huts in Kowloon, was able to bring a protracted and highly publicized law-suit against the Government, claiming damages for the closure, an action that would be at least unusual among the newspapers of the mainland.

There were some military clashes. Guns from neighbouring Communist-held islands occasionally opened fire on naval or other vessels that passed too near. In July, 1950, there was an exchange of fire at the border when Hong Kong police tried to arrest a suspect seeking to enter British territory. Later the same year a Hong Kong border patrol strayed over the frontier, were captured by Chinese forces and were later released. Similar incidents have occurred from time to time ever since. The Communists have shown themselves neurotically jealous of the security of both territory and waters. Pleasure yachters who have strayed into Chinese waters have been held for several months before being returned. But both sides have clearly been anxious to evade any wider conflict. With a little patience and some allowance for Chinese susceptibilities, such difficulties have always been resolved in the long run.

The Chinese Government never made in their public statements any overt claim for the return of the colony. Occasionally scantily-veiled threats against the island were used as an inducement to Britain to yield in some negotiation being conducted between the two sides. During the negotiations that took place on the establishment of diplomatic relations in the spring of 1950, Peking radio declared that Britain "should remember how Hong Kong was ceded as a result of a war of injustice" and that the prosperity of Hong Kong "depended entirely on the materials and manpower of the Chinese people". On the other hand various statesmen declared in public speeches that the Chinese People's Army had "liberated

HONG KONG 187

the entire area of China except Tibet and Taiwan", so apparently excluding Hong Kong and Macao. After the beginning of the Korean war it became apparent that no frontal assault was to be expected. Residents of Hong Kong began to breathe more freely.

But the situation was still a delicate one. It remained vital that nothing should be done to provoke unnecessarily the new force that had presented itself on the colony's doorstep. It was widely recognized that Hong Kong's future depended to some extent on the goodwill of the mainland government. Even if no military assault was to be made there remained the danger of investment by political infiltration or by economic blockade.

The Government tried so far as possible to insulate the colony from the disputes of rival political factions. But in the existing political conditions this was an impossible ambition. The civil war, already lost and won on the mainland, was still waged with ferocity in Hong Kong. And inevitably incidents arose.

The first of these concerned the ownership of the civil aircraft that had formerly belonged to the Chinese State airlines, the Central Air Transport Corporation (wholly owned by the Government) and the China National Aviation Corporation (in which the Government held an eighty per cent interest). In July and August, 1949, when the war was all but lost, the Nationalists transferred seventy-three aircraft belonging to these organizations to Hong Kong. Soon after the foundation of the People's Republic, the President of the C.T.T.C. and the majority of the Corporation's employees in Hong Kong defected to the Communists, taking two of the planes with them. In December the Nationalist Government sold the seventy-one remaining planes to General Chennault, formerly Commander of the U.S. 14th Air Force in China, and a staunch supporter of Chiang Kai-shek. He in turn transferred them to Civil Air Transport, Inc., a company formed for that purpose and registered in the United States. These transactions were generally regarded as a means of ensuring that the planes should no longer be legally regarded as state property.

There were various clashes at the airport between supporters of both parties, seeking to secure control of the planes. In May, 1950, the Hong Kong Government took custody of the aircraft until ownership should have been finally determined. C.A.T. then applied to the Hong Kong courts for a declaration that it was the rightful owner of those planes that had formerly belonged to the C.A.T.C. In May, 1951, the Chief Justice of Hong Kong gave judgement dismissing the application, on the grounds that the sale to General Chennault was only a device to prevent the aircraft from falling into the hands of the C.P.G.; that at the time in question the Nationalist Government had already ceased to be the *de facto* government of China; and that in any case British recognition in January, 1950, was retrospective in effect to October 1st, 1949, the date when the C.P.G. was established; thus, in the eyes of the British law, the aircraft no longer belonged to the Nationalist Government at the time when they were disposed of. The judgement was confirmed by the Hong Kong Appeal Court. But when a further appeal was made, the Judicial Committee of the Privy Council, in July, 1952, reversed the judgements, declaring that there was no basis for saying the sale was made for an improper purpose, as found by the Chief Justice of Hong Kong; and that the legitimate sale of State property by what was at the time the *de jure* government of the country could not be invalidated retrospectively by the act of recognition. In the light of this decision a similar judgement was brought in the case of the remaining aircraft.

The Communist Press and radio had throughout denied that the British courts possessed any jurisdiction. They were for a time appeased by the favourable judgements of the Hong Kong courts. But when the Judicial Committee of the Privy Council gave judgement, the Chinese Government issued a strong protest, demanded that the aircraft should be "immediately returned", and accused Britain of "encroachment on the sovereign rights of the People's Republic of China". In August, 1952, in retaliation, the military authorities in Shanghai requisitioned the two main British-owned dockyards in the city, then still functioning under British control and valued at about £4 million. And in November, after a similar judgement had been brought over the remaining thirty-one aircraft, the Shanghai water, gas and electricity undertakings, all British-owned, and a big British shipping company in the city were taken over in their turn.

There were various other cases of retaliatory confiscation as a result of actions by the Hong Kong Government. When a Chinese oil tanker, formerly Nationalist-owned, came under the control of a Communist crew, and seemed likely to be of assistance to the Chinese war effort in Korea, it was requisitioned by the Hong Kong

HONG KONG 189

authorities. In reply equipment and installations belonging to a British oil company in Shanghai were requisitioned by the authorities there. And when a fishing trawler claimed by the Nationalists was held by the Hong Kong Government pending judgement, the Chinese Government took possession of British-owned wharves and warehouses in Canton.

On three occasions more serious disturbances took place in the colony as a result of the political warfare raging beneath the surface. The first occurred in March, 1952, after a disastrous fire which broke out, as periodically happens, in one of the squatter villages of home-made shacks in the colony. The Communist authorities in Canton sought, as their predecessors under previous régimes had sometimes done, to send a "comfort mission", to bring sympathy and relief to the victims. The mission was refused permission to enter the colony. The Communist-led reception committee nevertheless sought to make its way to the border as arranged, and when they returned, a crowd of about 10,000 sympathizers who had assembled to meet them at Kowloon station, proceeded to march round that town, soon disintegrating into a riotous mob which, armed with clubs, rocks, and bottles, proceeded to destroy shops, over-turn and burn vehicles, and attack passers-by. Twelve people were injured, one of whom subsequently died. The *People's Daily* published an article, complaining in virulent terms of a "prearranged slaughter", and accused the Hong Kong Government of having deliberately provoked the riots by attacks from police and soldiers (in fact no soldiers had been involved at all). It was said that the British imperialists, at the dictate of the United States, were turning Hong Kong into a base of imperialist aggression against China. And the mission from Canton, when they were later given permission to enter the colony, refused, declaring ominously that they would be back "some day" and expressing the hope that local Chinese would continue their struggle against the British.

The next occasion on which the colony found itself seriously involved in Chinese political conflicts was in 1955. On April 10 of that year, immediately before the Bandung Conference, the Chinese Government informed the British Embassy in Peking that they believed that Nationalist agents in Hong Kong might seek to make trouble for Chinese delegations passing through the colony. This information was passed on to the Hong Kong Government and certain precautions were taken to protect the party. Nevertheless, next day, an Indian airliner, which was carrying eight Communist Chinese journalists, two Polish journalists and a North Vietnam delegate to the Bandung Conference, crashed off Borneo with the loss of fifteen lives. Peking radio immediately declared that the crash was due to sabotage. On April 13 the Chinese Government presented a Note to Britain, alleging that the plane had been sabotaged by United States and Nationalist agents who had hoped to assassinate Chou En-lai and other members of the Chinese delegation. The Note charged the British Government with "grave responsibility" for not taking adequate heed of the warning that had been given. And it demanded thorough investigation to secure the arrest of those responsible. The British reply said that the aircraft had been under police guard all the time it had been in Hong Kong, and that the British Government could not take responsibility for an accident to a foreign airliner outside British territory and British territorial waters.

However an official inquiry next month found "irrefutable evidence" that the airliner had been destroyed by the explosion of a time bomb. The Hong Kong Government accepted that the bomb had probably been placed on board at Hong Kong. They instituted searching inquiries. On May 18, as a result of information provided from Communist sources, their suspicion fell on a former aircraft cleaner at the airfield. On the same day the man concerned escaped to Formosa, apparently forewarned. The evidence suggested that he had been bribed by a K.M.T. intelligence organization to offer his services in sabotaging the aircraft. In September a warrant was issued for his arrest by the Hong Kong Government, and a request made to the Nationalist authorities for his extradition. The Nationalists claimed that they had no knowledge of the man; that in any case they had no diplomatic relations with Britain; and that, finally, there was no extradition treaty between the two countries. A series of further requests produced similarly unco-operative answers. The Chinese Press welcomed the efforts of the Hong Kong Government to bring the accused man to book, but demanded that the Hong Kong authorities should also punish all the other "Chiang Kai-shek espionage agents" who had been involved.

These political conflicts came to a head in the riots that occurred in Kowloon in October, 1956. On October 10, the day observed by the K.M.T. as the Chinese national day, disturbances took place after a Government official removed Nationalist flags which, con-

HONG KONG

trary to regulations, had been posted on the walls of Government buildings. Crowds began to set fire to cars, schools and other buildings, to loot shops and to attack Europeans in the streets. A Nationalist-led mob raided the offices of Communist trades unions and official premises of Chinese Government organizations. Disorders continued for two days. There was recurrent fighting between Nationalist and Communist supporters. The opportunity was taken by various secret societies and racketeering organizations to settle old scores. Police had to open fire. Troops with tanks and armoured cars were sent to assist them. Altogether 51 people were killed, including the wife of a Swiss consular official, and several hundred injured. An official statement on October 12 announced that the major responsibility rested with the secret societies, and that there was no evidence that the riots had been deliberately planned by any political organization.

On October 13 Chou En-lai expressed his "indignation and concern" at the riots, which he attributed to K.M.T. agents; and demanded that the Hong Kong Government should take immediate steps to bring them to book and to provide protection for the Chinese population and Chinese Government organizations. At a Press conference next day the Chinese Prime Minister said that the Chinese Government would "not permit such disorders on the doorstep of China". He rejected the British explanation that gangsters were responsible. He alleged that the Hong Kong authorities planned to use Nationalist agents to weaken the influence of the C.P.G. in Hong Kong. And he said that the Chinese authorities were watching to see what attitude the British took towards the K.M.T. agents, and whether the British were capable of maintaining order in Hong Kong and Kowloon. The *People's Daily* declared that the Hong Kong authorities had connived with K.M.T. agents in order to create the disorders. The British Government replied that the Hong Kong authorities had done their utmost to protect domestic and foreign interests, and that they could not accept any charge of negligence.

There is no need to doubt that the Chinese Government were seriously concerned over the power that Nationalist elements had acquired in Hong Kong. They had for long, especially during the campaign against counter-revolutionaries in 1951–2, accused the Hong Kong Government of allowing the colony to be used as a hotbed of conspiracy and intrigue against China. The warnings were no doubt mainly designed to stimulate the Hong Kong Government to more effective control of Nationalist agents who, it was widely agreed, were extremely active among the secret societies. In face of all such accusations, the Hong Kong Government had to seek to appear firm in suppressing mischievous political activity within the colony, and yet to remain independent of influence from the mainland government.

The colony had other difficulties in its relations with the mainland. From the very beginning of its existence there had been some ambivalence in the national status of its Chinese residents. When the colony was founded it was still regarded as in some sense a part of China. Chinese customs duties were levied. For long Chinese law was applied to those of Chinese race. When the New Territories were ceded, Chinese officials continued to function in Kowloon city for a year or two. And until fairly recently most Chinese in the colony certainly thought of themselves as no different in nationality from their cousins on the other side of the hilltops.

Today the rules governing nationality in the colony are the same as in other colonies, that is, all Chinese born in the colony, and all who are the offspring of a citizen of the U.K. and colonies, are themselves eligible for citizenship of the U.K. and colonies. But at the same time, under Chinese nationality law, which is based on *jus sanguinius*, nearly all the Chinese residents of the colony are regarded as Chinese nationals. Under a regulation passed in 1951, all those in the colony who wished to claim British citizenship were required to register and to substantiate their claim. Failure to register was regarded as implying abandonment of British status. It was thought that perhaps one-fifth at the most of the Chinese residents might be eligible for U.K. citizenship. In fact many of those that were eligible failed to register. Thus today by far the greater part of the colony's inhabitants are not U.K. citizens. They are, however, claimed by China as Chinese nationals.

This causes many complications. On a number of occasions since the present Chinese Government came to power, it has made representations to Britain, claiming to act on behalf of the Chinese residents of the colony. These protests represent something of a dilemma to the Hong Kong authorities. After the Kowloon riots of 1956 the *People's Daily* indignantly rejected suggestions that the Chinese Government had no standing to make protests over

HONG KONG 193

such internal affairs of the colony, declaring "the Hong Kong authorities must understand that the Chinese Government have every right to demand the protection of Chinese people in Hong Kong and Kowloon". Peking radio said that China could not "sit with folded hands and watch its compatriots slaughtered". Because Britain herself accepts that a majority of the inhabitants of the colony are not British subjects, she has never attempted formally to resist such claims. Yet at the same time, since there is almost no matter within the competence of the Hong Kong Government which does not in some degree affect the welfare of Chinese nationals, there is a danger that the way may thus be laid open for almost unlimited interference by the Chinese Government in the domestic affairs of the colony.

In order to carry out their functions on behalf of Chinese nationals, the Chinese Government have put forward requests for consular representation in the colony, just as other powers have consuls there to protect the interests of their commerce and nationals. This again raises delicate issues for the Hong Kong Government. When, in 1883, Lord Derby suggested that the Chinese imperial government might be represented by a consul in Hong Kong in order to help reach a settlement in cases arising over Chinese customs dues and extradition, the Hong Kong Government opposed the suggestion on the grounds that the Chinese population might begin to look to the Chinese consul rather than the colonial government as the source of authority. This is precisely the problem that is presented once more today. The position of a foreign power claiming to represent the great majority of the inhabitants of a colony is not analogous to that of other countries. A Chinese consular office might gradually assume the status of a universal patron to whom all Chinese residents might bring their problems, and who might act as an agency to bring pressure on the Government on every conceivable problem of administration. It could make itself the focus for the loyalties of most of the Chinese inhabitants. And it could become a more effective centre for Communist propaganda and agitation than any of the existing agencies of the C.P.G. within the colony. As a result Chinese requests for consular representation have been consistently turned down.

These approaches nevertheless have a quite separate importance. For the request for consular representation involves in the most unequivocal form recognition of full British sovereignty in the area. The National Government, for instance, dealt in many matters concerning Hong Kong through the Governor of Kwangtung province. After the war their representative in Hong Kong was entitled "Special Commissioner in Kwangtung and Kwangshi". This carried the implication that the colony and its peoples were a part of China. Chou En-lai himself, in an interview with three Labour M.P.s in June, 1957, acknowledged the significance of the Chinese Government's request from this point of view. He claimed that his Government nevertheless wanted a consul in order to develop more friendly relations with the Hong Kong Government, and because the greater part of the population of Hong Kong were Chinese.

Somewhat similar difficulties have arisen over the question of immigration. When the island was ceded, it was provided, under a supplementary treaty, that all natives of China were to have unrestricted access to it. This provision was until recently scrupulously observed by the Hong Kong authorities. It was for this reason that the population of about 5,000 Chinese on the island before the British came had grown to more than one and a half million (in the whole colony) by 1940. By the end of the war this number had dropped to about 600,000. But with the regrowth of the island's prosperity, the provision of rice at subsidized prices, and the disturbed conditions on the mainland, it rose to about two million by the summer of 1947; and continued to rise rapidly. The refugees began to become an impossible burden on the colony's economy. There was no work for them in the island. The colony was dependent on outside supplies for most of its food and some of its water. And there was simply no physical accommodation for the refugee population, who lived in appalling conditions in overcrowded tenements, on rooftops and home-made shacks. Eventually, in May, 1950, the Government were obliged to place restrictions on entry from the mainland, except for the local traffic between the colony and Kwangtung which was allowed to continue unhindered. A brief relaxation was attempted in 1956, but the flow quickly became so great that controls had to be reimposed.

The Chinese Government immediately protested against the restrictions. They recalled that for a hundred years Chinese nationals had never been treated as foreign immigrants in Hong Kong, and described the new regulations as unreasonable and unfriendly to the People's Republic. In fact, however, the continued

HONG KONG

ebb of population was not a good advertisement for the régime, and the Government may not have been altogether sorry that it was stopped. Certainly they have never put much heat into their protests. And even now some refugees continue to reach the colony from China.

The Hong Kong Government have always recognized that the effective administration of Hong Kong depends to some extent on the goodwill of the mainland. They have consistently sought to avoid action which might be considered to be provocative. There have even been some attempts at co-operation. In September, 1955, the Governor of Hong Kong paid a private visit to Peking, during which he was entertained to lunch by Chou En-lai, and there was some discussion of problems affecting relations between the colony and the mainland. During 1956 there was a series of talks between the railway authorities of Hong Kong and Canton about the resumption of through train services. Though all the technical arrangements were satisfactorily completed, it proved impossible to reach agreement on a system which would have given the Hong Kong authorities adequate control of the numbers of Chinese arriving, and the discussions were finally abandoned. Finally, during 1960, an agreement was reached with the Chinese authorities in Kwangtung on the supply of water from a recently completed Chinese reservoir to supplement the inadequate water resources of the colony.

But Hong Kong's relations with the mainland have always centred principally around trade. The colony's dealings with the mainland recovered fairly rapidly after the war. Both European and Chinese merchants in the island fairly quickly re-established their old contacts. A large proportion of Chinese exports of traditional products continued to flow through the colony. The regrowth was not even much checked by the course of the civil war. By 1949 the trade was already running at over £35 million in each direction, besides a fairly large invisible trade in shipping, insurance and banking.

At first the victory of the Communists brought increasing prosperity to the colony. In the first place there was a large inflow of capital, both Chinese and European, from the mainland to Hong Kong. Many wealthy Chinese families settled in the island and established their businesses there. Some of the European firms that had previously been based in Shanghai now centred their activities in Hong Kong.

At the same time trading activity, after a brief slump early in 1950, became brisker than ever. Hong Kong merchants benefited more than any from the boom that resulted from more stable conditions in China and the spate of Chinese purchases at the beginning of the Korean war. As a result total trade in 1950 was higher than it had ever been before.

But this was not to last. China's entry into the Korean war brought increasing restrictions on the trade. Hong Kong, whose livelihood at that time still depended largely on its trade with China, was somewhat reluctant in its approach to these controls. Until December, 1950, two months after China's entry into the war, there was no restriction on the export of arms, aircraft, military equipment or the machinery for making them. In that month, as a result of this over-tolerant approach, the United States included the colony in its total embargo of trade with China. This was a severe blow to the colony, since its textile industry had been largely dependent on imports of United States raw cotton. For the moment, however, oil, rubber tyres, scrap iron and steel plates continued to be exported to China. Shipments of some kinds of oil were not controlled until February, 1951, and not finally brought to a halt till June of that year. Exports of rubber and many metal products were banned from March, 1951. And from about half-way through 1951 the Hong Kong authorities made strenuous efforts to ensure full compliance with the U.N. embargo, though the colony remained subject to sharp and usually ill-informed criticism from United States senators and others.

As a result of the controls, trade with China slumped catastrophically. In 1952 exports to China, at just over £30 million, reached only a third of the previous year's volume. They have continued to decline ever since, even after the embargo was relaxed. By 1959 they were only worth £8 million including re-exports. Trade in the other direction was maintained and has even increased. In the last two or three years the Chinese have conducted a considerable export drive in Hong Kong, as in other parts of South East Asia. A large number of Chinese exports of native products, as well as such new exports as textiles, bicycles, torches, sewing-machines, and similar light industrial products, continue to be channelled through the colony. In addition the colony remains dependent for some of its own needs, especially meat, vegetables, fish and other food products, on exports from the mainland. The trade is of considerable value to the Chinese Government since, from their favourable balance, they obtain sterling worth over £50 million a year.

The continued decline in the colony's exports to China is a result of a general shift in the pattern of trade. It was believed at one time that there was a deliberate effort by the Chinese authorities to bypass Hong Kong for political reasons. During talks with the Chinese trade delegation in London in the summer of 1954, intensive efforts were made to persuade the Chinese representatives of the advantage of dealing through Hong Kong, and it was thought then that these had had some success. But exports through the colony have continued to go down. It is doubtful in fact if political considerations have been the over-riding ones. The Chinese State agencies order in large enough quantities to be able to deal direct with manufacturers in Europe, so cutting out the profits of the Hong Kong middlemen. Some of the requirements formerly met by Hong Kong are now satisfied by East European countries. The Chinese have developed the former French concession port of Kwangchow, now renamed Tsam Kong, about 250 miles southwest of Hong Kong; and developed a rail link to Amoy: so that some trade has been diverted to these ports. And in the last year or two they have chartered and bought a number of ships that trade direct between European and Chinese ports. In addition Hong Kong's merchants, who usually have no assured market for the goods they buy, deal mainly in commodities that are cheap, easily stored, and have a fairly rapid turnover, offering a steady profit on a small price margin, without tying up a large volume of capital. Their methods are not suited to trade in capital goods, such as China chiefly imports. Thus the whole balance of Hong Kong's trade has been changed.

The China trade, which represented about a third of the total before the Korean war, now represents not much more than an eighth. Re-exports to China are only about a thirtieth of the total; and direct exports to China have almost ceased. To compensate this there has been a considerable development of trade with Japan, South East Asia and the U.K.

But the big change in trade results from the huge growth in Hong Kong's native industry, as a result of which the colony's own products take up a far higher proportion of the trade. In 1950

Hong Kong products represented only five per cent of the colony's total exports; today they represent seventy per cent. This development is likely to continue in the future.

In many ways, therefore, in political sympathies, in commercial contacts, in personal intercourse, Hong Kong is more detached from the mainland today than ever before. Yet such isolation can only be relative. Geographically, ethnically, culturally, Hong Kong is a segment of China. And the inhabitants of the colony can never for a moment remain unaware how far its existence remains dependent on the favour of the giant beyond its borders.

Yet Hong Kong has itself brought much that is of value to China. For, if it is in many ways a part of China, in some sense it is equally a piece of Europe. It has helped to bring European culture, European merchandise, European nationals, and European values to the frontiers of China. Although this may not recommend it to the present rulers of China, it has in fact proved a more fertile and more stable meeting ground of East and West than almost any other city of the world. In its streets, Chinese and Britains meet and exchange ideas as they can do almost nowhere else today. In its university the learning of England and China is transmitted in the English and Chinese languages to Chinese and English alike. Even the now isolated Chinese on the mainland are probably more conscious of the European voices in Hong Kong than those of any other Western centre. Nowhere else is the Far West and the Far East within speaking distance of each other.

The agreement by which the island was first transferred was repudiated by both government and public opinion on either side. For it the two negotiators were, equally, disgraced and dismissed. Yet it is hard to doubt that, however brazen the original annexation, the intercourse, of trade, of ideas and of human beings that that cession made possible, has been of some value to both the parties to it.

10

THE TWO CHINAS

IN recognizing the People's Republic of China, Britain argued that she was acknowledging a fact. But she could not, in so doing, obliterate another fact, less compelling perhaps but no less incorrigible, the presence of eight million people of Chinese origin on an island, once part of China, but not now under the effective control of the Communist Government. Nor could she unmake the further reality that a majority of the nations of the world, including her closest friends and allies, continued, in the teeth of the evidence, to acknowledge the ruler of this island as the Government of China.

The reconciliation of these three states of affairs posed difficult problems for British governments. These centred round two main questions: which of the contending governments had a legal right to the territory of Formosa; and which should occupy the seat at the United Nations reserved for "the Government of the Republic of China".

The Declaration signed at Cairo by Mr. Churchill, Mr. Roosevelt and General Chiang Kai-shek in 1943, had asserted that "all the territories Japan has stolen from the Chinese such as Manchuria, Formosa and the Pescadores, shall be restored to the Republic of China". After the war, the Allied Powers permitted Chiang Kai-shek's forces to return to the island pending the conclusion of a Japanese Peace Treaty. But until such a treaty was signed, Chinese sovereignty was still not formally restored to the island. During 1949, when a Communist victory began to be imminent, some of the Nationalist troops were transferred to Formosa. Chiang Kai-shek himself, having relinquished the presidency for a time, transferred his headquarters to the island. So long as Britain recognized the Nationalist Government, the terms of the Cairo Declaration could be quoted as confirming British recognition of the Nationalist claim to Formosa. When a Conservative M.P. asked in the House of Commons what steps the British Government were taking to ensure that Formosa remained in the hands of the only Chinese Government they recognized, Mr.

McNeil, the Minister of State, replied that the British Goverment could take no unilateral action as the issue "would be a matter for the Cairo Powers".

This situation was altered by the British recognition of the Chinese People's Government in January, 1950. For if they adhered to their view that Formosa should be returned to the "Republic of China", the British Government would, it was generally felt, be obliged to hold that Formosa should be returned to the Central People's Government. This position was not vitally affected by the decision of the British Government, on recognition, to retain a consul in Formosa. The consul was accredited to the provincial and not the National Government in Formosa, and it was made clear that the appointment was made on a *de facto* basis.

For a time after the Communist victory even the United States Government appeared to abandon faith in the future of the Nationalist Government. Although they continued to recognize them, military and economic assistance came to an end, and some concluded that it was only a matter of time before the Nationalist régime fell. In the early part of 1950, it was doubtful whether the United States Government would have intervened had the Communists launched the assault on the island they were then apparently preparing. But by his decision at the outbreak of the Korean war to instruct the United States Seventh Fleet to prevent hostilities in either direction across the straits, and so "neutralize" the island, President Truman not only guaranteed its security but drew a clear dividing line between the island and the mainland, so underlining its existence as a separate entity. In this decision the "two China" policy was already implicit.

It was for this reason that the Chinese Government's reaction to the move was so violent. For the United States' action not only made the recovery of the island by military means, never easy, out of the question. More important, it transformed it from an internal into an international affair. So long as Formosa could have been regarded as a purely domestic matter, the final stage of the civil war, there remained at least some hope that eventually they might, if not by invasion, then at least by political blandishments, regain possession of the island. Once it came to be regarded as an international problem, justifying foreign, or even United Nations, intervention, this possibility became remote. And it was only too obvious that the United States, which publicly declared that Formosa was

THE TWO CHINAS 201

essential to her own defence, would never voluntarily cede it to the Communists.

Thus the Chinese propaganda organs launched an all-out attack at United States' "interference in China's internal affairs". On August 24 Chou En-lai wrote to the Secretary-General of the United Nations, accusing the United States Government of "aggression" against Formosa and calling for "complete withdrawal of all United States armed invading forces from Formosa". On August 28 Mr. Malik, as Chairman of the Security Council for the current month, sought to place these charges on the Council's agenda. The United States representative agreed to discussion of "the Formosa question". At the same time he called for a general renunciation of the use of force. But he resisted the suggestion that a representative of China should be invited to take part in such discussions. Britain, however, supported the proposal. And it was passed by the Council as a whole.

The Chinese Government, while protesting against a discussion of the "Formosa question", which they claimed was an internal affair that the United Nations was not competent to consider, agreed to come to New York to discuss "U.S. aggression against China". The British Government were placed in a difficult position. They acknowledged that Formosa should, under the terms of the Cairo Declaration, be handed over to the People's Republic. By a strict interpretation of international law it could have been argued that, by acknowledging that Formosa was a part of China, they accepted that the efforts of the legal government to recover that territory were an internal matter, which should not be subject to interference either from outside governments or from the United Nations. But they recognized that for the United States both the legal and the strategic position was entirely different. And they certainly had no wish that the problem should be solved by other than peaceful means.

These differing positions were reflected in the communiqué issued after Mr. Attlee's talks with Mr. Truman on December 8, 1950. This said: "On the question of Formosa we have noted that both Chinese claimants have insisted upon the validity of the Cairo Declaration and have expressed reluctance to have the matter considered by the United Nations. We agreed that the issue should be settled by peaceful means and in such a way as to safeguard the interests of the people of Formosa and the maintenance of peace and security in the Pacific, and that consideration of this question by the United Nations will contribute to these ends." On December 14, 1950, Mr. Bevin said in the House of Commons that while the Government adhered to the Cairo Declaration, they were bound to recognize that this was not the appropriate moment to settle the matter. But the problem might eventually be solved either by the United Nations, or by the Five-Power Conference to settle Far Eastern problems that was then envisaged.

In fact the discussions of the matter in the United Nations soon proved abortive and the matter was submerged in discussion of the more urgent questions of the Korean war. But the difference between the United States and British attitudes to the problem came to a head in the discussions for the conclusion of a Japanese peace treaty during 1951. During the early part of that year the United States Government initiated discussions with various governments, including that of the Soviet Union, to bring about the conclusion of a treaty. On April 3 the British Government proposed that the Peking Government should be consulted about the terms of the peace treaty. The United States Government replied that they recognized only the Nationalists and did not contemplate discussion of the treaty with the Peking régime. Yet, the British Government contended, a Japanese peace treaty must certainly have to be signed by the principal protagonist in the war against Japan.

For two months deadlock on the issue continued. On June 3, Mr. Dulles, then President Truman's special representative on Far Eastern questions, flew to London to try to iron the matter out. On June 14 a joint statement by Mr. Dulles and Mr. Morrison, the Foreign Secretary, declared that the two ministers had reached full agreement. They agreed to go on disagreeing. The agreed draft of a treaty was circulated among other interested governments, but neither to the Chinese Communists nor to the Nationalists. In a subsequent statement to the House Mr. Morrison said that both governments had accepted that if the treaty was not to be indefinitely delayed the best solution was that China should not be invited to sign the treaty at all. He thought that Chinese interests had been protected in the draft and once the treaty had been signed it would be for Japan herself to decide her future relations with China.

The United States draft of the treaty made no reference to the final disposition of Formosa and the Pescadores, providing merely

THE TWO CHINAS

that Japan renounced all sovereignty in these areas. The draft was for this reason among others, rejected by the Soviet Union. After some further discussion and amendments, the treaty was nevertheless finally signed at San Francisco on September 8 by representatives of forty-nine nations. The Soviet Union, though they attended the conference, refused to sign the final treaty.

The Chinese Government denounced both the treaty itself and the fact that the C.P.G. had not been invited to the San Francisco conference. On August 17 they delivered a Note to this effect to the British and other diplomatic representatives in Peking. The Nationalists were equally indignant at not having been asked to take part at San Francisco. They declared that without them the treaty would be "lacking in moral force and legal justification". And on September 3 they issued a formal statement that the Nationalist Government would not consider the provisions of the draft treaty sponsored by the United States and Britain as binding on them.

Yet in fact the treaty was highly favourable to the Nationalists. So long as either Japan, or the Allied governments as victors, continued to hold any residual rights in Formosa, the Nationalist Government might have found the island suddenly whisked from beneath them and handed over to some rival authority. By depriving Japan of all further rights and leaving the island in a kind of legal vacuum, the treaty gave the Nationalists the opportunity to establish themselves as the *de facto* government within that vacuum. The longer they remained there the more firmly they might be able to establish, in the eyes of international opinion, their existence as an independent entity.

The second major problem that the existence of two rival Chinas posed concerned their representation in the United Nations. This was equally thorny; and equally invited dissension between Britain and the United States. At the time of British recognition of the People's Republic, there was already some criticism in the United Kingdom that the British Government had failed to keep in step with the United States. In the subsequent months the Government were especially anxious that their policies on Far Eastern questions should not be too far out of line with those of the United States. When, on January 13, 1950, only seven days after recognition, the question of replacing the Nationalist representative by a representative of the People's Republic came before the United Nations, the British delegate abstained. The same policy continued to be followed throughout the next few months. When questioned on the matter in the House of Commons, ministers declared that it was the Government's policy to wait until there was a majority in favour of the admission of representatives of the C.P.G. before they themselves voted in favour of this.

The question became one of intense controversy at the United Nations. The Chinese Government appointed a member of their Politbureau as their delegate at the United Nations and Security Council, and as the time of their annual meetings approached, similar representatives to all the subsidiary organs. On February 3, the Nationalists announced that they would veto any attempt to award the China seat to the Communist Government. The veto could certainly be used to prevent new admissions to the U.N. (though some Western governments had held, in the face of Soviet attempts to veto admission, that the question of entry was a procedural question, which was not subject to veto). In China's case the question was not one of admission. It was recognized that a situation in which a government representing one of the permanent members might be able to retain its seat in perpetuity by use of the veto was an absurdity which the West could not seek to sustain. And it was thus generally held that the question was a procedural one which could be decided by a simple majority.

There were various opinions on how this question should be tackled. According to the Charter, admission to the United Nations takes place on a vote by the General Assembly "on the recommendation of the Security Council". It was generally considered that a similar procedure must be followed in deciding which of two contending governments should represent a member State. The Secretary-General, Mr. Trygve Lie, proposed the general adoption of the principle that any government that exercised effective authority over a country, and was habitually obeyed by the bulk of the population, should be admitted; and that in any case representation in the United Nations should be kept entirely distinct from the question of diplomatic recognition. He suggested that a committee should be set up to determine which government was in control of China and so in a position to represent China at the United Nations. The Indian Government proposed that a poll

THE TWO CHINAS

should be taken of all United Nations members on the matter. Britain held that the Security Council could decide without guidance from the Assembly. This was the way most likely to be favourable to the Chinese Government, since it so happened that at the time in question five members of the Security Council, the Soviet Union, India, Yugoslavia, Norway and Britain, had already recognized Communist China.

Thus, from about March, 1950, onwards, the British delegation at New York began to lobby the delegations of other members of the Security Council on the admission of Communist China. France did not commit herself, but was thought to be less likely to support the admission of the People's Republic as a result of Soviet recognition of Ho Chi-minh. Egypt and Cuba were reported to have refused to support admission, while Ecuador was likely to abstain. The question was discussed at a meeting of the Foreign Ministers of the United States, Britain and France in May, but no agreement could be reached and each government decided to maintain their own position. On May 24, Mr. Bevin said in the House of Commons that "we think it is better for the new China to be inside the United Nations". On the other hand this was not yet the general opinion and the Government "could not, in the transition period, come to a conclusion to throw out one representative, and to take on another".

In July the Soviet delegation returned to the United Nations. At this time both Egypt and France were thought to be wavering on the question of Chinese representation. If both were to vote in favour of the Communists, the necessary seven votes would have been obtained. But when, on August 1, Mr. Malik, the Chairman for that month, introduced a resolution calling for the expulsion of the Nationalist delegate and the admission of one from the People's Republic, the proposal was rejected, by eight votes to three, as precipitate. Britain voted against the resolution; but soon afterwards voted in favour of another Soviet proposal that the question of Chinese representation should be included in the Council's agenda. A series of telegrams was received from the Chinese Government demanding representation, naming China's representatives, and calling for an immediate reply.

In September the Indian delegate introduced a resolution asking the General Assembly, on its own initiative, to recognize the Communist Government's delegate as the Chinese representative in the

Assembly, and recommending that other organs should adopt a similar course. Britain, for the first time, voted in favour of this proposal. The vote was nevertheless lost, by sixteen votes to thirty-three with ten abstentions. But on the same day, the General Assembly adopted a Canadian proposal to set up a special committee, consisting of the President of the Assembly and six others, to consider the whole question of Chinese representation and to report back to the Assembly with recommendations. As a result of China's participation in the Korean war and her rejection of all United Nations peace proposals however, the committee only met once and then adjourned, pending a Korean settlement. In 1951 when the committee met again the Polish delegate proposed recognition of Chinese Communist delegates. The committee as a whole reported to the Assembly that "in the present circumstances it had been unable to make any recommendation on the question". But one effect of these discussions was that it was decided that the Assembly, alone, could in future decide which of the contending governments should be represented in it.

For the moment Britain continued to uphold the right of the People's Republic to the Chinese seat. In a debate in the House of Commons on November 29, 1950, Mr. Bevin said that he had always believed that "it would be better for us to help to shepherd China into the United Nations rather than to oppose her entry and cause unnecessary frustration". In the statement issued after their talks in Washington on December 8, 1950, Mr. Attlee and President Truman declared: "On the question of the Chinese seat in the United Nations, the two governments differ. The United Kingdom have recognized the Central People's Government and consider that their representative should occupy China's seat in the United Nations. The United States have opposed and continue to oppose the seating of the Chinese Communists' representative in the United Nations." Thus for nearly a year in the various organs of the United Nations (each of which can decide for itself on questions concerning the credentials of its delegates), Britain continued to vote, in opposition to the United States and some other Commonwealth countries, in favour of China's admission.

On June 5, 1951, in the Trusteeship Council, the British delegate, for the first time since September, 1950, voted in favour of postponement of any discussion of the question of Chinese representation. The British delegate, Sir Alan Burns, said that the British

THE TWO CHINAS

Government had been voting for the admission of the People's Republic to the Chinese seat in the hope that the Chinese Government would "recognize the obligation of a member of the United Nations not to support aggression, and to settle their disputes by peaceful means". They still hoped that China would agree to an honourable settlement in Korea, but in the present crisis the British Government thought it appropriate that the question now raised should be postponed for the time being. On June 11, Mr. Younger, in a written reply in the House of Commons, stated that "H.M.G. still believed that delegates from the C.P.G. should represent China in the United Nations. In view, however, of that government's persistence in behaviour which is inconsistent with the purposes and principles of the Charter, it now appears to H.M.G. that consideration of this question should be postponed for the time being". And when the question was again raised in the General Assembly in the autumn, Britain voted against the inscription of a Soviet motion calling for the seating of representatives of the People's Republic. The British delegate announced that the British Government (now a Conservative one) supported the policy of a moratorium on discussion of the question until the conclusion of the Korean war.

So long as the Korean war continued this remained the Government's policy. Conservative ministers were at pains to point out that they were merely continuing the policy of their predecessors. And in the existing circumstances it was not seriously opposed by the Opposition. But it was generally assumed that as soon as the war was over the matter would come up again. Already on November 19, 1951, immediately after he had ceased to be Foreign Minister, Mr. Morrison said in the House of Commons that the Opposition trusted that "as soon as circumstances change and the possibility of Chinese admission emerges", H.M.G. would seek to bring about the admission of the effective Chinese Government to the United Nations. On July 2, 1952, Mr. Selwyn Lloyd the Minister of State, said that he thought that "when an armistice was concluded [in Korea] we may hope to make progress over this difficult matter". And during the next year the Government's arguments against consideration of the matter continued to be based on the grounds that at that time the C.P.G. was "participating in aggression in Korea".

In July, 1953, when an armistice was on the point of conclusion,

Mr. Butler, in answer to a question, announced that the Government's policy on Chinese representation in the United Nations would have to be reconsidered "at the appropriate time after an armistice". When the terms of the armistice were announced a few days later, Mr. Selwyn Lloyd said that the matter was one which must be considered and dealt with by the United Nations, and the Government would "certainly see that it was discussed even before open negotiations took place". Other Government spokesmen declared that the question would have to be discussed at the Political Conference which was to be called after the armistice.

Opinion in the United States was still firmly opposed to consideration of the matter by the United Nations. The communiqué issued at the end of the meeting of the A.N.Z.U.S. Foreign Ministers in September, 1953, said that agreement had been reached to oppose the seating of Communist China pending the results of the Korean peace conference. And at the 1953 session of the General Assembly, the British Government agreed to cooperate with the U.S. Government in tabling a motion for a further moratorium though this time, on British insistence, consideration of the matter was postponed only for the "current year", i.e. till the end of 1953, instead of for the "current session" as before.

In October, 1953, Chou En-lai issued a statement in which he said that for the United Nations to safeguard peace and international security effectively, it was essential to restore to the People's Republic of China its legitimate rights in the United Nations. Public opinion in Britain generally assumed that the matter would have to be brought to a head the next year. In January, 1954, Sir Gladwyn Jebb, on the eve of his departure from the United Nations, said that, if the United Nations was to be a world organization, Communist States must be represented. The absence of China "imposed a considerable strain on the organization". There were reports in March and again in June that Britain, with the support of India and Canada, was pressing the United States to reconsider their attitude. Mr. Webb, the New Zealand Minister for External Affairs, declared in favour of Chinese admission. A public opinion poll in Britain showed that over sixty per cent of those questioned favoured Chinese admission while only twenty per cent were opposed.

Opinion in the United States, however, was very different. A public opinion poll there showed only eleven per cent for and fifty-

THE TWO CHINAS 209

eight per cent against the admission of Communist China. The question of Chinese representation at the United Nations was never even considered at the Korean peace discussions at Geneva in April–May, 1954, as had earlier been suggested by British spokesmen. And, in July, 1954, on his return from a visit to the United States, Sir Winston Churchill said that the question of Chinese admission was "not of immediate importance".

Many might perhaps have considered that the question was in fact of more immediate importance then than at any time since the autumn of 1950. For now the circumstances that had previously been quoted to prove the ineligibility of the People's Republic for membership of the United Nations no longer obtained. The Chinese Government were no longer, as so often proclaimed in the past, "participating in aggression against United Nations forces". But now that the old arguments for opposing Chinese entry no longer had any force, new ones began to be brought forward. On July 14, Mr. Selwyn Lloyd told the House of Commons that before the question of the Peking Government taking the China seat was considered, "good faith should be shown by deeds and not just words", for example, in the consolidation of the armistic in Korea and Indo-China. And at the meeting of the General Assembly in September, Britain again supported a United States proposal to postpone discussion. Mr. Selwyn Lloyd said that while the Government lost no opportunity in pointing out to American audiences the advantages that might be gained by the admission of Communist China to the United Nations, it would be foolish at that moment "to seek to force this view through against the wishes of their American allies".

It is not clear why the Government thought it more foolish for Britain to seek to uphold her own views against those of the United States than for the United States to follow the same policy. In fact, however, by the next year there were new reasons to make it even more difficult for the United Kingdom to resist supporting United States policy and opposing those they themselves professed. In April, 1955, the Eoka rebellion in Cyprus broke out. The Greek Government sought to bring the matter to the United Nations. There was no doubt that the bulk of world opinion was hostile to the United Kingdom. If inscription of the item was to be resisted, the support of the United States delegation, usually bringing with it a majority of the Latin-American and some other nations, was essential. On August 20, diplomatic correspondents reported that

O

it had been agreed between the United States and the United Kingdom to defer discussion of Chinese representation for another year. And on September 21, the Assembly again voted to postpone consideration.

Yet again the arguments used to justify the vote a year before had now become invalid. The peace settlements reached in Korea and Indo-China had proved reasonably secure. Chinese troops were being withdrawn from Korea altogether. At the Bandung Conference China had shown herself accommodating and conciliatory. She had opened negotiations with the United States on measures to relax tension in the Formosa area. Yet again British ministers found new arguments to justify their vote in favour of the resolution. Mr. Nutting, the Minister of State, now claimed that Britain had voted for postponement of discussion on the grounds that "though Chinese representation in the United Nations was one of the issues that would have to be settled before normal peaceful relations could be re-established in the Far East", the Government had not thought that the present moment was timely, since differing views on it were strongly held and debate would "place an intolerable strain on the United Nations".

For the next five years exactly similar votes took place. Each year the United Kingdom supported proposals of the United States that consideration should be deferred until the next session. The fact that Britain had recognized China did not prevent her from following an identical policy with that of the United States. Even in 1961, when a refusal to consider the matter would certainly not have been entertained, Britain joined with the U.S. in support of a resolution whose effect would be to require a two-thirds majority to secure Chinese admission. And she was reported to be supporting a further delaying measure by which the matter would be considered in conjunction with other proposals for amending the composition of United Nations bodies. The Chinese press repeatedly protested violently at these decisions. It declared that, by excluding the 600 million people of China, the United Nations was excluding a quarter of the human race; and proclaimed that China was being illegally deprived of her rights under the Charter.

The United Nations has had to face few cases where two rival governments have disputed the same seat. The other divided nations of the world do not aspire to admission. Credentials of the revolutionary government in Iraq were accepted almost immediately.

THE TWO CHINAS 211

Mr. Kadar's representatives were speaking and voting within a few weeks of the Hungarian uprising. For in both cases the government concerned exercised effective control over their territories. Discussion of China's case in fact has merely turned on whether the People's Republic had a right to the China seat on the criterion that should be applied to such cases. The matter has been determined almost entirely on the grounds of expediency. Almost every year new arguments have been evolved to justify postponement. The recent influx of new members to the U.N. makes it unlikely that the matter can be shelved much longer; though whether a decision acceptable to the Chinese Government can be reached in the near future seems unlikely.

British policy has been largely governed by U.S. sentiment. But even in the U.S. there are now some who favour recognizing the reality of "two Chinas". There are some who would even be willing to accept the admission of the People's Republic to the United Nations. Indeed, as long ago as 1950, when the Democratic administration was resolutely hostile to any move for admission, there were already some in America who advised a more flexible approach. In his book *War or Peace* published in April, 1950, six months after the establishment of the present government of China, Mr. John Foster Dulles wrote that if "the Communist Government of China in fact proves its ability to govern China without serious domestic resistance, then it too should be admitted to the United Nations. . . . If we want a world organization, then it should be representative of the world as it is". It is unfortunate that, during recent years, British governments have apparently been almost as reluctant as Mr. Dulles himself to put into effect this excellent advice.

The differences that arose over Chinese representation in the United Nations were only one facet of the general problem presented by the existence of the two Chinas. During the time of the Labour Government in Britain, Britain and the United States had in effect, for example over the Japanese Peace Treaty, agreed to differ. After the Conservative Government was elected in November, 1951, Britain began to move further towards the United States position. In January, 1952, after a visit to the United States, Sir Winston Churchill said he was glad that the United States "did not allow the Chinese anti-Communists in Formosa to be invaded and massacred from the mainland". Even after the Chinese Government agreed to set up a diplomatic mission in London, Britain continued to maintain a consular post in Formosa. An official of the Board of Trade paid a visit to the island to discuss commercial matters. From about 1957, there were brief visits by British M.P.s of both parties, journalists and other figures to Formosa. An organization called the "Friends of Free China" became vocal in advertising the claims of the Formosa régime. During the disputes over the offshore islands, the British Government, though they did not conceal their opinion that it was unwise to hold the islands, made it apparent that they would not apply the same considerations to Formosa itself. And the mere passage of time tended to establish in the public mind the existence of an individual entity, Formosa, separate and distinct from the mainland.

The Chinese Government, however, have at all times based their claims to Formosa on the grounds that the island was indissolubly a part of China. The Government in Formosa have based their claims to the mainland on identical grounds. The Chinese Government were thus implacable in their hostility to any attempt to dissociate the two. In particular they have been violently hostile to all efforts to find some reconciliation of the conflicting views about Chinese representation and other matters by the adoption of a so-called "two China" policy, by which, for example, both the Nationalists and Communists might be represented in the United Nations. When for the first time since the civil war, a British M.P. visited Formosa early in 1957, the *People's Daily* declared that the activities of such people, "interested in creating two Chinas", could only "damage Sino-British relations and harm the Far Eastern situation". Chou En-lai expressed his indignation to a party of Labour M.P.s who visited him in 1957, at the recent development of relations between Britain and Formosa, and the tendency to "treat Formosa as a government". In January, 1958, in an interview with the Reuters' correspondents in Peking, he said that the United States were seeking to use Britain and Japan in order to put into effect its two Chinas policy, and that if in fact Britain used its vote at the United Nations to bring about this result, relations between China and Britain would be seriously impaired: if on the other hand, Britain would once more vote to seat the People's Republic,

THE TWO CHINAS

the two countries could exchange ambassadors and establish full diplomatic relations.

In April of the same year he repeated this promise to Mr. Harold Wilson, M.P. He declared categorically that China would not take a seat at the United Nations if the Nationalists were also represented there. In his report to the N.P.C. in February of that year, he said that the "flirtation between the British Government and the Chiang Kai-shek clique" had recently notably increased. Britain had become a "propaganda centre for the absurd contention that the status of Formosa was undetermined". China would never tolerate the British practice in following United States attempts to create "two Chinas".

These attacks were extended even to those who believed that they were making proposals favourable to the Chinese Government's case. Thus when Lord Attlee made a speech recommending United Nations trusteeship of Formosa, the official Labour Party policy, the Peking Press reacted with a violent denunciation of the "Dulles-Lloyd-Attlee line" for dismembering China. When Lord Landsdowne remarked in the House of Lords that the signing of the Japanese Peace Treaty had not conferred any rights of sovereignty over Formosa, either to China or to anyone else, the Chinese Press, declaring that it was a fundamental right of a victor to recover lost territory from a defeated State, warned that, by aiding American aggression against China, Britain would "swallow a bitter bill of its own making and get its due punishment in the end". And when Mr. Selwyn Lloyd referred to the Formosa question as an "international one", the *People's Daily* said that this "demonstrated clearly the unscrupulous perfidy of British imperialism and its violation of international obligations". For it was a vital element in the Chinese attitude to Formosa that the problem is not an international, but a domestic one.

The real difference between the Chinese and British Governments over Formosa today stems from their different interpretations of the effect of the Cairo and Potsdam Declarations. These both declared that Formosa was to be returned to China. The Chinese Government claim that, since Britain now acknowledges them as the legitimate government of China, she must automatically accept that it is to them that Formosa must be returned. The British Government, however, contend that the question can no longer be solved "merely by reference to the Cairo and Potsdam Declarations". In a statement in the House of Commons on November 19, 1958, Mr. Selwyn Lloyd said that both these declarations had been made at a time "when there was only one entity claiming to represent China". Since there were now two such entities and international opinion differed as to which should represent the Government of China, the problem of returning Formosa to "China", was one that inevitably aroused differences among the governments charged with carrying out the Declarations. The statement's accompanying, and by no means necessary, conclusion that "the problem of Formosa has become an international one", contained the important implication that the existence of the Formosa régime was itself a factor affecting British attitudes on the question of sovereignty.

Similar problems arise over the United Nations. So long as different governments are recognized in different quarters as the "Government of China", it will prove difficult to reach international agreement on which should be seated in the United Nations in that capacity. On both problems, while Britain's own viewpoint is not far different from that of the Chinese Government, her position has been conditioned partly by the views of her allies. The fundamental difference between Britain and China, therefore, has concerned not the merits of the two cases, but the extent to which Britain has been ready to seek to make her own opinion prevail over those of other governments.

THE FUTURE

II

CHINESE ASPIRATIONS AND BRITISH INTERESTS

TODAY a hundred years have been obliterated. For a century, after Britain first prised open the reluctant oyster-shell of the Celestial Empire, China was constrained to submit to invasion by Europe and to adopt, eventually, in many fields the manners and modes that were acceptable to Europe. Today the oyster-shell is almost as tightly shut as ever, and China is able to develop, within this barrier, a way of life indifferent, often hostile, to the values imposed briefly by the West. For a century, all Chinese actions in the field of foreign affairs had to be adjusted to the power of the Western nations camped round her shores. Today the nations of Europe have retreated to their own continent once more. For a century, Britain was able to secure favourable conditions of residence for her subjects and special juridical arrangements in cases where these were involved. During the last ten years conditions of residence for British people in China have been almost as constricting, and the legal procedures to which they have been subject almost as fierce and unpredictable, as a hundred and fifty years ago. For a century, Britain secured permission for British traders to traffic freely, first in designated areas, later all over China. Today British businessmen are once more almost totally excluded from China. For a century, Britain obtained authority for British missionaries to travel and preach throughout the country. Today there are none left.

The British position in China began to be liquidated long before the Communists arrived there. Some of the privileges which she enjoyed were no longer compatible with the twentieth-century world. Semi-colonialism was bound to go the same way as colonialism itself. But today Britain could no longer impose her will over China's even if she would. For the most fundamental of all the changes that have transformed the relations between the two countries concerns their relative power. When Britain could subdue she could dictate. Now that Chinese power has become formidable, it is Britain's turn to view with apprehension the aspirations of China's new rulers.

THE FUTURE

Dissensions persist. Among these, some of those very issues over which two hundred years ago friction between the two countries first arose, differing views of diplomatic procedures, conflicting attitudes to commercial intercourse, rival national pretensions, have continued to bedevil their relations even within the last few years. And the difference in world-view that first gave rise to conflict has now been replaced by an ideological gulf that is hardly less fundamental. Today once more the two countries view the world scene with divergent visions. These are conditioned by the different historical experience, geographical viewpoint, strategic interest, commercial advantage, as well as the ideological conviction, of each.

China's historical experience is dominated by the memory of subjection at the hands of the Western powers over the last century. For more than fifty years the fundamental object of all Chinese statesmen, of whatever political persuasion, has been to evict the foreigner from China and to re-establish China's power. One of the main aims, therefore, was to reassert China's sovereignty over areas where Chinese authority once prevailed but had since been challenged. To most Chinese the natural frontiers of China were those that had been reached at the height of China's power in the early Han, early Tang and early Ching times. But only within the last few years has a Chinese government possessed the power to satisfy such an ambition.

The present government of China, as soon as they acceded to power, restored full Chinese sovereignty in Manchuria, Sinkiang and Tibet. They have been assiduous in seeking to reacquire Formosa. They have re-established Chinese vassal-States in Vietnam and North Korea; and perhaps seek to do the same in Mongolia. For Britain this irridentist movement can be a direct threat in so far as it may be directed towards Hong Kong. Indirectly it may affect her interests in other parts of the Far East.

But China's experience of European usurpations has stimulated among her present generation, not only the particular urge to reassert China's former greatness, but a more generalized resentment against all forms of colonialism wherever they may occur. Such anti-colonial sentiment has a particularly powerful appeal to the present rulers of China, for whom Leninist theories of imperialism provide the appropriate ideological argumentation. To the outside observer this emotion may appear increasingly remote

CHINESE ASPIRATIONS 219

from the actualities of the present-day world. An examination of the fulminations against British imperialism in the Chinese Press today might lead one to suppose that the progressive dissolution of British imperial dominion during the last fifteen years had been kept a closely guarded secret from the present rulers of China. Yet such sentiments are not necessarily entirely contrived. Just as the behaviour of individuals may be influenced for long by events that lie deep in the past, so the mentality of nations sometimes remains for many years under the influence of traumatic experiences that stand a generation back. And to those peoples whose thinking is closely prescribed by ideology, international realities are themselves an irrelevance: the scriptural assertion of colonialism is alone sufficient to evoke the requisite emotional response.

Even for those quite unmoved by dogma such sentiments may still have some reality. New events may serve to reinforce pre-existing attitudes. The sense that during the last ten years the nations of the West have conspired to exclude China from international councils; the feeling that they have been motivated, in the Korean war, in U.S. support for the Formosa régime and the mobilization of anti-Communist power in S.E.A.T.O., by a desire to frustrate legitimate Chinese ambitions; a general impression that international deliberations are still unduly dominated by the West, all these may have helped to perpetuate inherited resentments among many Chinese who are not Communists.

Indignation against the iniquities of imperialists is particularly attractive to the Chinese rulers since it serves, incidentally, the objects of Chinese foreign policy. It may win favour from other peoples, enflamed with similar passions. It may serve to weaken the position of the West in areas where colonialism persists, or is only recently extinct. The Chinese Government have sought to identify themselves with all once-subject peoples as fellow-victims of brutal European colonialism. They have attempted to mobilize Pan-Asian sentiment in resistance to the West. "Anglo-American imperialism" has become a universal imprecation, a kind of all-purpose swear-word, devoid of any precise intellectual content, but full of the required emotive power. For China, even more perhaps than for the Soviet Union today, an attitude of militant hostility towards colonialism has become a basic principle of foreign policy.

The heritage of the past has affected British attitudes to China in complex ways. Imperialism in China, as in other areas, left behind it for a time a complex sentiment, in which both sympathy and guilt played their parts. The elimination of Britain's special privileges was greeted by many almost with relief. The decline of British dominance in China was viewed with the same realism as the disintegration of British power in other parts of the world.

But the experience that most influences British minds and Government policies in dealing with China today are those of the last ten years. Chinese actions in Tibet, Korea, the offshore islands, the Burmese and Indian frontier areas, the implacable hostility of her rulers towards the West and all it stands for, provoke a mood of acute apprehension in many British minds. Chinese leaders habitually pronounce on international affairs in terms considerably more ferocious than their Soviet colleagues. The isolation of China, the sense of mystery that once more surrounds her affairs, the hidden menace of her gigantic population, all these serve to intensify the trepidations of the outside world. The Chinese dragon appears no longer the benevolent beast of Chinese mythology, but rather some dark and dangerous monster, at present, for the most part, still brooding within its cavern, yet which may at any moment, once aroused, suddenly emerge, lashing its tail, to terrorize the country all around.

Geography conditions the two countries' relations in divergent senses. China is basically a continental power. The ocean has never been a vital element in her existence. Her conquests, both in the distant past and in recent years, have been of territories adjacent to her own. Her power and interests even today remain concentrated at the eastern end of the Eurasian land-mass. And any enlargement of these which she may seek to accomplish is likely to take place mainly in the proximity of this region.

Britain has sought her fortune always beyond the seas. As a result she built up interests all over the globe. Today she is beginning to withdraw within her own boundaries once more. She has been ejected from some areas by the achievement of independence by once-subject peoples. She understands that military power, even if it were available, is no longer an effective means of maintaining influence. She is able, with modern methods of communication, to conduct much of her trade within her borders. These developments have vitally affected Britain's position in the East. In many parts of the area formerly under British rule, the Indian sub-continent,

CHINESE ASPIRATIONS 221

Burma, Malaya, Britain no longer has a footing. Some of her former military outposts, airfields in Malaya, the naval dockyards at Hong Kong and Trincomalee, have been abandoned. Commitments and power, equally, have contracted. The process is likely to continue in the future. And in the long run Britain will no doubt find her interests centred more and more in Europe.

Thus in some senses Britain and China have become further apart than before. But this process has been counteracted by other influences having a contrary effect. On the one hand the general shrivelling of space; on the other the new expansion of China's power. While at the beginning of the opium wars British warships were a six months' journey from China, today the distance can be measured in hours. Militarily, politically, economically and culturally the world has become a single organism. And all the time that British power has been withdrawing from the East, Chinese has been extending towards the West.

Today, therefore, the point of contact between the two powers has moved westwards. Britain and China are now contiguous not on the coast of China itself but in South East Asia. For many of the nations of this region China once drew tribute. During the last ten years she has done much to reassert her position there. She has set up a client-state in North Vietnam. She has encouraged the emergence of neutral buffer-zones in Cambodia and Laos. She has seen the establishment of a predominantly Chinese city-state in Singapore. And she has wooed the allegiance of nearly twenty million overseas Chinese settled in the region. Even within the Chinese borders the centre of gravity has moved west. For the first time in her history, stable and effective centres of Chinese power have been established in Central Asia and Tibet.

But Britain too still maintains a considerable interest in South East Asia. She still has colonial possessions in North Borneo and Sarawak (where there are substantial Chinese populations), and, further afield, in the Pacific islands. She has close Commonwealth links with Malaya, Singapore, India, Pakistan and Ceylon. She has extensive commercial interests all over the region, especially in Malaya. She still maintains armed forces in Malaya, naval facilities in Singapore, and air staging posts in other parts of the area. And she is committed, as a member of S.E.A.T.O., to the defence of the region against outside aggression.

There is one point where the contact is even closer. This is Hong

Kong. Hong Kong was acquired more as a seat of military power than as a commercial centre, since it was believed that the access acquired to Chinese treaty ports sufficiently secured British trading interests. Today the naval dockyard has been abandoned, though the harbour continues to be used by warships. A military garrison is still maintained; and the colony could still serve, as it served in the Korean war, as a rear position and staging post for operations conducted in other parts of the region. But the experience of the Pacific war unmistakably demonstrated, if it needed demonstration, that today the military effectiveness of the island in any operations conducted against the Chinese mainland is nil.

Thus for Britain Hong Kong is now mainly valuable as a trading post. The total value of the trade of Hong Kong is £500 million a year, of which a fairly substantial proportion is earned by British firms. The United Kingdom's own trade with the island is worth about £60 million a year. British firms play a dominant part in the entrepôt trade with other parts of South East Asia. There is also some British participation in Hong Kong's native industry, whose exports are worth nearly £100 million a year. There are today about fifteen thousand British residents in the colony, almost all drawing support from it in one way or another.

Thus, even from a purely commercial point of view, British interests in Hong Kong are substantial. Yet it could be argued that the most important function of Hong Kong for Britain lies neither in its military nor in its commercial capacities. If it is accepted that Britain has an interest in the progressive penetration of the barriers that at present curtain off the Communist and non-Communist hemispheres from one another, Hong Kong has a unique part to play. While almost everywhere else the world is rigidly partitioned between the domains of the two world blocks, Hong Kong remains, like Berlin in the West, as one small transparent chink in this sombre series of barricades. In Hong Kong about ten thousand people freely penetrate the bamboo curtain every day. In Hong Kong East and West still conspire together to defy the gloomy generalization of Kipling. Here it is possible, on the very threshold of the greatest power of Asia, of the most rigidly totalitarian régime now existing, to advertise to its peoples the virtues of British thought, culture, values and political ideals. While everywhere around Europe is retreating to its own borders, Hong Kong remains, one last outpost of Europe in the East.

CHINESE ASPIRATIONS 223

In 1997 the New Territories, comprising a large part of the area of the colony, will revert to China. The colony will then be confined to the island of Victoria, one or two other small islands and a tiny foothold on the mainland. It will become more than ever dependent on the mainland for food, water and other resources. Perhaps more important, the return of the New Territories may well stimulate pressure for the return of the older portion of the colony, if that still exists. Yet Britain has many good reasons for wishing to remain in the island so long as possible. And it will be an important object of her policy to seek means of achieving this.

Here, therefore, in South East Asia and Hong Kong, is where British interests and the aspirations of a powerful, resentful and expansive China come most acutely into conflict. Eventually China's influence will without doubt spread further afield. Already she has shown some interest in the affairs of the Middle East and Africa; even, to a lesser extent, those of Europe and Latin-America. She appears to be aspiring to ideological hegemony within the Communist world. In the long run it seems likely that China's power and numbers may come to dominate the earth even more overpoweringly than the United States or the Soviet Union can today. If the Chinese population continues to grow at its present rate it will reach something like fifteen hundred million by the end of the century, or more than half the present population of the world. Although estimates of China's resources, both agricultural and industrial, are highly problematic it seems doubtful how easily these could support a population approaching that magnitude. Such factors may affect Chinese attitudes to the outside world. Without presupposing any overt attempts at expansion, China may at least come, like Italy in Europe, to be a powerful advocate of the maximum possible mobility of populations.

Certainly, by whatever means, China's power and influence will continue to surge outwards from her present borders. It must be Britain's purpose to ensure that this process occurs in such a way as will not disturb the stability of the region nor threaten British interests.

Among the factors that may affect Britain's capacity to achieve this will be the strategic relationship between the two powers.

Strategy depends on imputed strength as much as on the concentration of power immediately visible. Throughout the nineteenth century Britain was able to attain her ends in China, not through the force actually at hand in the area, but through the power that China knew to be at call when required. Successive humiliations at the hands of the armed forces of the West had taught her that she was powerless to resist any exaction that was proposed to her. Even under the Nationalists the position was basically no different. China could protest, as loudly as she dared. But both sides remained well aware where in fact the balance of power lay.

The position is today transformed. With all its limitations China's power no longer needs to take any serious account of British military force, considered in isolation. British naval power in the Far East is not such as could exert any great effect on the vast land-mass of China. The British garrison and airfields at Hong Kong could be swallowed in a day. Only if Britain were believed able and willing to launch the full weight of her nuclear armoury— from carriers, submarines or by an initial strike from Hong Kong —might Britain, unhelped, bring any effective military pressure to bear against China. In the lesser wars that alone today are thinkable, Britain could not begin to match the forces available to China.

There are in fact only two powers which, from a military point of view, today present any problem to China, the United States and the Soviet Union. Against the Soviet Union, China is at present indefensible. Even if there were no ideological reasons to unite them, China would be bound to remain in alliance with that country, as Chiang Kai-shek, for all his political hostility, twice demonstrated. Today, the two countries are also united, in despite of differences in other fields, by their common antipathy to the United States. All their interests lead them to hold together in defence of the Eurasian land-mass.

For, from the Chinese point of view, the fundamental change that has taken place in the Pacific since before the war is the emergence of the United States as a West Pacific power. In the pre-war period, the United States had no naval force in the Pacific that could match the Japanese fleet; and no naval base west of Hawaii. Today she has naval bases at Wake Island, Guam, Okinawa and other places. The Seventh Fleet patrols the waters between Formosa and the Chinese mainland. She has powerful air forces within a few hundred miles of China, in Formosa, Korea, Okinawa and Japan. She has land forces in Korea and Okinawa. She has supplied guided missiles to the Nationalist forces in Formosa. She has concluded a series of mutual security pacts with South Korea,

CHINESE ASPIRATIONS

Formosa, the Philippines, Australia and New Zealand, and other non-Communist countries of the region. And, finally, she has built up a defensive alliance of European and Asian countries in S.E.A.T.O.

This combination of circumstances means that in any conflict in which the United States becomes involved, China would start off at an insuperable strategic disadvantage. She has no forward bases from which she can threaten the United States. She is unlikely to be given intercontinental ballistic missiles or submarine missile-launchers by the Soviet Union. She is thus completely powerless, unaided, to make her power felt against the United States; still less against Britain. And although nuclear weapons are probably today nowhere regarded as practical weapons for use, their mere possession makes available to other powers an ultimate sanction that could leave China at a grave disadvantage, whether in negotiations or in war itself.

Yet while China is powerless, alone, to win a war against the West, it is almost equally difficult for the West to inflict defeat on her. For although China has little in the way of a navy or an air force, her leaders can be fairly confident that no invading army in the world could overcome a slow attrition by Chinese miles and numbers. Thus China is probably today, in a purely conventional war, unconquerable. And her leaders are reported to believe that, even in a nuclear war, China may be better equipped to survive, because of the dissemination of her population in tiny villages over huge areas, than most other peoples—a confidence which, if sincerely held, is almost certainly misplaced, and could be highly dangerous. This invulnerability could encourage an aggressive attitude towards the outside world. And were China in the near future to acquire nuclear weapons, her demeanour might well become even more disquieting. How soon such a development might take place it is idle to predict. What is almost certain is that the Chinese Government are devoting massive resources to the attempt. And it would be foolish to assume that by the end of this decade China will be without such an armoury.

Meanwhile China will undoubtedly continue to seek to push back from her borders the hostile forces that now ring her. If these seem likely to constrict her even more closely, she may be prepared, as once before, to engage in limited war to cast off the pressure. She will be ruthless in asserting her will over weaker neighbours in

P

matters under dispute. She will seek by propaganda, by cajolery, threats, perhaps subversion, to persuade neighbouring states to throw off their allegiance to the West. She will continue to discredit S.E.A.T.O. in the eyes of her neighbours. She will try to bring about the establishment of neutral buffer states, as she has succeeded in doing in Indo-China. And she will continue to seek to extend her own influence throughout Asia in such a way as to counteract so far as possible that of the Western Powers.

Thus while, on the one hand, the available British potential in the Far East has continued to decline, China's power on the other has immeasurably increased. Even before the war, Britain was unable to exert any effective military influence in the East. Today, her power still further diminished, she is even more driven back towards her continent. At the same time the evolution of colonies and the withdrawal of British residents means that she no longer has the same responsibilities within the area. Because of greater military mobility the presence of forces on the spot is of less importance. Finally, today Britain is able to rely increasingly on collective measures to ensure the defence of her interests in the region.

In fact relations between China and Britain are no longer seriously influenced by strategic factors. Fifty years ago, China became the battlefield for Europe's domestic struggles. Today Europe has almost entirely vacated the scene. The Far East is now an independent sphere of action in which Britain can play little part. It is no longer conceivable that China and Britain should again, as a hundred and twenty years ago, become engaged in single combat. The two countries enter into the strategic calculations of the other not individually, but collectively, as members of opposing coalitions. The Chinese objective may be to destroy the coalition to which Britain belongs. Britain's own interest, in default of private sanctions, must be to find collective means to ensure that the peace of these distant regions shall remain secure.

The commercial relationship between the two countries has in the last few years, been changed equally radically. The most apparent symptoms of this change are perhaps the least significant. The form taken by Western, and especially British, participation in China's economic existence was already something of an anachronism before the Communists came to power. As in other

CHINESE ASPIRATIONS 227

parts of the world, growing political independence would almost certainly have brought with it increasing economic autonomy. In any case the ruthless ejection of the foreign businessman and the appropriation of his assets did not fundamentally affect the most important of the outside economic links with China. Most of the foreign business community were interested, directly or indirectly, in Chinese trade with the outside world. This trade, though no longer carried out on Chinese soil, is maintained still under the new conditions. Trading negotiations take place today, not in the business houses of Shanghai, Tientsin and Hankow, but in the offices of London, Peking and Hong Kong; the myriad individual Chinese traders of former times have been replaced by the officials of government import and export corporations. But the transactions that these undertake have not themselves been fundamentally altered.

There have, however, been other important changes. On the Chinese side the mentality of those who determine the course of the trade has altered. The fact that all transactions are now conducted by the state means that they are subject sometimes to the demands of state. While still conducted so as to bring the maximum advantage to China, this advantage may occasionally be assessed from a political, as well as a strictly commercial, standpoint. Such factors have undoubtedly influenced the transfer of three-quarters of China's foreign trade to the Soviet *bloc*. They probably account for the radical drop in Chinese imports from Hong Kong. They no doubt affected the Chinese decision to establish control of her own shipping facilities in competition with those of the West. Yet all these were partly influenced by sound commercial considerations. The political effect of governmental control of trade remains largely potential. Perhaps its most significant result is the adverse position of foreign traders in negotiating not merely their sales and purchases, but the conditions under which this commerce is conducted.

A more important change has affected the composition of the trade. Until recently the basis of Western dealings with China was the exchange of Chinese agricultural products for manufactured articles, mainly consumer goods from the West. British imports from China are today largely the same as before the war. The chief items remain such commodities as egg products, bristles, soya beans, goat hair, tea, vegetable oils, and other Chinese native products. But within China's total exports there has been a significant increase in the total represented by manufactured goods and minerals: these now make up nearly one-third of the total. And among exports to Britain such items as cotton cloth, tinned food, household goods and the like form a significant proportion. Chinese imports have been even more affected. China is today primarily interested in the import of capital goods and raw materials to build up her industrial potential. The leading items among her imports from Britain today are iron and steel products, copper wire, wooltops, chemicals, fertilizers, machinery, motor vehicles and tractors, and similar articles.

Another new development has affected Britain's long-standing interest in the carriage of goods to and from China. A large proportion of Chinese trade with Europe now travels overland across the trans-Siberian railway. Many other exports from the Soviet *bloc* are carried in Polish vessels. Comecon, the agency for co-ordinating the economies of the Soviet *bloc* (to which China sends an observer), intends eventually to provide joint services to China. Since 1958, the Chinese Government, apparently dissatisfied with the prevailing conference prices, have themselves chartered a large number of vessels in Hong Kong and Europe, so as to present competition to the conferences. They have bought a few new and second-hand merchant ships, which they are running with Chinese crews. And they are themselves building merchant ships of over twenty thousand tons displacement. British ships will probably continue to carry a good proportion of shipments from West Europe. But there is no doubt that in the long run they will have a diminishing proportion of the total carrying business.

Finally, yet another change affecting British commercial interests concerns the third markets, especially in South East Asia, in which both countries are interested. The development of China's economic capacity has made her into an important competitor with Britain in the export of consumer goods, and especially of low quality textiles. In the last few years, and especially since 1958, China has conducted a vigorous sales drive in such goods in the Far East, partly no doubt to acquire foreign exchange for purchases of capital equipment. Low wage costs make these exports almost impossible for Britain to compete with effectively. And in the long run there is little doubt that China, without the large resources of exportable raw materials such as rubber, oil or copper, that some other underdeveloped countries possess, but with a huge labour force working

CHINESE ASPIRATIONS 229

at low wage rates, will become, like Japan, an increasingly dangerous threat not only for such traditional British exports, but for sales of capital goods as well.

For generations the potentialities of the China trade have been painted by enthusiastic British traders in the most spectacular, and improbable, colours. During the nineteenth century the myth of a bottomless market of 400 million consumers for cheap British textiles became an obsession with some (though to their credit British officials always showed considerably more realism than British merchants). Within the last few years once more, the vision of a huge demand from a rapidly developing economy for British machinery, chemicals, tractors and other commodities has once more lured eager British exporters. The opportunities of the trade for Britain have probably been magnified on the one hand by the extremely vocal commercial organizations engaged in this field, and on the other by the exhortations of political elements, with little knowledge but considerable enthusiasm. In fact British trade with China has never in its history been more than two and a half per cent of total U.K. trade. Today it represents about 0·7 per cent.

The drastic remoulding of the Chinese economy that is now taking place will inevitably transform the nature of British commercial contacts with China. At the same time this resurgence of China's economic power will inevitably make China once more, as two thousand years ago, a decisive force in the trade of South East Asia and perhaps further afield. The new situation will represent an important challenge to British commercial enterprise.

International relations today are dominated more than all else by ideological conviction. Britain and China are thus divided now above all by conflicting political persuasions. Since such persuasions have been elevated in the modern world, like religion in the medieval, to absolutes, whose truth is sustained by categorical imperatives, ideologies themselves become by nature exclusive and so aggressive. Thus while once it was the military and economic colonialism of Britain and her friends that evoked the fears of Chinese rulers, today it is the ideological imperialism propagated by China and her allies that arouses apprehension in Britain.

The vision of the world preserved by the present-day mandarins of China is obstructed by a stigma almost as distorting as that which afflicted their predecessors two hundred years ago. Like those they are convinced that the ways which they value are essentially superior to those of the benighted regions of infidel capitalism without. Like those, they have therefore sought to deprive their peoples of all contact with such pernicious outside influences. And like those, they have no doubt whatever that the forces at work within the universe are favourable to their own claims and that the ultimate triumph of their cause is sealed and sanctified by the holy laws of history. For the rule of Communism is assured by a Mandate of Heaven, spelled out with an authority more secure than any of imperial days, the unchallengeable certainty that only dialectic can provide.

The British, for their part, view the philosophy of the new Chinese rulers with almost as much impatience and distrust as they once viewed the arrogance of an earlier generation of Chinese officials. They consider, like Lord Palmerston, the manner of Chinese pronouncements often overbearing, and the matter contumacious. Like him they have resented insults and humiliations to British national pride which were the visible expression of these attitudes. And they have feared above all the barbarous and pagan creed by which such actions were inspired.

In Britain ideological faiths are various and vague. But in so far as any general political faith can be made explicit at all, the polity that has been set up in China is entirely repugnant to British attitudes. The absence of any genuinely free system of elections or parliamentary government, the lack of independence of the judiciary and the arbitrary, sometimes ruthless methods of the courts, the rigid inhibition of freedom of speech, press and assembly, the inexorable pressure of the propaganda machine in seeking to instil one unique opinion on all major political, social and international problems, the universal assertion of state power over individual rights, above all the ubiquitous supremacy within the state of a single sect and a single dogma, all these are the negation of the political ideals that the British people have been brought up to respect, and that they themselves did much to propagate all over the world. While they may recognize that, in tackling the fundamental problems facing China, in re-establishing an effective administration, in developing the Chinese economy, in building China into a great power once more, the ruling oligarchy in China have shown themselves able and energetic, they feel less sympathy with the methods by which this has been achieved. Both peoples speak much of "democracy". But while to

CHINESE ASPIRATIONS 231

the ruling caste in China, the system of elections and parliamentary government in Britain is only a facade, in which the true interests of the working classes can never be assured because of the domination of the state machinery by the *bourgeoisie*, to most British people, the system set up in China, in which the mass of the population can have no effective control over the way they are ruled, is the very antithesis of all that they understand by democracy.

The outside world has always felt a special distrust of the creed now upheld in China from a belief that it is indissolubly associated with aggressive and subversive designs. Communists in all countries have readily provided evidence that their parties favoured the overthrow of the existing political structure in every country of the West. When the present Chinese Government came to power there were some signs that China was seeking to play a dominant role in disseminating the creed they professed to the peoples of other lands, especially in Asia, as once the Comintern did in Europe. Not long after the establishment of the new government, a conference of Pacific and Asian peoples was held in Peking. A bureau of Asian and Pacific peoples was established, which has from time to time pronounced on international affairs. There have been continual visits of trades unionists and other political personalities to China from these and other regions. For a time, during the mid-fifties, China's efforts at evangelization became more discreet. The interests of the Chinese state sometimes seemed to take precedence over those of world Communism. The Chinese Government showed themselves willing to conciliate governments and parties, for example in Cambodia, Laos, the U.A.R., Iraq, Latin-America, even reactionary autocracies, as in the Yemen, which professed creeds entirely hostile to their own. But during the last two years, China has shown herself, more perhaps than any other Communist power, rigidly uncompromising in her determination to preserve the purity of the Communist faith, and to oppose attempts to reach accommodation with the heathen forces of capitalism. In the establishment of the communes China has seemed to set herself up as a model, to be imitated by other powers passing on the road to Communism. Finally, in her disputes with the Soviet Union on the inevitability of war, she has seemed to seek to wrest from that country spiritual authority within the Communist world.

Thus Chinese ideology has become to Britain as grave a threat as

THE FUTURE

Chinese armies. The rivalries of ideology in fact spill over imperceptibly into those of national power. China's ideological challenge may be a means of promoting purely national Chinese interests. The spread of Communism in Asia would further displace British commercial interests. It would bring about a significant alteration in the world balance of power to Britain's detriment. But it is a threat, not merely to the national interests of Britain, but to the principles and ideals that she believes in. The defence of such a faith may perhaps be regarded today as an interest no less urgent and compelling than those of the nation-state itself.

British political creeds can present no corresponding threat to China. Britain today has no ideological ambitions in that country. The Christian churches are resigned to the exclusion of foreign influence from the development of Christianity in China. In the countries that lie between them Britain has sought to contain, but rarely to suppress, the dogmas that China now proclaims. Indeed the most fundamental of all the ideological differences that divide them perhaps lies in Britain's faith in the value of tolerance.

The clash of ideologies is thus the most fundamental of all the differences that today divide Britain and China. All religions must seek to destroy their rivals. This is especially true of one which is regarded with the fanatical devotion of that professed by the reigning sect in China. While the political faith of the British may permit that those who profess the Communist faith are not perhaps all irrevocably doomed to perdition, even to allow such heretics to propagate their beliefs throughout the land, the creed of the Chinese priesthood is one that will permit no rivals, that must find any other faith by definition blasphemous and sinful, that will admit no doubt whatever that their own ways are the ways of righteousness, and that for those who do not see this one true light there can be no redemption.

Whether seen in terms of history, geography, strategy, commerce or ideology, the relationship that now exists between Britain and China is thus very different from what it was thirty years ago. This is a result of changes at both ends of the earth. The really significant alteration in the relationship between the two countries has come in fact, not in the last twenty years, but in the last five. This is only partly due to the change of government in China, and the time-lag before this could bring any fundamental access of Chinese power.

CHINESE ASPIRATIONS

It is equally true of the position of Britain. The decline in Britain's power and influence in the world came not as a result of the war, but of the events that followed it. Britain ended the war a great power. She was a victor nation, the only one, with China herself, who had fought in her own battlefield, from beginning to end, undefeated. She still held direct administrative responsibility for vast areas of the world containing nearly a quarter of its population. She still had military installations, naval bases, airfields, strung across the entire globe. She received one of the first permanent seats on the U.N. Security Council without question or dispute, at a time when India, Indonesia, Germany and Brazil were not even considered, and when China and France were only grudgingly accepted. For years afterwards, she took part, regularly and automatically, in exclusive "summit" gatherings convoked to settle the fate of the entire world. She wielded influence without power, because she still possessed prestige. She has lost that influence today, partly because prestige without power is necessarily a waning asset; and partly because of the rise or recovery of other nations. For two hundred years Britain has occupied a position in the world out of all proportion to her size. In the last five years alone she has been cut down to something nearer her true proportions. This must exert a decisive influence on her future policy to one of the world's natural giants.

China is today the most powerful nation in the Far East. Britain's influence there is negligible. China may soon be the most powerful nation of the world. Britain is already now only a second-class power. British interests in Asia are today only marginal. Though China has as yet little interest or influence in Britain's hemisphere, as her strength increases it will no doubt come to be increasingly felt there too. The growing power of China is indeed perhaps the most significant world event within the present generation. If Britain is to adjust herself to the facts of international life today she must learn how best to accommodate herself to this gathering force.

12

BRITISH POLICY AND THE FUTURE

BRITAIN'S two most immediate interests in conducting relations with China are the promotion of British trading interests and the preservation of Hong Kong. She has a more important interest in the preservation of peaceful conditions throughout the Far East; and, in particular, the prevention of any aggression against British possessions or interests there. She has a more remote concern to ensure that governments within the region remain well-disposed towards Britain, and so to prevent the adherence of rulers and peoples there to any political faith which may represent a threat to her own interests or to the values that she upholds. But her ultimate object must be, in China as elsewhere, to secure that improvement of understanding and reconciliation of interests, above all between the two great ideological blocks, which alone can secure the future peace of the world.

In seeking to expand her trade with China today, Britain faces various difficulties. First, there is a limit to the extent to which China's exports to Britain can be raised. The availability of Chinese goods is conditioned by commitments to the Soviet Union, not only for current sales, but for repayments of Soviet economic assistance over the last ten years. It is doubtful how far imports of the highly specialized Chinese native products can be expanded. Some British imports of manufactured goods, such as cotton cloth, linen, rayon and other artificial fibres, have during the last few years been limited by British Government quotas. Such measures, which are of course designed to protect British and Commonwealth manufacturers, have aroused some apprehension not only among the British consuming industries, but among some British exporters to China, who fear they may ultimately affect their sales.

Despite these handicaps to Chinese exports, China today has a trading surplus with the United Kingdom. She has an enormous surplus in trade with Hong Kong. And she gets fairly large volumes of exchange in overseas remittances. Thus the difficulty

BRITISH POLICY AND THE FUTURE 235

which British exporters face in increasing British sales to China does not lie in any shortage of sterling on the Chinese side—though it may be conditioned by the proportion she makes available for purchases of British goods.

Basically British exporters face the same problem in China as elsewhere, intense competition from their commercial rivals. At present these are mainly the Soviet Union, West Germany, France, and other West European countries. For the moment she is, in fact, in a favourable position in that, for political reasons, the United States at present engages in no trade with China at all; and Japan in little. Yet during the last few years Britain has not been able to increase her trade so fast as either West Germany or France (whose commercial activities are not hampered by the fact that they have no political relations with China). China is still an importer on a large scale of many goods which Britain is well equipped to sell. But unless their prices and delivery dates compare favourably with those of other European nations, including the Soviet Union, British manufactures will continue to lose ground. If they are to make use of the opportunities that exist in China there will be a need for a vigorous effort by British exporters. An important advantage might be gained by the establishment now of personal relationships with the Chinese trading agencies, and, where possible, with the end-users in the Chinese economic machine. Finally, the British Government for their part may have to consider how far restrictions that have been placed on China's textile exports are damaging British export interests in the Chinese market.

One new form that British business with China might take is the sale of technical information. Negotiations for the sale of certain patents have already taken place. There has been discussion about the sales of complete plants, such as have been made to the Soviet Union. As the Chinese economy develops and becomes able to undertake large-scale production of consumer goods, there may be more scope for business of this sort. In this field, as in others, success for Britain will depend on her ability to maintain a level of technical achievement and of prices comparable to those of her rivals. British shipping, which has for so long enjoyed a dominant position on the China coasts, will also have to be prepared to face more intense competition from both Chinese and foreign vessels. And it may find itself obliged to seek to bring about a less restrictive attitude on the part of the Far Eastern shipping conferences.

Finally, British commercial interests will have to adjust themselves to the increasing manufacturing capacity of China herself. It is likely that both in China and elsewhere in the East, they will find that Britain's advantage lies in concentrating on exports of capital goods and other commodities in which a high level of capital investment and technical accomplishment is concentrated. Only Japan at present among Far Eastern countries can meet such needs. And despite high British labour costs there will continue to be a good prospect for sales of such equipment for some years to come. But it would be foolish to suppose, as many have done, that there is room for a startling development of British trade with China. It will no doubt continue to grow, but increases are unlikely to be sensational.

Hong Kong cannot be defended from direct attack from China. Nor, if it were once lost, could Britain, unaided, recover it. Hong Kong was deliberately omitted from the area covered by S.E.A.T.O., so that no assistance would be automatically available from that source. In such an event in practice Britain would, of course, appeal to the United Nations. She might hope that the United Nations could, by recourse to the General Assembly if necessary, be induced to seek to remedy the aggression as effectively as once they did in Korea. The likelihood that the United Nations, dominated as it is by anti-colonial sentiment, might accept such responsibility would depend to some extent on the readiness of the United States and fellow-members of the Commonwealth to use their influence in this direction. Thus Britain might be well advised to ensure in advance that such co-operation would be forthcoming.

It is most unlikely, however, that any attempt by China to recover Hong Kong would take the form of direct aggression. Ninety-nine per cent of the population of Hong Kong are Chinese by race and culture, and most of these by nationality. If the Chinese Government wished to annex Hong Kong, they would almost certainly try to achieve this by the subversion of this population, rather than by a direct assault—hoping that, by such means, they could quickly make the colony ungovernable. They could also cause considerable embarrassment by cutting off supplies of vegetables, meat and water from Chinese territory, an action which could only be met by an operation comparable to, but far more costly than, the Berlin air lift.

BRITISH POLICY AND THE FUTURE 237

It is perhaps doubtful how far Britain would be able effectively to counter Chinese action along these lines. That no such action has so far been taken probably indicates that the Chinese Government see no great urgency in securing the return of the colony. Possibly they are glad of the very substantial supplies of foreign exchange (something like £50 million a year) which they acquire through their trade surplus with it. Perhaps they are not sorry to have some means of contact with the outside world, for example with the Chinese in Formosa. But the continued existence of Hong Kong will certainly remain to some extent dependent on the goodwill of the Chinese Government. Thus, in its actions in Hong Kong, Britain will have to continue to carry out the present policy of the Hong Kong authorities in avoiding any step which could be interpreted as provocative to China. Thus they will probably wish to discountenance all those activities, such as seditious operations by agents hostile to the Chinese Government, which might lead the Chinese Government to doubt the value of the colony to them; and to encourage all forms of activity, commercial and political, which the Chinese Government could regard as commending its continued existence under British rule.

If it is permitted to subsist, Hong Kong could be made the most important of all channels open to Britain for influencing Chinese opinion. There is constant traffic between the colony and the mainland. Students resident in Hong Kong travel to universities in China and back for their vacations. Traders from Canton visit Hong Kong almost at their pleasure. Hong Kong broadcasts are almost certainly widely listened to in south-east China. The news and views that are current in Hong Kong thus almost certainly percolate to many parts of the mainland otherwise completely shut off from Western contacts. And the picture that Hong Kong presents of British policies, culture and values could be a significant influence in the limited political life of the Chinese mainland.

The first need, if Hong Kong is effectively to advertise a non-Communist way of life, is that it should be able to secure an adequate standard of living for its population. That it cannot do so today is no fault of the Hong Kong Government. The colonial authorities have devoted intensive efforts to coping with the million and more refugees within the colony. They have succeeded in rehousing three hundred thousand of them in special resettlement accommodations. But about the same number still remain without any kind of regular housing at all; while very many others live in appallingly overcrowded conditions, in shacks, or in rooftop penthouses. At the moment the burden of these falls entirely on the colony itself. If, in future, the colony is going to be able to assure to all who dwell there a standard of life that can be compared without fear of disparagement with that of those beyond the border, the British Government may have to decide whether, for this, if not for purely humanitarian reasons, they should not begin to undertake some part of the burden.

Britain must also of course continue by other means to help maintain the prosperity of the colony. During the last ten years the industrial capacity of Hong Kong has grown at phenomenal speed. But this development still only scratches the surface of the colony's employment problem. British industry understandably fights shy of investment in an area whose future is so hazardous. This is especially true of the New Territories, where much development is today concentrated, and where the returns can in any case not be long-lived. In these circumstances the British Government should perhaps consider whether they might not do more, by direct aid, to assist the Hong Kong economy. In the year 1959–60 the Colonial Services vote for Hong Kong was only £150,000 against over £3,000,000 for the Aden Protectorate. In that year the colony received £218,000 worth of Colonial Development and Welfare funds against nearly £3,500,000 for Sarawak, and over £5,000,000 for British Guiana. With the decline of the China trade and the development of direct commercial contacts all over the world, Hong Kong's value as an entrepôt may continue to decline, and its prosperity will increasingly depend on its own industrial resources. Thus British Governments will have to continue to resist attempts to secure special protection against the colony's exports in Britain and elsewhere in favour of home producers.

Next, British Governments should perhaps consider the possibility of some political development within the colony. The reasons preventing any effective degree of political evolution so far are self-evident. Yet it should surely be possible to provide that the Chinese population of the colony are presented with a comparison with conditions on the mainland more provocative than that with which at present confronts them: that between a Chinese autocracy and a European. There seems little reason why they should not be in a position to participate, at a local level and in limited fields, more

BRITISH POLICY AND THE FUTURE 239

effectively than they can at present in the decisions of government within the colony. A constitution, such as was for a time considered during the late forties, could scarcely seriously endanger the foundations of British rule, and might achieve much as an exercise in political education.

For an understanding among Hong Kong residents of at least the basic rudiments of democracy could be a legacy more valuable to Britain, when the colony is finally lost, than any other product of British rule. For, whatever policy the British Government adopts, the long-term future of Hong Kong cannot be anything but precarious. The island's future prospects must be considered within the context of the likely disintegration of the colonial system throughout the world within the next few years. In these circumstances the determination of policy must at least anticipate the situation that will come about when it finally returns to China. There is no doubt that at that time the final impact of the colony's three million inhabitants could have a significant effect on the Chinese body politic. This may indeed be one of the factors that have prevented any Chinese move to recover it. In the long run it is more important that the effect of British rule in Hong Kong should leave some permanent imprint on the society of the Chinese mainland than that during the next few years the commercial prosperity of the island should be maximized.

For this reason, even more important than either the political or economic development of the colony, is the need to make Hong Kong a more effective centre for projecting alternative cultural and social values throughout the area. If Hong Kong is really to be as some proclaim, the shop window of the West, it is important to ensure that the West's best wares are displayed there. In these circumstances the broadcasting and radio-diffusion services in the colony should perhaps be more carefully considered than at present. The activities of the British Council, at present still operating on a shoestring should be expanded. More British literature and textbooks must be made available at accessible prices. Educational facilities should be improved. Hong Kong University could, with assistance, be brought to play the role its founders envisaged for it in bringing together the cultures of East and West. Indeed, now that European scholars are excluded from the mainland, Hong Kong could be of as much importance in bringing increased knowledge of China to the West as of projecting European values in the

East. Britain is spending vast sums of money all over the world in improving her information services. Such investment would be nowhere more worthwhile than in Hong Kong.

In seeking to prevent any threat to the peace in the Far East, Britain will no doubt continue to rely mainly on measures of collective defence. She will be principally concerned with the danger of aggression from China. In most of the areas where this is likely to occur (though not in Hong Kong or Formosa) such an event would automatically call forth retaliatory action by S.E.A.T.O.

Britain may have to consider, however, whether the ends of collective security which she seeks are not better secured by recourse to the United Nations than to some limited organization of limited membership such as S.E.A.T.O. All military pacts, however defensive in intention, are distrusted by wide sections of opinion throughout the East. The most important and influential nations of the area, including some of Britain's close associates, have never concealed their hostility to S.E.A.T.O. The degree of military co-ordination that has been brought about is extremely limited, and could easily have been secured without formal association, for example by the type of bilateral agreement that the United States has entered into with members of C.E.N.T.O. United Nations action, if achieved, would probably bring a wide measure of military support, and would certainly enjoy greater moral authority, than action under the pact.

Any treaty organization which provides for action in advance of, and irrespective of, United Nations decisions in fact not only serves to derogate from the authority of the United Nations which the British Government profess to uphold, but makes it impossible for that organization to take effective action in any situation where such an alliance is involved. Only if recourse to the United Nations failed should it be necessary to consider the desirability of alternative action. If any regional defence agreement is nevertheless felt necessary, this should certainly explicitly acknowledge the prior responsibility of the United Nations in meeting any breaches of the peace. In South East Asia, it is doubtful if, in fact, there is much to be gained by spelling out such commitments in advance. Military co-ordination, anti-subversive activity and economic assistance, such as are provided for under the treaty, could quite as well be afforded by other, less politically damaging means.

BRITISH POLICY AND THE FUTURE 241

Britain's reliance on collective defence in meeting a threat from China should have produced a complete reassessment of her own military requirements within the area. In any major conflict in which she may be involved, she may be reasonably assured that she will enjoy the military support of a number of allies, including, almost certainly, the United States. At the same time the increased mobility that modern military methods, aircraft, long range supply ships, carrier-borne commandos, allow, makes the establishment of large permanent garrisons and supply bases considerably less necessary, even from a purely military standpoint, than they once were. In addition, the political odium which in almost every case attaches to such bases, detracts from their military value at the same time as their political expediency. In many cases such political factors will in fact prove finally the marginal consideration. So long as Britain can continue to enjoy the use of military facilities in Singapore and Malaya, without paying a political penalty disproportionate to their value, she has no reason to give them up. But she would certainly be wise to consider in advance whether they are likely in fact to remain at her disposal much longer than many others that have had to be abandoned in other parts of the world. The reduction of British commitments, for colonial defence or colonial security, has in any case reduced the need for facilities on the spot. Perhaps the garrison in Hong Kong will continue to be maintained, as a symbol as much as a serious threat (though it is a symbol increasingly expensive to project). Eventually there is little doubt that Britain will have to seek to bring about such an improvement in the mobility of her forces both by air and by sea, that she becomes, so far as possible, independent of the precarious assurance afforded by insecure land establishments set on distant shores.

At the moment the most acute danger of aggression from China arises in the Formosa Straits. In fact it is most unlikely that China will ever attempt a direct assault on Formosa, a difficult enough operation at any time, but now rendered almost impossible by the security pact between the United States and Formosa. She may, however, continue from time to time to launch assaults against the offshore islands, especially those most exposed, since, even if unsuccessful, these cause a certain political embarrassment to the United States.

Unfortunately although everybody becomes acutely aware of the danger such conflicts provoke at the time when they are taking

Q

place, so soon as the firing dies down it tends to be forgotten again. Retreat, while attacks continue, is ignominious; and when they cease, unnecessary. Britain should consider whether she might do more to bring about, between the rounds, some adjustment of the present anomalous position. Matsu is about 20 miles from the Chinese coast and 150 from Formosa; Quemoy about 5 from China, nearly 150 from Formosa. Both, unlike Formosa and the Pescadores, have always, even before the last war, been a part of the Chinese mainland. So long as the present situation continues, not only the Chinese Government themselves but many outside observers will consider that China has a legitimate grievance. During the first Chinese assault in 1954–5, it was confidently predicted, that so soon as the immediate threat was removed, the United States would be able to secure a Nationalist withdrawal from these provocative positions. After the 1958 attack it was believed that some settlement might be reached at the Warsaw talks. On neither occasion has anything been done. It is wiser to meet such threats before, rather than after, they became menacing.

The other main fields of Chinese belligerence in recent years have been in Tibet; and on the borders of India. Britain no longer seeks seriously, any more than the Indian Government which inherited her position there, to maintain the anachronistic distinction between a Chinese suzerainty over Tibet and Chinese sovereignty there. The Tibetan appeal to the United Nations in 1950 was studiously ignored by that body, then in any case much preoccupied with other affairs; and recent appeals have not even attempted to assert the separate national identity of Tibet. In these circumstances, there is little that Britain can do to meet renewed outbursts of violence in Tibet or other minority areas of China, except to seek to bring the force of international opinion effectively to bear on China.

British Government spokesmen have never pronounced on the merits of the frontier disputes between China and her southern neighbours. This is no doubt the attitude favoured by the Governments mainly concerned themselves. The true facts in the different areas concerned are in any case complex and obscure. In such cases the parties concerned have preferred to deal by direct negotiation than to become embroiled in acrimony at the United Nations, to which China does not even belong. Both here and in other parts of South East Asia where China seems bent on forcible

BRITISH POLICY AND THE FUTURE 243

expansion Britain will no doubt continue to deplore, and where necessary to resist, the use of armed forces to seek to impose settlement of such disputes; and, where desired, to invite effective measures by the United Nations to remedy such action.

But in considering the possibility of aggressive action by China, Britain should perhaps direct her policy as much towards influencing the attitudes of the Chinese Government as towards seeking to meet their actions once these have already been precipitated. Defence policy itself, in the nuclear age more than ever, is concerned rather with preventing war than with making it. In the political field British actions may be of vital importance in influencing the mood of the Chinese leaders. As the only major Western power in relations with the present government, she might perhaps have done far more than she has done, at least in recent years, to improve the channels of communication between China and the West. That opportunity still lies open. The need is greater than ever.

China's present mood is an ugly one, arrogant and self-righteous. It derives to some extent from the fact that China is still in an early, Stalinist phase of her revolution. But it may derive too, in part, from the frustration born of exclusion. Treated as an outlaw, China is tempted to behave as an outlaw. More closely in touch with international opinion, China would become more accessible to its influence; in particular to the goodwill or disfavour of the uncommitted nations. At the same time China's participation in world councils would allow at least the discussion of some of the international disputes in which she has recently become involved.

Today there are, indeed, more urgent reasons for securing China's entry into the family of nations. China has already announced that she will not regard as binding any agreement on disarmament to which she is not a party. Yet it is obvious that all the labours of the negotiations that have already taken place on this subject, and of all those that are to come, will have been in vain if any control system which they contrive is not extended to one of the world's major powers. Should China appear to be about to produce nuclear weapons, this need may become of immediate urgency.

The principal means for securing these objects must be to bring about Chinese membership of the United Nations. Although this would not probably bring about any immediate modification of the

Chinese mood, it would reduce the sense of exclusion and bring China more closely in touch with international opinion. China is perhaps more likely to show respect for the rules of an organization to which she belongs than of one from which she is excluded. But the strongest arguments for China's admission concern the organization itself. For better or for worse the Central People's Government is the effective government of the entire Chinese mainland, exerting authority over 700 million people. It may be doubted whether any body which excludes the representatives of a quarter of the world's population can properly describe itself as a world organization.

So far the United Nations has not even begun to face the problem. Until recently a majority of its members, including Britain, have continued year after year to support a resolution refusing even to consider the question. The British Government justified their decision to support such a resolution on the grounds that, as Mr. Selwyn Lloyd stated in 1959, though Britain believed China should be admitted, she felt that discussion of the subject would "split the organization up the middle". This is a curious argument to use. If no subject were to be discussed except those on which agreement was assured, it is difficult to know what the organization could effectively achieve. In fact a change in the British Government's attitude might long ago, given the present sentiment within the United Nations, have secured the solution which they themselves profess to favour. Very shortly there will almost certainly be a majority in favour of discussion; and quite possibly in favour of China's admission. It is perhaps better that the final decision to admit should come with the acquiescence of the West than in such a way as to represent a defeat for their policies.

Even, however, if a majority of United Nations members were to vote in favour of some representation of the C.P.G., the problem would not be solved. At present it is quite certain that the Chinese Government would not accept representation at the United Nations so long as another government purporting to represent China were allowed to retain membership. It is unlikely that she would do so if a separate government representing Formosa remained a member. The Chinese Government, like the Nationalists themselves, have always been insistent that Formosa is only a part of China, and to accept a dual representation, even under protest, would be to acknowledge the "two China" policy which they have so ferociously opposed.

BRITISH POLICY AND THE FUTURE

Some such solution is, nevertheless, the only logical one in the present situation. It is also that most likely to commend itself to a majority in the United Nations. And it is towards a solution along these lines that Britain should perhaps seek to move. The best hope would be to arrive at some formula which might satisfy the pride of both parties. This could perhaps be met by the provision for temporary, "exceptional" representation of "Formosa" in the special circumstances following the civil war. The People's Government would, of course, occupy China's permanent seat in the Security Council. It is by no means certain that either party would accept this solution. But it would be at least a first step towards the rationalization of existing absurdity.

The problem of United Nations representation is only one aspect of the whole question of the conflicting claims of both Communist and Nationalist Governments to represent the one legitimate government of China, having legal authority over all those areas now under the control of the other. In Britain, neither Government nor people are prepared to acknowledge Formosa's claims to rule the mainland. Some have more sympathy with the claims of the Chinese Government to Formosa. But few would seriously support that the inhabitants of the island should be handed over to the mainland irrespective of their own wishes. At the same time the legal as well as the practical difficulties of enforcing United Nations trusteeship of the island, or the holding of a referendum, against the wishes of its present government, are such as to make such proposals, in theory admirable, of doubtful practical value.

The simplest, and indeed self-evident, solution of the problem would be similar to that within the United Nations; international recognition of the C.P.G. as the Government of China, and of the Nationalists as the Government of Formosa. The Nationalists would be required to withdraw from the offshore islands. And the Communists would be required to renounce any claim to recover Formosa by force.

There are signs that such a solution is becoming increasingly acceptable to international opinion. Unfortunately the countries that are least likely to accept it willingly are those which it chiefly concerns. No United Nations resolution, however widely supported, is likely at present to induce either Communists or Nationalists to renounce their existing claims. The Nationalists at present may well refuse to acknowledge recognition as the Government of Formosa alone. More important, they will not, merely because the United Nations so decided, withdraw their troops from the offshore islands. Only the most ruthless economic pressure from the United States, and perhaps public repudiation of responsibility for the islands' defence, could induce them to do this. Britain should perhaps use her influence to persuade the United States to exert some such pressure. Certainly it would be wiser to withdraw from such positions voluntarily than to be evicted from them by force of arms.

The Chinese Government have for long sought to achieve "the peaceful liberation" of Formosa. They have appealed to the patriotic family sentiments of the Chinese who now inhabit the island to induce them to return to the mainland. They have offered them an amnesty and positions of authority in China. They have even given some indications that they might accept a continuation of effective rule by the Nationalists in the island if these would acknowledge the nominal sovereignty of the mainland government: Chou En-lai told three Labour M.P.s in 1957, "I have co-operated with [Chiang Kai-shek] twice and I can co-operate with him again." It may be that ultimately some such solution of the Formosa problem may come about. But it will be long before any in Formosa are ready to acknowledge Communist suzerainty. And meanwhile the Communists will no doubt continue to resist any "two China" policy that seems likely to make its achievement more difficult.

What, therefore, seems almost certain is that neither government will be ready to make formal and explicit renunciations of their own claims (such as the United States have sought to pursuade the Chinese Government to enter into at the Warsaw talks). They might perhaps accept some such solution as a *fait accompli*, which they themselves were not required to endorse. And the most immediate object of British policy should probably be to secure increasing international recognition that the Nationalist régime is the Government of Formosa and the Pescadores, not that of China. So long as Chiang Kai-shek continues to assert his claim to the mainland, so long as he can be portrayed as a new Koxinga, representing lawful authority throughout the land, and seeking to harry the mainland authorities in support of this contention, the peace of the Formosa Straits is likely to remain in danger. For this reason a fundamental object of British policy must be to encourage in world opinion a more realistic acceptance of the facts of international life in the area.

The next object of British policy, to seek to prevent the spread of Communism and of governments sympathetic to its objects, is surrounded with difficulties. To secure the continued authority of governments sympathetic to Britain's aims, all that can be done is to continue to cultivate friendly relations at all levels—not merely the governmental. Any policy, such as has sometimes been followed during the last fifteen years, that may appear designed to support a particular régime, rather than a nation as a whole, will prove disastrous. Governments must inevitably eventually fall. Popular moods persist. Such policies in the past in the Far East as in the Near, have served to identify the West with right-wing, or otherwise unrepresentative governments, so that, when these are replaced, their authors have drawn corresponding odium from the new ruling class.

This danger is especially present when assistance, military or economic, is to be given. In this sense Britain is perhaps less subject to guilt by association than the United States. But it is important to ensure that any aid which is given is clearly seen as designed to promote the economic welfare of the people as a whole rather than as assistance for the government itself. In the Far East, as elsewhere, Britain will have to be ready to live with whatever authorities may be established, however inimical these may at first seem to her interests. Friendship that is sufficiently disinterested and deeply-based will prove better able to transcend the vagaries of political change than friendship that is too closely conditioned by political sympathies.

It will of course remain the case that the accession of Communist governments, wherever it may occur, will normally prove damaging, not only to the national interests of Britain, but to the political ideals for which she stands. In Asia the example of Chinese Communism will remain a challenge to both interests and ideals. It is a challenge that will be promoted as much with economic arms as political. At present the peoples of Asia are inevitably more concerned to eat than to vote. And if the Chinese system seems to possess the recipe for even one square meal a day, they may well forego the pleasures of the ballot box for those of the rice bowl.

Such arguments must not be over-simplified. The process of

political change is certainly not so rational nor so self-conscious as such models sometimes presuppose. Widespread recognition that a Communist government can provide rapid economic growth will not in itself ensure the access to power of Communist governments, nor even the adoption by existing governments of Communist economic methods, still less the political institutions. All that can be said is that if the discrepancy between the economic achievements of the two systems becomes too great, it is probable that the basic premises of parliamentary forms of government will become increasingly challenged, and those of the Communist system increasingly accepted.

The supreme economic asset of the Communist system is the high level of domestic accumulation it makes possible, an advantage that probably more than outweighs the greater flexibility in distribution that non-Communist societies achieve. One of the most important contributions which the West can make will be to help the non-Communist underdeveloped countries of the area to find ways, especially in the early phases of development, of achieving high levels of domestic savings, without adopting the political formulae that Communism prescribes. Until this is achieved the West will have to ensure that their total level of economic assistance to non-Communist nations is such as to achieve as high a rate of investment *per capita* of the assisted population as those attained in the Communist countries of the area. And it will be equally necessary to ensure that the level of technical knowledge, and of its application, are as high in non-Communist countries as in Communist.

But it is of vital importance for Britain and the West that the political aspects of this struggle should be clearly disentangled from the economic; and that both of these should be removed entirely from their European context. It is essential that developing nations should be clearly aware that, if Communist systems do show a rate of growth that is attractive, it will be because of differences in the volume of investment and methods of industrial organization, rather than in the political system by which these are accompanied. Many countries of Asia may in fact come to adopt economic methods reminiscent of those applied in Communist countries. So long as these are not accompanied by the political adjuncts with which they are associated in the Communist world, they represent no threat to Britain. On the other hand if the policy of the West towards these lands appears directed to seeking to preserve the economic system

BRITISH POLICY AND THE FUTURE 249

that is established in Europe and North America, they may well only ensure that Western economic methods and political ideals are together rejected. Similarly, on the political side, the West must accept that the systems adopted in newly emerging countries will not necessarily be those that have recently become the norm in Western countries, having entirely different historical, social and economic backgrounds. The basic political objective of the West should be that the forms of government adopted, whether left-wing or right-wing, nationalist or neutralist, are broadly representative of the aspirations of the peoples concerned. An ideological war waged on behalf of Western democratic forms would be as chauvinistic, and as suicidal, as one waged on behalf of Western capitalism.

Thus to meet the political challenge of China, Britain must be ready to seek the appropriate political weapons. For it is on this plane that the basic contest, if contest there must be, will be carried on. Most countries today, even while they still seek to find a defence in military weapons they dare not use, recognize at bottom that, since the real prize is human hearts, not patches of earth, future wars must be waged on the ideological, rather than the military, level. Any struggles that Britain and China become involved in today are more likely to be conducted with leaflets and broadcasts than with bullets and battleships. Already Peking radio transmits a powerful barrage of verbal missiles across the Middle East, Africa, and Latin America. The B.B.C. counterattacks with cannonades all over the Far East. By propaganda, cheap literature, the successful exploitation of Chinese economic, cultural, sporting and other accomplishments, China will continue to seek to expand her influence in Asia. In Hong Kong, Singapore, Malaya and other parts of Asia, Britain will seek to establish outposts for the non-Communist cause.

So long as the pretensions of Chinese ideology continue to represent a threat to British interests and values, Britain will have to seek the means of effectively containing them. In the long run perhaps such verbal battles will come to assume less importance. Possibly the first fine fervour of Chinese evangelism will be softened. Faiths on both sides will no doubt evolve. The final object of such battles is indeed not to win victories but to reach settlements, not to conquer but to convince. Thus the real problem for Britain is the same in facing Chinese creeds as in facing Chinese power. If the dragon of Communism can only be tamed, there will be no need to vanquish it.

A reduction of the existing isolation of China on the plane of international relations is only the beginning of the breakdown of the more fundamental isolation of the Chinese mind. Most of the countries that came for a time under Western domination or influence, in the Indian sub-continent, in South East Asia, in Africa, have remained, even after the imperial power was ejected, in some contact with the mind and manners of the world they have cast off. Most of the Communist powers, even, inherit a common European culture with the nations of the West. In China, however, links with the former European occupiers have now been totally rejected. Even her ties with European Communists are today tenuous. This total isolation of the Chinese mind, taken in conjunction with a certain mental arrogance natural to the Chinese people, could serve to induce a still more uncompromising mood among the Chinese leaders which, if it were to be accompanied by a considerable increase in Chinese power, might prove highly dangerous to the outside world.

One important way in which Britain might try to lessen Chinese isolation would be to seek increasing contacts between the Chinese people and her own. Considering how much has been done at the official level to encourage contacts between Britain and the Soviet Union, and to direct these into politically neutral channels, it is surprising that so little has been done so far to achieve the same objects in relation to China. Contacts with that country are at present even more restricted and still more subject to political considerations than those with the Soviet Union. Yet the long-term need for communication is certainly greater. There is an urgent need for some body, similar to the Great Britain–U.S.S.R. Society, to undertake similar functions for contacts with China. This should do all it can to secure visits to this country by groups of Chinese students, technicians, artists, academics, trade unionists and others; and seek to ensure that they acquire a more objective picture of Britain than they could receive from the Chinese Press. Visits in the opposite direction should be fostered for the same purpose, as well as for making opinion in Britain more aware of a vitally important part of the world about which it still tends to remain unhappily ignorant. The Chinese groups will inevitably be

BRITISH POLICY AND THE FUTURE 251

dominated by members of the Communist Party and others who are regarded as politically reliable. But since it is these who at present exert most influence in Chinese society, it is perhaps worthwhile seeking to make some effort to influence their thinking. An important start might be made by taking up the invitation of the Chinese National People's Congress for a visit by a joint parliamentary delegation which was earlier, in somewhat off-hand fashion, rejected.

Most fruitful of all would be an attempt to induce some of the Chinese leaders to travel to the West. No leaders in any country of the world reveal so blatantly, in all their public utterances, their baleful ignorance of the world beyond their borders and the thinking processes of those who live there than the present rulers of China. At present the majority of these, including Mao Tse-tung and Liu Shao-chi, the President of the Republic, have never travelled outside China at all, except on one or two visits to Russia. In societies where the reporting of embassies and the pronouncements of the Press must of necessity be mainly the confirmation of a preconceived image, the educative value of foreign travel is especially important. There can be little doubt Mr. Khrushchev has learned more during his widespread visits to non-Communist countries, peering into cafés, strolling along pavements, chatting with farm workers, than from all the diplomatic dispatches he has studied in his life. The dogmatic and uncompromising tone of current Chinese interventions in world affairs constitutes one of the major disturbing factors on the international scene today. Any move that Britain might make which could cause the Chinese leaders to see a little more of the world than they have knowledge of at present—whether in Britain or elsewhere—might be of profound value in helping them towards a more realistic assessment of the facts of the existing world.

It would be rash, however, for Western statesmen to suppose that, by drawing China more out into the international scene, they may have better opportunities for exploiting differences of opinion between China and the Soviet Union. There is little doubt that the recent ideological dispute between China and Russia has exerted a very profound influence on relations between these two countries. It is doubtful whether the Communist *bloc* can ever again be such a cohesive entity as it once appeared. As China's power increases, she will inevitably seek still more independence from the Soviet

Union. But it is important for the West to accept the fact that both countries have at present everything to gain by continuing to stand together, especially on any matter affecting their relations with the West. Their common hostility to the United States, their common economic ties, their common strategic interests, their common frontiers, their common—or at least similar—ideology, all these continue to bind them together. They thus have a mutual interest in sinking their differences in the face of outside forces; just as the United States and Britain, in similar circumstances, have a mutual interest in sinking theirs. All attempts to exploit such issues as divide the two will be easily seen through, and may well only have the effect, like attempts to divide the United States from her allies, of drawing them closer together. At the moment, in any case, the Soviet Union may well be exerting a restraining influence on Chinese policy. To isolate China further might only increase the instability of her behaviour. Only at a later stage, when Chinese power and numbers come to be a dominating force throughout the world, is the Soviet Union likely to modify significantly her relationship.

Britain has a long and honourable tradition in promoting knowledge and understanding between China and Europe. Today, as the only major Western power in relations with the new China, she could play a vitally important role in helping to integrate that country into the community of nations. To do this effectively she may sometimes need to show independence from some of her major allies, as once ten years ago. She must be ready to meet China as an independent and adult member of the society of nations. She should be clear about the nature of the underlying grievances, and of the ideological predilections, which condition much of Chinese behaviour. She should be ready to acknowledge China's legitimate national interests. Until she is accepted by others on equal terms as a full member of the community of nations, China may remain reluctant to accept the norms of behaviour that community seeks to impose. In the longer term a more difficult effort at reconcilation may be required. While Britain must certainly continue to resist any attempts at the forcible export of China's present ideology, she may need to accept that it is likely to remain the dominant force within China for many years to come. If the West is to come to terms with China it will need to acknowledge and to understand that creed. So long as political passions on both sides are directed at the destruction of the dominant ideas of the opposing society, the acerbities of the cold war are unlikely to be abated. Truly peaceful coexistence will require a readiness to respect—if not to accept—the ideological convictions of others. For the cold war is perhaps more likely to reach conclusion through the reconciliation of the two great ideologies than through the conquest of one by the other.

There is no part of the world today where British policy might exert such an important influence as in her relations with China. There the largest aggregation of people in the world are working with fanatical energy to build up a super-power of huge proportions. There the concatenation of an intensely inflamed national sentiment, acute intelligence, formidable industry and overwhelming numbers provide a combination that will not be easily denied. The nation they are creating is at present still uncouth in the conduct of its relations with its neighbours. It remains aloof and inaccessible even from its closest allies. And unless assimilated into the world community it could become an increasingly unstable element in international society.

If Britain is to be in a position to cope intelligently with this new force, she will have to show herself more conscious of its importance. Government departments will have to show some awareness of China's stature: the strength of the diplomatic staff of the British Embassy in Peking is at present seven, against twelve in Moscow, twenty in Bonn and thirty-four in Washington. British academic institutions will have to be prepared to devote as much, or more, time and resources to the study of Chinese language, literature, history and institutions as they do now to those of European nations: at present only three or four universities in the whole country take an academic interest in Chinese culture, while no schools teach even a romanized form of the Chinese language. When we possess a better understanding, we will be better equipped to respond intelligently to the challenge that China represents.

Britain's ultimate aim in the Far East is, as elsewhere, to seek to reduce the underlying tensions that still imperil man's future. Since human consciousness remains largely conditioned by national loyalties, the achievement of this aim will involve in the first place adjustments of national differences, sometimes concessions to national susceptibilities. In the longer term, divisions of thought and culture—in which ideological allegiances will certainly play their part—may be even more dangerous. It must be the object of British policy, not merely to alleviate the national frictions and resentments that could make China a dangerous force today, but to remedy those more profound alienations as well, by seeking yet again, as once a century and a half ago, to free channels of communication between China and Europe; to reopen a trade in persons and ideas; and so perhaps, eventually, to achieve a more enduring meeting of minds between East and West. East will remain East, and West, West. But somewhere, if the world is to be one, they must meet.

INDEX

Aircraft, Chinese, in Hong Kong, 83–84, 86, 187–8
Amethyst incident, 68–73
Anglo-Japanese alliance, 36–37, 38, 39
Assistance,
  British financial, to China, 43, 49
  British military, to China, 49–50, 53, 58
Attitudes:
  British to China, 10, 12–16, 20–23, 30–31, 36, 40, 48, 59, 65–67, 78–82, 154–8
  Chinese to Britain, 10, 12–16, 30–32, 37, 40–41, 46, 59, 86–87, 159, 173–4, 212–13
Attlee, C. R., visit to Washington, 1950, 94–95

Banks, British, 129, 139–40, 152–3
British Council, 57, 239
Burma Road, 49
Business,
  British, 128–54, 226–9, 234–6
  decision to withdraw, 138–9
  difficulties under Communists, 132–4, 135–40
  under Nationalists, 57, 130–2

China Association, 145–6
Christianity, arrival of, 104
Civil War, 1946–9, 60, 64–69, 131

Concessions, leases and settlements, 29, 34–35
Consulates, British, 76, 155–6
Contacts,
  British with China, 11–16, 19 ff.
  earliest European, 9–11
Crime and Punishment, 21–22

Delegations,
  British, 145, 167–8, 173
  Chinese, 146, 168–9
Diplomatic relations, early differences, 13–14, 23–24

East India Company, 19, 23–25
Embargo, 10, 141–3
Extra-territorial rights, 29, 50–52

Foreign residents, detention of, 121–3, 156–7
Formosa:
  British relations with, 83–84, 86
  international position, 200–3, 212–14, 245–8
  neutralization, 88, 200–201

Geneva Conference, 140, 160–7

Hong Kong, 29, 58, 75, 78, 84–85, 155, 176–98, 221–3, 236–40
  acquisition, 29, 176–7
  constitution, 179, 238–9
  disturbances, 183, 189, 190–1

immigration, 194–5
trade, 195–8

Indo-China War, 160–4, 167
Investment, British, 130, 131, 141

Japan:
  British alliance, 36–37, 38, 39
  British conciliation, 43–48, 49
  Japanese encroachments in China, 39, 43–45
Japanese Peace Treaty, 202–3

Korea:
  aggressor resolution on, 98–100
  Commonwealth Prime Ministers' initiative, 96–97

Missionaries, 29, 104–27, 156–7
  affiliations of converts, 107–8
  catholic, 122–3
  Chinese attitudes towards, 108–10, 115, 120–2
  conditions of residence, 104, 107–8, 112–14
  decision to withdraw, 110–12, 118–20, 124–5
Moscow Declaration, 65, 67
Municipalities, foreign, 56

Nationalist Party, British dealings with, 38–39, 41, 42–60, 181–4

Off-shore islands, 169–72, 241–2
Opium, 25–28, 128
Opium Wars, 28–29, 30–31

Overseas Chinese, 73

Parallel, 38th, 89–91
Property, British, 55, 152–3

Recognition, 74, 76–79, 81–82, 158
  British attitudes, 65–67, 75, 77–79
  communist reaction, 83–85
  foreign attitudes, 74, 76, 79–80
  Nationalist attitudes, 80
S.E.A.T.O., 165–6, 219, 221, 240–41
Shipping, British, 56, 57
Sino-Japanese War, 44–47, 49, 53–54, 108, 130
Strategic position:
  British, 36, 42–43, 223–4, 240–41
  Chinese, 92, 224–6

Tibet, 77, 87
Trade, 14–15, 19–20, 32–34, 128–54, 226–9, 234-6
  commercial procedure, 147–50
  organization, British, 20–21, 128–30, 143–7
  organization, Chinese, 134, 150–2

United Nations, Chinese membership of, 83–84, 86, 203–11, 243–5

War-time alliance, 48–53
Washington treaties, 38, 44

Yalta agreement, 54